Disruptions as Opportunities

CHINA UNDERSTANDINGS TODAY

Series Editors: Mary Gallagher and Emily Wilcox

China Understandings Today is dedicated to the study of contemporary China and seeks to present the latest and most innovative scholarship in social sciences and the humanities to the academic community as well as the general public. The series is sponsored by the Lieberthal-Rogel Center for Chinese Studies at the University of Michigan.

A complete list of titles in the series can be found at www.press.umich.edu

Disruptions as Opportunities

GOVERNING CHINESE SOCIETY WITH INTERACTIVE AUTHORITARIANISM

Taiyi Sun

University of Michigan Press
Ann Arbor

For questions or permissions, please contact um.press.perms@umich.edu

Published in the United States of America by the
University of Michigan Press
Manufactured in the United States of America
Printed on acid-free paper
First published March 2023

A CIP catalog record for this book is available from the British Library.

Library of Congress Cataloging-in-Publication data has been applied for.

ISBN 978-0-472-07563-8 (hardcover : alk. paper)
ISBN 978-0-472-05563-0 (paper : alk. paper)
ISBN 978-0-472-90330-6 (open access ebook)

DOI: https://doi.org/10.3998/mpub.12326710

The University of Michigan Press's open access publishing program is made possible thanks to additional funding from the University of Michigan Office of the Provost and the generous support of contributing libraries.

To my wife Tingting, our son Jinyu, and my parents

Contents

Digital materials related to this title can be found on
the Fulcrum platform via the following citable URL:
https://doi.org/10.3998/mpub.12326710

Figures

Tables

Acknowledgments

I began the research that launched this book in 2012, and I made my final edits in 2022. During this decade-long journey, I have received guidance, support, and assistance from an enormous network of people and institutions.

To Joseph Fewsmith, my dissertation committee chair, thank you for protecting my curiosity and confidence when I was newly acquainted with the field of Chinese politics, and not only for teaching me that research in politics is about understanding the people involved but also for involving me in your own projects. After equipping me with the relevant theories and tools, you also provided ample room for me to carry out my research with great flexibility and autonomy. This project would not have happened without you.

To Jessica Teets, who has played several significant roles in my academic career, thank you for being a constant source of intellectual generosity, inspiration, and encouragement. The critical commentary and helpful suggestions you provided at every stage of this book were influential and fundamental. And thank you for helping to choose the title of the book.

To Quansheng Zhao, my mentor and advisor for over a decade, thank you for guiding me through academic terrains and empowering me to be outspoken with my ideas in the public sphere. It was also during our discussions about the censorship regime in China that you came up with the term "interactive authoritarianism"—the central theme of this book.

Thanks to my dissertation committee—Joseph Fewsmith, John Gerring, William W. Grimes, Taylor Boas, and Robert Weller—for continuously bringing refreshing and rigorous ideas, suggestions, and guidance to my project and challenging me to be a better scholar in the meantime. To the native speakers who helped me perfect my written English and poured edit marks onto the pages of various chapters of this book—Jessica Teets, Daniel Whitman, Chris Carothers, Benjamin Lynerd, Sydney King, and Mary Hashman —I thank you for your generosity and support.

To the scholars and colleagues who were never reluctant to share your intellectual power with me, thank you for your kindness and inspiration. I have benefited greatly from discussions with Ezra Vogel, Roderick MacFarquhar, Karla Simon, Elizabeth Perry, Yuhua Wang, Marshall Ganz, Adil Najam, Min Ye, Michael Swaine, Amitai Etzioni, Philip J. Crowley, Caroline Reeves, Reza Hasmath, Quansheng Zhao, Cheng Li, Zhiqun Zhu, Xiaoyu Pu, Guoli Liu, Jennifer Pan, Yue Hou, Greg Distelhorst, Yiqing Xu, Chris Carothers, Diana Fu, Iza Ding, Jany Gao, Ling Chen, and Yichen Guan. Also, thanks to Xiaojing Tang and Kara Greenberg for providing technical support during my research.

To the numerous Chinese scholars, incredible research team members, and candid interviewees who made my fieldwork possible, especially Qiang (Braven) Zhang, Qibin Lu, and Hong Guo, thank you for your unwavering support and sometimes taking risks to help me succeed. For reasons that readers will understand, many of you are recognized in the endnotes simply as "interview #X" or remain anonymous at your request, but your observations, thoughts, and analyses grew into this book.

To the institutions that have provided me with resources and platforms while I was researching and writing this book—Christopher Newport University, Boston University, Harvard University, Massachusetts Institute of Technology, American University, George Washington University, Brown University, the University of Michigan, Beijing Normal University, Peking University, Sichuan University, Southwestern University of Finance and Economics, Sichuan Academy of Social Science, Zhejiang University, Nanjing University, Fudan University, Nankai University, and the Global Forum of Chinese Political Scientists—thank you for providing the institutional support to make this book possible. This book also benefited from Christopher Newport University's Faculty Development Grant, Boston University's Graduate Research Abroad Fellowship, and YiFang Foundation's Jing'E Fellowship.

This book includes excerpts from the author's following articles, reprinted with permission. Chapter 3 is a slightly altered version of my article "Deliberate Differentiation by the Chinese State: Outsourcing Responsibility for Governance," published in *The China Quarterly*. Chapter 5 contains revised sections from "Earthquakes and the Typologies of State-Society Relations in China," published in *China Information*. Chapter 6 includes material from a co-authored paper with Quansheng Zhao, "Delegated Censorship: The Dynamic, Layered, and Multistage Information Control Regime in China," published in *Politics and Society*.

To my parents, Jianguo Sun and Meiyun Jiang, thank you for having the vision and insight to always let me push my boundaries and step out of my intellectual comfort zones while not letting me forget my grass roots and culture. To my American host parents, Yvonne and Gary Nehring, thank you for hosting a boy from China twenty years ago, always challenging me to think critically with multiple perspectives, and insisting on supporting my intellectual journey in the United States. To my wife, Tingting, and our son, Jinyu, thank you for being my source of happiness and keeping my world joyful, meaningful, and rewarding.

Sara Cohen and Anna Pohlod at the University of Michigan Press and China Understandings Today series editor Mary Gallagher have been a pleasure to work with, gently hammering the manuscript into a more readable book. The University of Michigan faculty Executive Committee has also provided constructive feedback. Unfortunately, I alone have to take responsibility for the remaining errors and lack of clarity.

PART I

Introduction

Introduction

In the summer of 2014, as I was interviewing Chinese government officials for my doctoral dissertation fieldwork, news broke out that in Zhejiang province officials were taking down the crosses of a few churches. I immediately became curious as to why such actions were taken, especially since those churches were still allowed to continue to operate as places of worship, and such initiatives would only anger their congregants. Of course, I could not resist this opportunity to explore the logic of how the Chinese authoritarian state governs its society while the actions are taking place, and, to my surprise, the officials candidly acknowledged that the government does not gain much utility when the crosses are taken down.

So why do it? Why do it at that specific moment? Why were the actions taken against those specific churches but not others? Also, wouldn't repression be more effective if churches were forced to close down rather than having only the crosses removed? If the state is against the crosses, why allow them to be put up in the first place? To say that there are unbiased policy variations does not do justice to the intricate mechanisms of how the Chinese authoritarian state governs the society, and there is a more systematic and nuanced logic to such state behaviors.

"It was to test the effectiveness of policy commands by the state," the officials—who would prefer to remain anonymous—began to explain to me in detail. The state typically tolerated the newly emerged organizations (churches in this case) and individual actors within the society even if the activities were perceived to have regime-challenging potentials. When the state needs to test its authority, it picks some targets to exercise its repression capacity, and as long as orders are adhered to, and all sides are unambivalent about who the boss is, the episode is temporarily over, and toleration continues. It is neither necessary nor cost-effective to spend additional resources and annihilate the churches when simply taking down the crosses would make the point, especially when such organizations could potentially become useful for effective governance down the road. The state also intentionally saves many targets for later so that such practices of testing the effectiveness of policy commands might be replicated in the future. Churches are also not all the same, and by tolerating their activities, the state also keeps a scorecard for such societal actors. The state is intentional in its differentiation of actors, of the measures used, and in the timing of when repressive steps are taken. The answers to the questions mentioned above are so intriguing that they motivated my research for the next few years and ultimately compelled me to write this book.

My curiosity first made me follow the developments of the cross-removal campaigns. There were rumors that the whole movement was initiated because the then Communist Party secretary of Zhejiang province, Xia Baolong, did not like crosses. The personal taste of a leader might have played a role in the policy implementations, but it was clear that there were more systematic drivers and logics at work, far beyond the personalist explanations—for one thing, the campaigns resurfaced on and off later, even after Xia was no longer working in Zhejiang,[1] and there were plenty of replications of similar behaviors in other provinces, such as Henan and Anhui,[2] with variations in places such as Xinjiang, where domes of mosques were removed.[3] And the direct results of these state actions were the legalization of the appropriate practices with the passing of the "2017 Religious Affairs Regulations"[4] and the "2020 Measures for the Management of Religious Groups."[5] These laws incorporated *a ban* on building large fixtures on the exteriors of churches and temples. The 2004 regulations—the previous version of these laws—stipulated *a process of approval* for building large fixtures on the exteriors of these places of worship[6] and clarified the National Religious Affairs Administration as the direct supervisory unit of all religious organizations. The cross-removal campaigns had directly led to an adjustment in the laws that turned an issue that was previously approvable into a ban. I was beginning to recognize a process from toleration to differentiation to legalization taking place.

Religious organization is only one type of many actors in the nascent Chinese civil society. It was clear that other experiences of state-society interactions that had originated in different provinces, such as the handling of the ethnic activities in Xinjiang, would also make their ways into the stipulations in the regulations mentioned above, through a similar but parallel process—although the timing, methods, and strength of intervention would vary based on local government capacity and circumstances. The more I investigated, the more apparent it became that the procedures and methods of managing civil society organizations (CSOs), even though dynamic and evolving, follow specific patterns. The underlying approach by the state could shed light on the broader question this book intends to address: How do the steps taken by the Chinese state in the above-mentioned example reflect the logic of how China governs its society and prolongs its authoritarian rule? And using China as a case, why are some authoritarian regimes more resilient than others?

CHINA AND AUTHORITARIAN RESILIENCE

Since the 1990s, with the collapse of the Soviet Union and the third wave of democratization of authoritarian regimes, scholars have shown increasing interest in explaining the resilience of those who remain in power, as well as the prospects of their regime transitions. Specifically, Barbara Geddes finds that noncommunist single-party regimes last longer than military and personalist regimes,[7] and Jason Brownlee asserts that uninstitutionalized or patrimonial regimes are not necessarily at a disadvantage, and undemocratic regimes are not inherently fragile.[8] Although some of the longest-running single-party regimes, like the USSR under the Soviet Communist Party or Mexico under the Institutional Revolutionary Party (IRP), have experienced regime changes, the Chinese state under the Chinese Communist Party (CCP) stands out to be a resilient one. What explains those variations?

The comparative authoritarian durability literature has provided three main explanations for authoritarian resilience: legitimacy, good governance, and social control. An authoritarian state could be resilient due to its legitimacy,[9] whether traditional, charismatic, or rational-legal.[10] The authoritarian state should either have decent performance or at least be capable of making people believe that it is performing well.[11] In China's case, legitimacy could be driven by nationalism, based on history,[12] ideology,[13] the state's co-optation,[14] and performance,[15] covering both physical and virtual spaces.[16]

The second group of explanations focuses on good governance, reflected in the policy-making process and the outcome of increased civic participation. Institutions are set up for political participation and appeal that show regime responsiveness and provide accountability.[17] Sometimes specific rules and norms are genuinely set up and followed that prolong the regime.[18] Other times institutions are simply set up as instruments to help the authoritarian rulers govern[19] and structure political power.[20] Good governance also means adaptability[21] and the continued provision of public goods[22] while utilizing sources for consultation.[23] A regime that is willing to experiment with different challenges at the local level,[24] differentiate actors,[25] tolerate civic engagement education[26] in order to increase participation in the political process,[27] and promote successful cases and best practices would also be more resilient.[28] The flexibility in political structure and the willingness to evolve and implement policy experiments could be a significant source of survival.

A third dimension explaining authoritarian resilience focuses on social control and repression. Fearing the threat from popular uprisings, dictators may share rent in exchange for concessions,[29] channel control of the society through "peak associations,"[30] and co-opt private entrepreneurs.[31] Of course, informal coercive institutions and organizations could also be employed to provide regime resilience.[32] The Chinese state has developed a unique repertoire of repression[33] that can range from buying off demonstrators,[34] muting rightful resistance,[35] tactically intercepting petitioners,[36] individualizing strategies to "nip elements of instability in the bud,"[37] and tackling a person's social network,[38] to using thugs,[39] among others that can vary from "soft" to "hard" repression tactics.

Although appealing, those theories are not without shortcomings, especially when examining long-lasting regimes such as China. The often credited revolutionary legitimacy is less and less applicable as time goes by—the younger generation never had any experiences or memories of the humiliations—and performance legitimacy, which benefited from several decades of near continuous growth since the late 1979s, has become a more prominent factor.[40] Yet, with China's gross domestic product (GDP) shrinking by 6.8 percent during the first quarter of 2020, the regime showed no sign of collapsing. More recently, scholars have asserted nationalism as a new source of legitimacy for the Chinese regime. Indeed, it is easy to use nationalism to mobilize support against foreign powers, given China's "one hundred years of humiliation." However, manipulatable incidents do not frequently arise to provide consistent regime resilience, and counting on nationalism could become a double-edged sword for the CCP.[41]

Good governance and policy making provide a sensible alternative in explaining authoritarian resilience in China. However, with the lack of consistent and meaningful vertical accountability,[42] the CCP, being a mobilizational party—as opposed to a rational-legal bureaucracy envisioned by Max Weber—relies heavily on loyalists to accomplish tasks and govern effectively.[43] Many of the rules, whether formal or informal, are not only used as tools by the political elites to govern and are not necessarily equally applicable to those in power, but such rules and laws are also manipulatable and malleable.

There are also certain more nuanced elements overlooked by the social control and repression explanations. The corporatist framework fails to capture the unique phenomenon of the plural and occasionally autonomous nature of many active CSOs in China. And co-optation is a choice with intentional targets and differences in timing; it does not apply to all elites (let alone all people), and only during certain phases of interactions would it be deployed. The plethora of studies that provide intricate depictions of various repression tactics often does not tell us when and why specific tactics are used toward different players.

The arguments connecting adaptability to regime resilience are primarily convincing. Undoubtedly, there were plenty of moments in the history of the People's Republic when the regime could have fallen--from the political and economic grievances that culminated in the 1989 Tiananmen Square incident, to the robust rise of civil society activities after the 2008 Wenchuan earthquake demanding accountability from officials, to increased collective actions by workers not getting paid as they demand their rights, to the age of the internet that facilitates information of official corruptions, and to the desperate calls of loosening restrictions and providing better services to maintain normal lives during COVID-19 lockdowns in cities such as Xi'an and Shanghai in 2022. Any of those moments could have ended the current regime. But the Chinese state was able to adapt and evolve whenever there was a substantive crisis or challenge. More importantly, the regime was not merely adapting to the changing environment and the rising challenges; it often was actively taking the initiative to interact with the societal forces to stimulate its governance apparatus to evolve further. The type of reforms and the space allowed for experimentation are also so mercurial and volatile that the conditions, timing, and scope of permitted policy innovations need to be further investigated to answer why and how they could sustain the resilience of the regime.

An important critique of this literature (including consultative authoritarianism, graduated control, contingent symbiosis, privatization, variations in government approaches, etc.) is that existing theories are often good at explaining the phenomenon, causal relations, and mechanisms when it is region-specific, level-specific, case-specific, and time-specific, yet they may be limited in terms of the ability to generalize across these dimensions. Theories that point out a combination of factors explaining adaptability, flexibility, and differentiation toward different CSOs are often vague in pointing out which factors would be applicable under which conditions. The different explanations mentioned above are not necessarily competing and are sometimes complementary, as they would be more suitable under specific conditions. Still, a multitude of forces could work together during varying phases of state-society interactions under different conditions, and we need a more holistic and interactive approach to map the systematic logic and process of such interactions in order to provide a clearer picture of when which forces are in play.[44] This book builds on this existing scholarship and intends to answer the question "why China's party-state has not collapsed" through the lenses of institutional disruptions; it also provides a unified and dynamic framework and explains the logic and process of how and when different forces become critical drivers of authoritarian resilience. The model proposed in this book differs from the institutionalist arguments in that the key to authoritarian resilience is not in selecting and enforcing the "right" institutions but, rather, in following a learning process that might result in institutions or might not. It is the process that is providing the resilience rather than one particular institution.

THE ARGUMENT IN THIS BOOK

Before elaborating on the core argument in this book, it is necessary to define a few key terms. First, the use of "civil society" and "civil society organizations" or "CSOs" is broader than the typical scope in social science literature. I define "civil society" as the intermediary sphere between the state and the private sphere that is populated by voluntary associations that empower individuals to build networks based on trust and reciprocity. Thus, it not only reflects the classical definition--which analyzes an assemblage of individuals associated by a common acknowledgment of right and by a community of interests--and the sociological definition, which examines an area of social life organized by private or voluntary arrangements between individuals and groups outside the direct control of the state (usually within the public sphere). It also encompasses the more normative and political definition, with the emphasis on legality, private property, markets, and interest groups as well as empowering groups prevented by allegedly prejudiced or selfish elites from interacting on the basis of equality with their fellow citizens. For example, as cases discussed in later chapters demonstrate, how the Chinese state governs private companies follows the logic of how it governs society more than how a typical state regulates its market economy. One could often think of "non-state actors" to conceptualize the term "civil society" discussed in this book, but the choice of the term "civil society" and "civil society organizations" or "CSOs" is partially a matter of convenience, as it is intuitively a well-recognized concept that is used in this sector. The actors within the civil society analyzed in this book thus include not only traditional social organizations (registered or not registered) but also include activities and speeches in the digital space as well as societal actors, such as ride-sharing drivers, who are actively engaged in civil society activities demanding their political and civil rights in both the digital and physical spaces. This book, therefore, recognizes that there are China-specific cases that may not be best described using the term "civil society" and I try to use it only to capture the overall pattern and logic of state-society relations.

In this book I provide a unified *interactive authoritarianism* approach to capture the logic of how the Chinese state governs its civil society. The word "interactive" does not mean the state and society are of equal power and status. In fact, the interactions between the state and society in China are often dominated by state actors; this is not surprising when studying authoritarian politics. However, within this unbalanced relationship, the state intentionally leaves significant operating room for social innovations and unprecedented societal behaviors. Furthermore, what is worth noting, and often not sufficiently captured in the existing literature, is that the Chinese authoritarian state is not only adaptive to new developments and the emergence of new players within the society out of inertia or habit but is also often actively choosing a course of governance that corresponds to the behaviors and influences of societal actors. Being authoritarian means not being responsible to the people while favoring a concentration of power in the controlling elite. Seemingly as an oxymoron, the framework of "interactive authoritarianism" acknowledges that power is still concentrated in a few elites in general but can intentionally be shared with societal actors or not be exercised based on different circumstances of interactions. Civil society can and often does have input in shaping the dynamic and evolving state-society relations in China, especially after major institutional disruptions.

It goes without saying that the Chinese political system is complicated, if not completely opaque. A scholar of Chinese politics would often differentiate the Chinese Communist Party and the state, particularly when discussing state-society relations. The party has survived and thrived in the past few decades, while the state has retreated from society, particularly in the reform era. What is worth noting is that it is not just a matter of state retreating but involves many aspects of society growing up outside of the state, such as private enterprise and intellectuals (not outside the universities but outside the strictures of party ideology and international influence). In order to most efficiently lay out my argument, with full acknowledgment of the party being in control of the state, whenever I use the term "state" in this book, I mean the party-state—a state in which power is held by a single political party, here the CCP. In addition, the term "government" is used to describe those individuals who occupy the ongoing apparatus of the state at various levels.

The interactive authoritarianism framework in this book argues that the Chinese state has adopted an evolving three-stage interactive approach toward civil society actors (individuals or organizations) when new phenomena/forces have been introduced to the society: toleration, differentiation, and legalization without institutionalization. The first of three critical stages of this interactive authoritarianism approach is *toleration*. The toleration stage allows the state to observe and learn specific new civil society activities so that it does not miss out on a suitable governance mechanism or resource. The new activities within the Chinese society are so dynamic and vast that state capacity would be too limited to control everything effectively. Thus, tolerating insignificant actors (whether the state is aware of them or not) and new actors becomes the status quo strategy. When a CSO is newly formed, and the state is unsure of the capacity and intention of the CSO, the state usually chooses to tolerate it with a "wait and see" mentality. Such toleration is usually at the local level when the CSO has limited resources and influence. The local government is confident that existing institutional constraints are sufficient to prevent the tolerated CSOs from mobilizing enough regime-challenging resources. On the other hand, these CSOs, even though they might not be very effective, are essential targets to which the state could shift accountability. By designating and outsourcing specific tasks to such CSOs, local governments maintain the right to claim the credit when tasks are effectively implemented and can blame and replace the scapegoated CSO when citizens are not pleased with the public goods and services provided, thus improving the state's legitimacy. It is a win-win situation for the state and CSOs, as risks are manageable for both parties.

Toleration is seen as the first of the three stages because the preceding "ignorance" stage, in which the state is not aware of the players and activities, is both extremely short and hard to measure. I argue that even "toleration" is often accompanied by an institutional disruption, because without one the state is likely already differentiating the actors or even preparing to legalize certain behaviors or domains. It is also unlikely for new players to keep themselves under the radar for an extended period of time—the state is watching.

While tolerated, local governments start to collect information from those who have the potential to either cause more trouble or provide more public goods and services. Even though specific actions may be taken later during the second stage, differentiation, CSOs may already be differentiated on the local governments' books. The governments might be watching social organizations and their interactions with others (see Case I from chapter 5), or reading online posts without censoring (see Case II from chapter 6), or actively tracking locations, activities, and conversations of ride-sharing drivers (see Case III from chapter 7). Local governments' capacity and the circumstances determine the degree of toleration of CSOs. Local governments that are incapacitated from an institutional disruption (for example, after a major earthquake) or are extremely capable (such as the governments from Zhejiang that removed church crosses) tend to tolerate more. This is true even though decisions from the former are passive ones and the latter are active; such conditions are all part of the interactive authoritarian strategy.

The second stage of this approach is *differentiation*. The differentiation stage allows the state to assess and sort out the intentions and capacities of different actors and try out potential interventions and collaborations. Differentiation includes the *intent to differentiate* (or differentiation on the state's books) and the *act to differentiate* (such as terminating regime-challenging CSOs' legal status or cutting off their funding while actively supporting regime-supporting CSOs). The intent to differentiate can happen throughout the three stages and as early as the state starts to collect information about a particular CSO. The act to differentiate normally happens by the end of the initial toleration stage or after the toleration stage, and this is when the implementation of graduated controls starts. Differentiation can be triggered by an institutional disruption, such as an event or project that requires state-society collaborations, or societal actors crossing some policy red lines. At this stage the local government is more aware of the resources and intentions of the CSOs and may become more familiar with the personnel of the CSOs as well as their political ties and networks. So the focus shifts to soliciting consultations while utilizing resources and expertise from the regime-supporting CSOs and collecting information from and repressing those regime-challenging CSOs, especially those with a collective action potential. The local governments are more responsive to regime-supporting CSOs for their consultative value and public goods delivery potentials. By differentiating the two types of CSOs, the state can better utilize productive forces within the society and reduce political risks for the future. Those seemingly regime-supporting CSOs can provide services, resources, and expertise at a much lower cost than if the government had hired a staff—sometimes it is free.

Nevertheless, those seemingly regime-challenging CSOs posed organizational, informational, and ideological threats. This evolving stage is an intermediary stage in which the CSOs' influences are still limited to a specific locality or a region and the government's confidence in the existing institutional constraints is still high. The government's priority remains to get help from the regime-supporting CSOs rather than to deter the regime-challenging CSOs. The local governments, however, may use this period to test and hone their "regime stability maintenance measures" (维稳手段) so that more effective measures can be used when real and significant challenges to stability occur. This institutional adaptability means differentiations not only happen horizontally between different CSOs but also longitudinally, so some low-risk (but still risky to a certain extent) CSOs might be "saved for later" when the state needs to test its policy effectiveness. The cross-removal campaign mentioned at the beginning of this introduction is an example. If removing the crosses could make the point, it would be neither necessary nor cost-effective to spend additional resources and annihilate the churches. These interactions between the state and society would also help the state better differentiate actors in the society—some could be further exploited; others may need to be contained.

The testing of "regime stability maintenance measures" is a signal that interactive authoritarianism has already entered the differentiation stage. And the exercise of such measures could effectively aid the differentiation process, for those who vehemently resist the state's actions would be seen as untamable and face more repression in the future, while those who obey signal their collaborative potential. Of course, local government officials are not naïve and are not easily fooled. Those who have regime-challenging intentions but choose to hide their aspirations to bide their time temporarily are eventually sifted through repeated state-society interactions with different tools, including those "regime stability maintenance measures."

The third stage, *legalization*, happens toward the end of the second stage when the regime-supporting CSOs have grown sophisticated with some prestige, or when the regime-challenging CSOs' intentions are now evident. The legalization stage solidifies some practices to create legitimacy for the state-society collaborations/co-optations that the state sees beneficial. At this point, policy tools have been accumulated and necessary internal debates within the government have occurred. The government then makes new laws to govern specific types of CSOs and their activities, using laws as instruments. Sometimes a different set of laws govern the differentiated groups. For example, the 2016 Charity Law is intended to govern the supposedly more reassuring and domestic CSOs with the intention to let such CSOs be service providers and policy pioneers, while the 2016 Foreign NGO (Nongovernmental Organization) Law, on the other hand, is intended to govern the supposedly dangerous and foreign CSOs to constrain their space for operations further. The evolving developmental paths of these two laws are discussed in chapter 4.

It is also important to point out that legalization does not mean institutionalization. Rules and laws are made as tools to help the state govern the society, rather than institutions that would also constrain the government's actions. Such rules and laws are, therefore, malleable and sometimes even ephemeral based on the specific conditions, the state's preferences at the time, and the experiences from continued state-society interactions. This means that this three-stage "toleration-differentiation-legalization" process is a continuously evolving dynamic process. When new CSOs join and grow after being tolerated, new dimensions of differentiation are created, and new rules and laws are introduced. Using the cross-removal campaign example, if a new church is to be opened, even after rules and laws have already been made (third stage), given that some other churches have already gone through the three-stage process, it would still experience the whole process, since the new church may be led by a well-connected priest, or it might be exceptionally resourceful, for instance, and thus tolerated at the beginning, although the length spent on each stage could vary. After the toleration stage, the state would then actively interact and choose a differentiation strategy to best outsource responsibility and learn the necessary lessons before adding new stipulations to rules and laws during the third stage. Since the latecomer church did not necessarily join after an institutional disruption, and since others in the same sector have already gone through the process, it may experience the three stages faster than others.

The three stages of interactive authoritarianism happen at multiple levels, with toleration commonly at the local level, then moving up with differentiation happening typically from local to provincial levels, and legalization mostly at higher levels, including the central level. Such a fragmented multilevel approach is part of the design, driven by both clear intentions of officials and constraints that exist in the system. Actors are initially tolerated by local governments partly because they are new and weak, and the state believes that existing institutional constraints are enough to contain any risks. Then, at the differentiation stage, CSOs are more resourceful and capable and thus require the attention from higher-ups within the bureaucracy so that repression can be applied when necessary. However, many of the interactions are still unusual and not widely replicated in the exact same way in different regions, and variations in timing, intensity, and judgment occur based on the individuals involved and the overall political environment. Eventually, at the legalization stage, practices from different localities are solidified into rules and laws that are applicable to the larger society and that require the mobilization of resources at the central level.

The transition between the aforementioned three stages is not marked by clear boundaries, and the stages sometimes overlap. For instance, during the "toleration" stage, the state may have already started accumulating evidence and developing intentions to differentiate without having to take actual actions. Some actors being differentiated might still encounter periods of toleration, especially if these actors are deemed helpful for maintaining regime stability. The pilot programs informing the legalization stage also usually start while the state is interacting with actors during the differentiation stage. Furthermore, the sequence of the three stages may not be strictly chronological but is logical. Major institutional disruptions can change the pace and timing of the three-stage progression, often enlarging the window for CSOs to operate, although tolerating CSOs after institutional disruptions, whether the state is temporarily incapacitated or not, is still part of the interactive authoritarian strategy. Triggers such as collaborations demanded by major projects or events, or regime-challenging actors crossing red lines, can push the process from the "toleration" stage to the "differentiation" stage. Other triggers indicating that certain non-state actors have grown sophisticated with some prestige or regime-challenging actors' intentions have become evident can push them to the "legalization" stage.

The interactive authoritarianism approach builds on the theories of graduated control,[45] consultative authoritarianism,[46] responsive authoritarianism,[47] and the larger "institutions as instruments" and "institutional adaptability" literature by unifying the strategies and behaviors of the Chinese state and pointing out exactly which strategy would be the dominant one in a dynamic interactive process. During different stages and under different circumstances, the state takes different control strategies on various social organizations (graduated control), utilizes citizen participation channels to improve policy making (consultative authoritarianism), increases actual or imagined regime responsiveness (responsive authoritarianism), and sets up rules and norms to govern specific societal domains while adapting whenever necessary (institutions as instruments and institutional adaptability). These strategies and behaviors can appear at different stages under the interactive authoritarianism model or coexist during the same stage.

The interactive authoritarianism approach also provides answers to the conflicting empirical evidence of the more plural nascent civil society activities existing alongside the more state-controlled corporatist mechanisms within the same country. The interactive authoritarianism approach can lead to the resilience of an authoritarian state, because the state can better time the moment and intensity of repression and more accurately target actors in the society for outsourcing responsibilities, leading to improved service provision, more effective propaganda, and more areas for economic growth, including job creation and industrial innovations. This approach is discriminatory, and it limits the costs of repression by targeting specific individuals under specific circumstances through frequent interactions while continuing to facilitate opportunities for activities and expressions for the clear majority of the nonthreatening public. The interactive authoritarianism approach does not, however, suggest that the interaction between the state and society is between relatively equal parties. On the contrary, the overpowering authoritarian state, which could have utilized complete repression against all potential regime-challenging actors at all times, chooses to take the time to proactively interact with—not just reactively adapt to—actors in the society, using different methods and intensity of controls to strengthen its governance capacity in the long run instead.

Of course, major geopolitical events, including changes in international environments or the top/provincial leadership, can accelerate, decelerate, or even reverse the three-stage process. Such factors are discussed further in the case studies in order to better conceptualize the conditions and dynamics of interactive authoritarianism. In the following six chapters, I explore each of those three stages for conceptual clarity before bringing them together and using three case studies in different regions and domains to illustrate how this dynamic and unifying framework could be applicable in various conditions and scenarios.

The interactive authoritarianism approach also reveals that the Chinese state is more resilient than its peers because of—not despite—the institutional disruptions (explained in the next section in this chapter), such as significant challenges and crises the state faces. Those institutional disruptions provide opportunities for adaptation, innovation, and renewal of the state. What doesn't kill you makes you stronger.

INSTITUTIONAL DISRUPTION AS AN IMPORTANT CONDITION FOR ANALYSIS

This book also explores how the Chinese state uses institutional disruptions as opportunities to adapt and enhance its rule. Thus, major shocks to the system are often not destabilizers but important learning catalysts. In this section, I first provide a brief summary of the terms "institution" and "institutional disruption" as used in this book. Then I provide reasons why institutional disruptions are important conditions for the analysis of authoritarian politics, especially Chinese politics.

Institutions, according to Douglass North, are rules of the game or, more formally, humanly devised constraints that shape human interaction.[48] A crucial distinction that North draws between institutions and organizations is that institutions are the rules that define the way the game is played, while organizations are the players. Institutions reduce uncertainty and provide stability to socioeconomic structures and human interactions.[49] Although a vast number of theories in social science are generated by observing the systems or structures when they are stable or undergoing gradual, incremental changes with a relatively high degree of certainty, there are also important benefits to studying them when the institutions (the rules and constraints) are disrupted. I call this moment an "institutional disruption," when the ongoing rules and constraints of a system (whether political, economic, or social) are disrupted by a shock (whether external or internal, human-made or natural), and the system undergoes a process of returning to an old equilibrium or not immediately arriving at a new equilibrium. In this book, I treat institutional disruptions as important windows of opportunity to analyze the logic and limits of authoritarian governance of the society, for many potential constraints may otherwise not be as visible or accessible, and actors, including individuals and organizations riding on inertia, may not be as active when institutional disruptions are not present.

An extensive literature in social science is relevant to the concept of institutional disruption. Two examples of institutional disruptions are disaster and crisis, both of which are unexpected, undesirable, unimaginable, and often unmanageable.[50] A disaster is seen in three major paradigms, including duplication of war, an expression of vulnerability, and an entrance into a state of uncertainty.[51] The taxonomy of crisis also has three types: sudden crisis, creeping crisis, and chronic crisis.[52] In the demographic theory in natural science, institutional disruptions can be captured in the punctuated equilibria model, in which species go through extended periods of stability that are punctuated by short, discrete periods of change caused by either catastrophic events or the steady buildup of stressors.[53] This concept has been adopted by social scientists to capture short-lived periods of uncertainty or conflicts disrupting perceived long eras of stability.[54] During such Knightian uncertainty, agents are sometimes unsure as to what their interests are, let alone how to realize them.[55] Other social scientists have referred to similar moments as "critical junctures,"[56] "moments of original sin,"[57] "external shocks,"[58] "focusing events,"[59] and "external perturbations,"[60] among an enormous literature with various aspects of unique features.

While the literature is extensive, almost all of the authors are examining the causes of such institutional disruptions or their consequences.[61] Rather than being an accident of reality, such moments could be the representation of reality,[62] a crisis in communication,[63] or the revelation of existing problems.[64] A key point of debate among scholars is whether such institutional disruptions would have policy implications and, if so, what type of implications. These moments could be windows of opportunity for reform,[65] and the wider the window, the more coherent the coalition of policy entrepreneurs and the higher the possibility for legally constraining norms to emerge.[66] Other scholars also discuss the opportunity for social organizations,[67] the introduction of new policy approaches,[68] radical changes,[69] centralization of decision-making,[70] heightened state power and control,[71] and catalyst for reform and changes[72] as potential consequences. On the other hand, scholars such as Gilberto Capano warn against the tendency to link policy changes to arbitrarily selected exogenous phenomena and, as a result, having these exogenous events easily become a sweeping explanation for policy change and a source of confirmation bias.[73]

Although the immediate consequences of institutional disruptions are of theoretical and empirical importance, [74] what I focus on in this book are the unique conditions that institutional disruptions can bring. At the moment of institutional disruption, existing institutional arrangements are under pressure, and previously unrevealed constraints may become visible. Actors, especially the state, could no longer operate with inertia, for inaction could be seen as a failure. The restitutive mechanisms of the system in place may no longer function well, and the state may be forced to make decisions and choices.

In the case of studying state-society relations in the Chinese authoritarian state, the benefits are threefold. The first benefit is data accessibility. During an institutional disruption, existing constraints could suddenly become ineffective or irrelevant. The state could either be bogged down with dealing with a crisis or disaster or, more simply, a new phenomenon in the society and could not immediately afford to assert as much control during normal times. Data access could be less restricted, and government officials could have more freedom to share their thoughts lacking strict orders that might otherwise forbid them to do so. More importantly, such moments allow researchers to observe the dynamic process of policy evolution from the moment of disruption to the point when it is back to normal.

The second benefit is that there are simply more activities within the nascent civil society when there is a power vacuum due to an institutional disruption. Since the subject of study is state-society relations and civil society, it is beneficial for researchers to capture the moment when there are nascent forms of civil society activities, which could be entirely interfered with or contained during regular times.

A third benefit, and probably the most important methodologically, is that such moments better mimic real conditions of interest. Quite often the purpose of the study for many scholars of authoritarianism is to look at potential changes and evolutions (topics such as democratization, authoritarian resilience, or even revolution). These conditions are possible only when the state is under high pressure or faced with unprecedented challenges with high degrees of uncertainty. By looking at institutional disruptions, researchers can observe such conditions (albeit under different circumstances) so that generalizability and the credibility of inferences are likely to improve because the data used for inference are also collected under similar conditions.

The three critical institutional disruptions I examine in this book include an earthquake and the rapid development of CSOs, a new type of self-media publication online, and social media–based guerilla protests in the newly developed ride-sharing industry. The first is an exogenous shock by nature, the second is a disruption to the CCP-dominated media field, and the third is a disruption to both the transportation industry and old ways of organized collective action. The details and the rationale for selecting each of those cases are discussed in the next section of this chapter. For each of those three cases, existing institutional arrangements were temporarily disrupted, and the state had no immediately adequate mechanisms to deal with the new activities and the new players systematically. Immediately after a major earthquake, the constraints of governance suddenly changed from the pressure to deliver high growth to the necessity to recover. Many operational rules and norms were abruptly altered, providing unique opportunities for societal actors such as volunteers and civil society organizations to play more active roles. At the same time, information control was a vital part of CCP governance and control, and the self-media publications, springing up rapidly during the internet age, fundamentally changed the rules and magnitude of censorship, creating new challenges and opportunities for both the societal forces and the state. Meanwhile, the transportation industry in China used to be limited to a few manageable state-affiliated or state-controlled entities. However, with the startling rise of the car-sharing sector, in which virtually anybody could easily participate and in which participating drivers have high mobility and are well-connected through the internet with other drivers, such arrangements quickly disrupted the old status quo constraints the CCP placed on this sector, thus creating another institutional disruption. Although I do not disagree with North in terms of the result over time producing a new equilibrium that is not that different from the status quo and far less revolutionary,[75] during that moment there were still meaningful insights that could be observed, analyzed, and evaluated. The difference between North's "discontinuous institutional change" and the "institutional disruption" discussed in this book is that the former refers to a process while the latter describes a point in time.

METHODS AND DATA

Getting data from an authoritarian state can be challenging, especially in a diverse and multilevel state such as China. Multiple empirical strategies were, therefore, utilized from 2012 to 2022 to collect the necessary data. Surveys were conducted in 126 villages in Sichuan province, and over twelve hundred responses were collected. About seventy interviews were conducted with CSO leaders and government officials in Sichuan, Guangdong, and Zhejiang provinces. Participant observation was utilized to closely follow the activities of CSOs and ride-sharing drivers' messaging groups. Several self-media publications were set up on WeChat, Weibo, and Toutiao, so that the mechanisms of censorship toward Chinese political scientists' commentaries could be documented. In the meantime, an experiment and a natural experiment were conducted. I briefly discuss each of these empirical strategies and the data collected here.

I became interested in this project immediately after the 2008 Wenchuan earthquake, an 8.0 magnitude earthquake that struck the western province of Sichuan, China. Just as I felt empathetic toward the families who lost loved ones, I was also inspired and touched by the rise of volunteerism and the civil society–like associational behaviors in the quake-stricken region. Many organizations that were unregistered, and therefore illegal, were filling the power vacuum where the government was incapacitated in delivering public goods and services. What I had in mind, therefore, was to compare whether the tolerance of such CSOs and individuals' attitudes toward those CSOs were different between the quake-stricken region and other regions that were not affected, assuming earthquakes create a series of institutional disruptions. This is a typical natural experiment design where the treatment (earthquake), even though not assigned by the researcher, was such an exogenous shock that we could assume the specific location and time to hit was "as if random." For logistical reasons, as well as the more apparent ethical reasons, I cannot control and introduce an earthquake. At the meantime, with the assumption that the earthquake was random, I could, to a certain degree, assume that any significant differences between the quake-stricken region and the non-affected region had something to do with the activities and developments within the condition, and institutional disruption, that the earthquake created.

This initial design covered forty-three counties—most of the counties accessible and being west of the Chengdu-Kunming railroad as well as the

The Post Treatment Study with the Wenchuan 08' and Lushan 13' Earthquakes

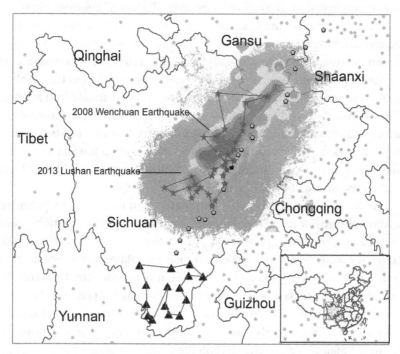

The lines connecting the stars and triangles (counties) are the travel routes the researchers took

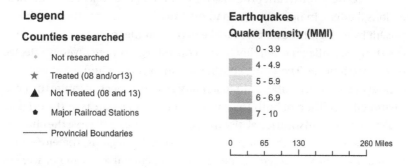

Figure 1. The region covered in the post-treatment study.

entire ethnic Yi region—from Sichuan province to mimic the remote rural population in China. The difference between these rural counties—in terms of economic development, social structure, and modernization level—is smaller than when urban counties and cities are also included.[76] The major reason to use the Chengdu-Kunming railroad as a cutoff line was that on the east side of the railroad, counties faced "contamination" from the development of the metropolitan city of Chongqing. In order to take into account different levels of access to transportation within the region mentioned above, counties were randomly selected within the block of counties that are less than 50 kilometers away from the nearest railroad station and within the block of counties that are more than 50 kilometers away (117km the farthest) both in the control and treatment region.

While the post-treatment observational data under a natural experiment setup could provide important evidence, there are crucial assumptions made that may not hold true. For example, one major assumption is that the villagers or communities before the earthquake would be almost identical or generally similar in both regions. However, it is unfortunate, theoretically, that the quake-stricken region (northern Sichuan) happened to be more developed on most economic indicators and also more diverse ethnically. For example, there were six different ethnic groups in my sample from the north but mainly one (ethnic Yi) from the south.

About two months after the first round of data was collected from those regions, Ludian, in northern Yunnan province bordering southern Sichuan, was hit by a magnitude 6.1 earthquake in the summer of 2014. Twelve out of the thirty-six villages originally in the control region were severely affected by the earthquake. Therefore, another round of surveys and interviews was conducted from December 2014 to January 2015 in order to capture the post-treatment condition of both the control and treatment areas in the original design. This new institutional disruption allowed me to observe the changes that occurred in both the affected and non-affected regions, therefore making it a difference-in-difference design. Just imagine if a researcher were to test the effectiveness of a new drug, and the original design measured two groups of people only *after* they took the drug or the placebo. The new design now provides information about participants both before and after taking the drug or the placebo—therefore considering the initial differences between the two groups—and allows the researcher to study the "change" (or improvement) that had occurred rather than the outcome (whether it is cure rate, mortality rate, or other indicators) only.

The Difference-in-Difference study with the Ludian earthquake 14'

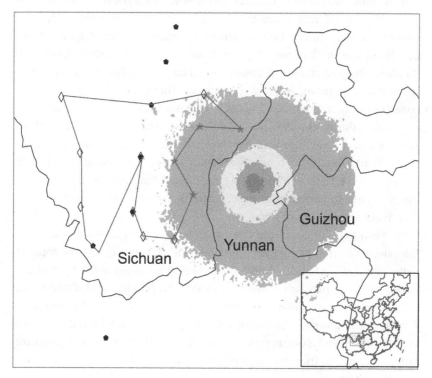

The lines connecting the stars and diamonds (counties) are the travel routes the researchers took

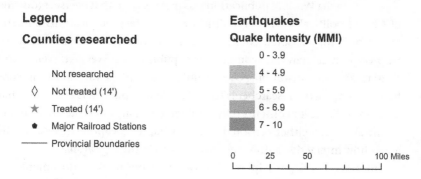

Legend

Counties researched

        Not researched

◇   Not treated (14')

★   Treated (14')

⬟   Major Railroad Stations

—— Provincial Boundaries

Earthquakes

Quake Intensity (MMI)

0 - 3.9

4 - 4.9

5 - 5.9

6 - 6.9

7 - 10

0   25   50   100 Miles

Figure 2. The region covered in the difference-in-difference study.

Furthermore, in my study both the post-treatment observational data and the difference-in-difference data were utilized for the observations that took place at different times in relationship to the earthquake. The two rounds of observations of the difference-in-difference study happened two months before and four months after the earthquake—relatively close to the incident. The post-treatment observational data was collected six years after the major earthquake, and one year after another big earthquake that happened in a similar proximity. The CSOs were able to develop, evolve, and professionalize during the five years after the 2008 earthquake and were able to practice and further improve what they had learned during the 2013 earthquake. Thus, the CSOs in these observations were more developed and effective in general. CSOs that initially were created but later failed or stopped operating due to various reasons were also included in the sample, making "survivorship bias" less of a concern.

Government officials from the village level to the provincial level were interviewed so that I could get the state's side of the story. On the topic of deliberate differentiation, I also made use of an experiment by sending emails to 114 county-level governors in Sichuan province, inquiring about setting up a new social organization. The governors were randomized into two different groups; the treatment group saw an additional sentence describing the social organization as politically sensitive, while the control group did not see that description. The results of this experiment are discussed in chapter 3.

A self-media WeChat publication was first set up so that overseas (outside of China) political scientists' political commentary publications and the record of being censored could be recorded, followed by publications of Sino-US political news and commentaries published in WeChat, Weibo, and Toutiao for comparison purposes. A unique advantage of publishing contents directly by the researcher is that the intent to publish is known so that data are available for contents that are at least initially attempted to be made public and then either censored or not. Chapter 6 captures those details about how interactive authoritarianism works in the digital space.

Interviews and participant observations were used to document the activities of various CSOs, including officially registered organizations, newly formed and yet-to-be-registered organizations, as well as loose networks of ride-sharing drivers who would share GPS (global positioning system) locations of themselves with other drivers within the network so that others who were also on wheels would immediately arrive on the scene to protest together in helping the original driver. The details of these guerilla protests are discussed in chapter 7.

After this introduction, in chapter 1 I first discuss the overall trend of civil society development in China and the key players in state-society relations. Then I use three chapters to capture the process of authoritarian tolerance, deliberate differentiation, and legalization without institutionalization. Chapter 2 provides the background and analysis of how and why the authoritarian state chooses to tolerate rather than completely block civil society activities. Chapter 3 uses interview evidence and the field experiment of sending emails to county governors to demonstrate how this deliberate differentiation exists on a systematic level and the logic behind such policy outcomes. Chapter 4 traces the process of lawmaking in the governance of CSOs and focuses particularly on the bifurcation of that process, leading to two different sets of laws (the Charity Law and the Foreign NGO Law) under two different departments (civil affairs and public security).

Subsequently, I use three cases to illustrate the logic of interactive authoritarianism in further detail. The cases are structured as a most-different-case design, for the cases are similar in just one independent variable (the three-stage approach of toleration, differentiation, and legalization) and in the dependent variable (authoritarian resilience in terms of improved service, more effective propaganda, and more areas for economic growth and job creation), while all other plausible factors show different values.[77] For the three cases discussed respectively in chapters 5, 6, and 7, their type of disruption, space occupied, administrative region, and key actors are all different. Yet, for each of those cases, there is the same pattern of toleration, differentiation, and legalization, and the state is prospering in those domains while the nascent civil society, after a few years, is severely constrained.

The state-society relations in China (and authoritarian countries in general) are complex, not just complicated. I, thus, follow Yuen Yuen Ang's approach by "systematically situating particular moments in a temporal sequence . . . and map the mutual adaptation"[78] to illustrate the dynamic nature of the interactive authoritarianism approach. The cases all focus on the period between the time when the institutional disruptions shock their respective fields and the time some laws and rules are made (what I call legalization without institutionalization), although some basic references to the paths the state-society relationship had taken in that sector prior to the disruption are also briefly discussed. I document the key adjustments in the state's approach in managing the society and capture reciprocal feedback

TABLE 1. The "most different case" design of the three cases in this book

Cases	Disruption (condition)	Space occupied	Difference in region	Different key actors	Tolerance	Tools and tactics for differentiation	Legalization and bifurcation	Outcome
CSOs in Sichuan	Earthquake	Physical space in localities	Rural	CSOs	Un-registered "illegal" associations allowed to exist	Crackdown vs. Registration, funding	Charity Law and Foreign NGO Law	More local public goods and service delivery
Self-media on WeChat	Technological innovation	Virtual space	National and international	Individuals, online communities, private companies	Critical thinking, diverse discourses, perspectives allowed	Censorship vs. ad. Revenue and influence (interview opportunities)	2017年6月1日,《互联网新闻信息服务管理规定》《网络安全法》	More supportive material, occasional policy recommendations
Ride-sharing communities	Market demand, technological innovation	Virtual + physical	Urban	Groups of (full-time and part-time) drivers	Individual anti-entrapment guerilla protest allowed	Harsher inspection vs. market revenue return	2018 年2月,交通运输部办公厅下发了关于《网络预约出租汽车监管信息交互平台运行管理办法》	More shared rides, service provided

from key parties involved, using both quantitative and qualitative data whenever appropriate. This book, therefore, considers the variations of different cases, different developmental stages of CSOs, different levels and departments of the government, as well as the policy-forming processes of the government.

The Sichuan earthquakes provide an opening—a case of "institutional disruption" that many predicted would generate civil society in China. Indeed, as we will see from the data, social capital was developed, but the state was able to evolve and adapt to maintain control of the public sphere. If we look at other aspects of Chinese society, we see similar processes going on. Look at "self-media" (explained in chapter 6 in detail) that operates in the virtual space and the ride-sharing sector (explained in chapter 7 in detail), which links both the physical and virtual spaces, parallel processes of interactive authoritarianism exist in those cases that had led to similar outcomes, despite their differences in disruptions, regions, and key actors involved (see table 1 below). The concluding chapter (Chapter 8) discusses the implications of such an approach and future prospects for civil society and authoritarian governance in China.

CHAPTER 1

Governing the Nascent Civil Society in China
Background and Key Players

The role of the state in society, especially charitable activities, has been crucial throughout Chinese history. State-stipulated charitable activities can be
traced back to 400 BC. "The Book of Rites" (礼记), a Chinese classical work
on royal regulations, includes details about where the elderly would have
received their nourishment:

> Those of fifty years received their nourishment in the (school of the) districts;
> those of sixty, theirs in the (smaller school of the) state; and those of seventy,
> theirs in the college. This rule extended to the feudal states. An old man of
> eighty made his acknowledgment for the ruler's message, by kneeling once
> and bringing his head twice to the ground. The blind did the same.[1]

Such ancient texts meticulously record the state's responsibility as the
preeminent humanitarian benefactor and establish that aid-giving is the
responsibility of the ruler, reducing "the people" to mere beneficiaries of the
imperial charity. Charitable activities serve as a tool to fortify the relationship between the ruler and the people. It is clear here that the process of
receiving nourishment is, on the one hand, an opportunity for the state to
provide public goods and services to its people and, on the other hand, an
occasion to affirm the state's legitimacy and absolute superiority over the
society. Such practices continued throughout Chinese history, such as estab-
lishing public hospitals (*pujiu bingfang* 普救病坊) in the Tang dynasty (618–
907 AD); the Futian institution (*futian yuan* 福田院), a temple run, state-
funded, charity in the Song dynasty (960–1279 AD); and many others since
the Song dynasty.[2] Historically, the Chinese people viewed the rulers as play-

ing the role of "parents" (*fumuguan* 父母官)—at least that was the expectation from the elites—so the informal institutions of "the state taking care of everyone" existed throughout history.

Unexpectedly, even though state activities in society have been dominant, they did not crowd out activities in society completely, for China has mostly been lightly governed. At first glance, one could be mistaken that imperial China seems to be a typical autocracy in which the supreme political power is concentrated in the hands of the emperor, whose decisions are subject to neither external legal restraints nor regularized mechanisms of popular control. However, the effect of such decisions has been drastically reduced as orders reach down through the administrative system.

Imperial China did not have a large formal bureaucracy to tightly control every aspect of society. The Confucian approach of small and frugal governance played an important role in leading to that outcome. As the population grew, the size of the bureaucracy did not change much. In the sixteenth century and the first half of the seventeenth, there were ten to fifteen thousand officials for the whole of the empire.[3] The Chinese population at the time was about 200 million,[4] so there were only 1–1.5 officials for every twenty thousand people. Such a ratio means that there were not enough civil servants to ensure effective control of the population, giving more flexibility for other social forces and informal institutions such as the scholar-gentry class and clan rules to be applied in governance. There are still legacies of such arrangements in local governance today. For example, temples and lineage systems still lead to government accountability and the provision of public goods and services, even without formal democratic institutions in rural China.[5] Therefore, most activities within the society are tolerated by the state, and there is a high degree of flexibility and variation by location and time, as long as the social forces are not interpreted as potentially challenging the authoritarian rule.

Since the People's Republic of China (PRC) was founded in 1949, due to the totalitarian nature of the Mao Zedong era, society is no longer lightly governed. The people of China were constantly mobilized for political campaigns for ideological unity, and any deviational thoughts and behaviors from the party-state line could be fatal. However, even under this totalitarian period, when there were factional conflicts within the top leadership, spaces in the society were occasionally created. For example, right after the Great Leap Forward and the famine afterward, the planners (such as Liu Shaoqi and Deng Xiaoping) wanted to try the household responsibility system even though Mao strongly opposed such attempts. As the top leaders debated, local villagers in Anhui secretly experimented with the household responsibility system. Peasants who met the grain quota could keep the extra beyond the quota, moving away from the collective corporative model, under which everything each household produced belonged to the collective. Even though these trials at the local level were short-lived, they paved the way for the promotion of the household responsibility system years later, which triggered the "reform and opening" era starting in the late 1970s.[6]

CIVIL SOCIETY OR CORPORATISM?

Since the 1980s there have been discussions about the emergence of civil society in China. Especially in the reform and opening era, with particular attention to the spring of 1989, for example, scholars observed a "sudden, massive spread of civil society," "nascent civil society," and "emergent civil society."[7] Chinese CSOs developed at a rapid pace in the three decades following the Tiananmen incident. Therefore, the question of whether civil society could emerge without formalized democratic institutions has been contested.

Optimists consider the progress made by China and many other authoritarian countries remarkable. Even though the state still, to some extent, represses civil society, the nascent civil society has overcome fear and is pushing against constraints and opening up spaces.[8] Pessimists, on the other hand, point out that the fundamentals have not changed and that there are limits and constraints that society has to face.[9] For scholars specifically studying China, theories of Sino-exceptionalism, graduated control, and consultative authoritarianism have been proposed to distinguish the Chinese model from Western liberal democracies.[10]

While the question of whether China has a civil society is already multifaceted, how civil society could be potentially organized also draws different frameworks. There are two major frameworks in conceptualizing civil society in China: the civil society framework and the state-corporatist framework. The civil society framework, tracing from Alexis de Tocqueville's *Democracy in America*, describes civil associations' relationships with democratization and how a robust autonomous civil society can check and monitor state power.[11] Proponents of this framework draw evidence from Chinese history,[12] as well as the rise of political liberalism in China in the early 1980s (with the 1989 Tiananmen student movement, in particular), to claim that there was once a nascent form of civil society in China and that we are seeing the resurgence of that society today.[13] The state-corporatist framework, on the other hand, asserts that the authoritarian state does not easily give up space. In fact, the state finds it effective to control society through "peak associations."[14] The state recognizes one and only one organization in each sector and creates an unequal relationship with them so that control can be channeled through this vertical hierarchy.[15]

The civil society framework underestimates the state's involvement and its dominant role in associational lives in authoritarian countries like China, yet the state-corporatist description also fails to capture the unique phenomenon of the plural and occasionally autonomous nature of many existing CSOs in China. The emergence of civil society is certainly a positive development in China. However, as discussed above, it is not clear whether the government will keep interfering from the top down with such developments and control such a space to the extent that it only helps the survival of the regime, or rather, allows a gradual freeing up of the space, both of which seem to be unfeasible for China's civil society.

A few scholars have discussed the possibility of looking at the local level rather than the elite level for civil society building in China.[16] Even at the local level, it is difficult to have meaningful reforms, because there are no incentives for the creation of meaningful constraints on actors, particularly stakeholders. Therefore, the literature points to limited space between the private sphere and the state in China. Institutions operating in such a space struggle for their legal recognition, autonomy, scope of influence, and their overall survival.

Alternatively, some scholars have pointed out the uniqueness of the China case—given Chinese CSOs' distinct relationship with the state—that CSOs may not be in their interest to defy the state and that strategic alliance with the state is mutually beneficial.[17] Blurring the boundary between the state and society is sometimes seen as the consequence of an assertive authoritarian state[18] and, in other times, a more nuanced caption of the state being a shifting, contradictory process in constant articulation with other social elements.[19]

The state-society interactions in China not only have a long history, but the above discussions also point out the complexity and diversity of how such relations are conceptualized, particularly at the local level. In order to provide meaningful and systematic analyses, the cases in this book focus on a few key actors from the society and the state. I discuss each of them briefly in the next section.

KEY SOCIETAL PLAYERS IN THE STATE-SOCIETY RELATIONS IN CHINA

CSOs

There are three main types of key players within the nascent Chinese civil society that figure prominently in the analysis to follow: CSOs, self-media, and ride-sharing drivers. These are actors that differ in their nature of operations, sizes, and goals and have been picked intentionally to construct the "most-different-case" design in order to illustrate that even with such different actors within the society, the logic of how to govern them is consistent.

CSOs, or civil society organizations, are voluntarily organized associational entities operating for the pursuit of shared interests by individuals within the civil society that are non-state, outside of the family, non-market, not for profit, and either officially registered or not. CSOs encompass a wide range of entities, including underground churches, community orchestras or dance groups, international aid organizations, and industry associations, among others. This means that CSOs could be local, national, or international; legal or illegal; political or nonpolitical.

CSOs are non-state actors, which means they are not organized by the state or don't belong to the state bureaucracy. Entities that have state affiliations or projects that provide services purchased by the state are still considered as CSOs in this book. Being "non-market" means CSOs are not businesses per se. Due to political and legal pressures, it is a common practice for CSOs to register as businesses, for businesses are treated more favorably than CSOs registered as social groups, social service groups (previously referred to as "People Run Non-Enterprises" 民办非企业), or foundations. Therefore, even when an organization is registered as a business, as long as the organization's work meets the definition provided above, it is still considered as a CSO. Being "not-for-profit" also does not mean the organization could not generate revenues or profits. Profit is the difference between revenue and cost. Since all operating organizations have costs, it is important to have some source of revenue (donations, funding, or fees for services provided.) Sometimes an organization does well and its revenue is much higher than its costs. As long as that profit is not distributed as dividends and is still used to further the mission of the organization, it is considered not-for-profit. In other words, a profit can occur as long as the purpose of the organization is not to maximize profit but to achieve the organization's specified missions.

NGO, short for nongovernmental organization, is a term that many researchers and practitioners choose to use when capturing organized activities in the third sector. In this book, I treat NGOs as a subgroup of CSOs that are formally organized. Informal entities such as a temporary community earthquake rescue team would be considered CSOs but not NGOs.

Self-Media

A second major category of key players in the Chinese nascent civil society is self-media (自媒体). Self-media refers to independently operated social media that publish text, audio, and video on various platforms. Although there are overlaps between self-media and CSOs, there are also self-media accounts operated by individuals or with for-profit motivations that may not be identified as a typical CSO but are still active players within the Chinese civil society. Self-media do not necessarily have to follow state media discourses and sometimes cover events and issues and provide commentaries in a way that is quite different from the official line. Such platforms include WeChat, Sina Weibo, Toutiao, Zhihu, and TikTok. The most popular platform was previously Sina Weibo (China's Twitter) because commoners could directly follow or even interact with celebrities. In the 2010s, attention shifted to WeChat because it combines features of WhatsApp, Facebook, Instagram, Twitter, and PayPal with additional functions in a single platform. Furthermore, Toutiao and TikTok are also becoming major self-media platforms that cannot be ignored.

WeChat broke the one billion active users per month mark at the end of 2018.[20] The WeChat official accounts platform allows individuals to publish original content (articles, often with pictures and videos) that could spread quickly among WeChat users, because users can subscribe to specific official accounts and share interesting content produced by others on their personal pages. Given the platform's popularity, many state media felt it was necessary to register their own WeChat official accounts so that they did not lose this important viewership on WeChat. Even though censorship has become stricter on self-media, especially if someone is producing original content, self-media continues to be an important player in state-society relations in terms of revealing scandals of officials, providing multi-perspective narratives on stories, or simply bringing people's attention to important public issues.

Ride-Sharing Drivers

Ride-sharing drivers are individuals who offer rides using their privately owned or rented vehicles for a fee. Through a transportation network company (like Uber), passengers can request rides in a taxi-like fashion through an app and over the internet. In this book, I distinguish ride-sharing drivers from taxi drivers, since with the former the method of getting the ride (only over the internet), vehicles used, the number of groups of passengers allowed (more than one), and flexibility in working hours (flexible) is significantly different. Ride sharing is a newly emerged industry based on technological innovations in the past few decades, while the taxi industry is well established and has been around for a long time. Ride-sharing drivers provide rides to others in a more casual way. For this book, the ride-sharing drivers' network is also a different political force than that of taxi drivers, even though the history of the ride-sharing industry originated from the taxi industry.

The ride-sharing industry came about in China around 2012 when Didi (aka Didi Chuxing or Didi Dache) started to test the waters in the city of Beijing. It was then designed as a platform for taxi drivers. Realizing that there might be a mismatch of the demand and supply of taxi rides, Didi provided significant financial incentives for taxi drivers who would install the app on their cell phones and use Didi's system for managing reservations and rides. The number of registered drivers on Didi grew to 350,000, with over 20 million users by the end of 2013.[21] By 2015 Didi had already covered 360 major cities in China, with 1.35 million drivers. About 80 percent of taxi drivers in China use Didi.[22]

About the same time when Didi was launched, another company called Kuaidi also started its service in the city of Hangzhou and was soon backed by Alibaba, one of China's most influential tech giants. The competition for market share led both companies to burn through investors' cash by offering drivers and riders bonuses when using their platforms. In July 2014 both Didi and Kuaidi launched a private car-sharing service called ZhuanChe (or specialized cars). Private cars that met the standards (usually luxury cars with a specified minimum wheelbase) were tapped by the platform, and targets for bonuses started to shift from taxi drivers to private car drivers. With Uber also entering the Chinese market in July 2014, private car owners started to enjoy the benefits that taxi drivers had been enjoying for the previous year and a half. Among various competing platforms such as Meituan, Shenzhou, Caocao, and Shouqi, Didi already had more than 550 million users and 31 million drivers in 2018.[23]

The ride-sharing drivers are different from CSOs and self-media because the drivers' priority is to make a profit, and they are connected because of a transportation network company. However, the focus of this book is their organized collective actions against government officials and the taxi industry. Their informal yet extremely effective networks are discussed, and I explain how such networks resemble CSOs in more detail in chapter 7.

The three key players within the Chinese nascent civil society being discussed here—the CSOs, self-media, and ride-sharing drivers—are neither mutually exclusive nor exhaustive in representing the players occupying this domain. There are aspects that they share, but they also have unique aspects in how they affect state-society relations in China. This book provides an in-depth analysis of these players and their direct interactions with respective government departments.

KEY STATE ACTORS THAT GOVERN THE SOCIETY

The Branches and Lumps of the Chinese State

When discussing the Chinese state, many people (including some scholars in academia) might automatically assume that it is one holistic player dealing with every issue like a Leviathan. This depiction could not be further from reality. Not only are there dynamics between the party and different branches of the state (the National People's Congress, the State Council, the Supreme People's Court, the Supreme People's Procuratorate, and the military), but factions within the party and each branch, the variations of policy implementation in a decentralized system, and the regional differences in circumstances make the approaches to governance diverse and complex.

If one tries to understand how the Chinese state governs the society, it is important to understand the "branches and lumps" (条条块块, or *tiaotiaokuaikuai*) of the government. *Tiao* (branches) refers to the vertical lines of authority over specific sectors reaching down from the central government to the local level. On each of those vertical lines, there are five and a half levels,[24] including the central, provincial, municipal, county level, townships, plus a quasi-official village level, which is referred to as a "half" level.[25] For example, on the issue of ecology and environment, there is the central government (which leads the Ministry of Ecology and Environment), provincial ecology and environment departments, municipal ecology and environment agencies, county ecology and environment bureaus, township ecology and environment teams, and relative individuals in charge of the issue within a village. The administrative systems that govern the nascent civil society are more complex than that of ecology and environment, and that particular structure is discussed in detail in this book. Along this vertical line of authority, each level listens to the orders given by the level above and gives orders to the level below or implements the orders.

Besides the branches (*tiao*, the vertical lines of authority), there are also the lumps (*kuai*, the horizontal lines of authority) that each level of government uses to coordinate. While the branches are organized based on functions, the lumps are organized based on the needs of the locality they govern. For example, a typical provincial government has about two dozen departments, such as the Department of Education, the Department of Science and Technology, the Department of Public Security, the Department of Civil Affairs, the Department of Finance, and many others. Such lumps exist at every level of the official government structure.

There are four intertwined and coexisting governing structures in China: the Chinese Communist Party (CCP) system, the state government, the National People's Congress (NPC), and the Chinese People's Political Consultative Conference (CPPCC). The first two are this book's focus, as they are more directly involved in day-to-day governance. At every level of the government, there are officials of the party and officials of the state. The CCP head of a province is usually ranked number one in a province, and the governmental head (or governor of the province) is usually ranked number two. While the party and the state's branch and lump structures generally mirror each other (the number one ranked official in the provincial ecology and environment department is the party secretary of the department and the number two ranked official is the department chief), the CCP structure does have its unique branches. For instance, the Office of the Central Cyberspace Affairs Commission is a CCP branch and has an office or staff at every level of the structure. At each level, the office is also part of the CCP propaganda department lump.

Such a complex multilevel branches and lumps structure creates conflicts within the hierarchy. Furthermore, some individuals hold concurrent positions at different levels of the hierarchy. Therefore, to make the ranking clearer, the Chinese bureaucracy came up with a nomenclature system that identifies each official at a specific administrative rank (national/central 国, central department/provincial 部, provincial department/municipal 厅局, municipal departments/county 处, department divisions/township 科). Sometimes, based on the number of people a person is supervising or the importance of the position, certain individuals may enjoy a higher or lower administrative rank than their peers within the same lump. Individuals outside of the government may also enjoy an administrative rank. For instance, presidents of the top thirty-one major universities enjoy the same ranking as a deputy governor of a province or a deputy director of a central department. However, even with this administrative ranking system, there are still problems and conflicts that can arise given this complex system. Under the branches system, a provincial Office of Cyberspace Affairs takes orders from the Office of the Central Cyberspace Affairs Commission. But under the lumps system, the same office should also take orders from the provincial CCP propaganda department. When the orders are different from the branches and lumps, there is a conflict, and there are no clear and standard mechanisms to resolve the conflict, since those giving orders enjoy the same rank and do not have to listen to each other. The lump usually reflects local interests, and the branch usually pays special attention to the functional specialty of the issue, so this dilemma is also a focal point of the center-local power struggle.

Civil Affairs

There are three main types of branches within the Chinese state and the CCP that figure prominently in the analysis to follow: Civil Affairs, Public Security, and Cyberspace Affairs. The first two are a part of the state structure, and the latter is a part of the CCP structure. The Ministry of Civil Affairs was founded in 1978, replacing the Ministry of Internal Affairs. Its jurisdictions include caring for the disabled, the homeless, senior care, child care, people in poverty, and people's livelihood and welfare in general, including disaster response. It also is in charge of family issues such as marriage and funerals. The most important function regarding governing society is its jurisdiction over charitable activities and social organizations.

The Office of Civil Affairs at every level of the government is where CSOs are officially registered. For a long time, China was a corporatist system where only one interest representing a group of a kind could be registered at each level within a locality. This means that Civil Affairs officials made sure there were no redundant existing CSOs that were already doing similar work before they would officially register a group. Before 2004, CSOs were under a "dual management system." They needed to find a Professional Supervisory Unit (PSU) as a sponsor, usually a government agency in a similar field, and then register with the Ministry of Civil Affairs. Therefore, that ministry also shared responsibilities with other government offices in regulating CSOs.

After 2004, with the passing of the 2004 "Regulation on Foundation Administration" (*jijinhui guanlitiaoli* 基金会管理条例, hereafter referred to as the "2004 Foundation Regulations"),[26] CSOs were given more freedom, and foundations organized by private individuals could register directly with the Ministry of Civil Affairs. A few years later, given the robust growth of CSOs after the 2008 Wenchuan earthquake, in 2011 the then minister of Civil Affairs, Li Liguo, said during the National Civil Affairs working meeting that certain social organizations' "affiliated authority" units (meaning the PSUs) should turn their role into "operational guidance" units and, in the meantime, encourage certain types of social organizations to be registered directly without having to find an "affiliated authority" to sponsor them. The four specific types that would qualify are industry associations, science and technology organizations, charities, and entities providing community social services.[27] When the state's grip on the society tightened again after President Xi Jinping took office in 2012, Civil Affairs was asked to share its jurisdictions with other ministries again. For example, with the increasing distrust of the activities that foreign NGOs are doing in China, the government announced in 2016 that foreign NGOs would be under the Ministry of Public Security's jurisdiction while domestic NGOs would still be under Civil Affairs. Chapter 4 provides a detailed account of key moments of the state-society interactions and the change of the laws and regulations.

Public Security

Another branch of the government that plays a key role in the analysis of state-society relations in this book is Public Security. The Ministry of Public Security is the principal police and security authority in charge of law enforcement in China. From individual affairs such as personal identification issuance and Hukou[28] registration to routine tasks such as border control and traffic control, as well as undertakings such as crime investigation, counter-terrorism operations, and drug control, among many other security-related jobs, the Ministry of Public Security is a police force with many additional functions.

Regarding the control of society, Public Security authorities often target CSOs that are not officially registered—therefore, treated as illegal. This is especially the case when associational activities have goals that are not aligned with those of the government. For ambiguous activities that public security is not yet sure about, there is usually a tolerated monitoring period, and collaboration between Civil Affairs and Public Security within this domain is quite common.

One of the newly acquired functions after the passing of the 2016 Foreign NGO Law (which went into force in 2017) is to supervise all overseas NGOs. NGOs from outside of China must register with the Public Security authorities instead of Civil Affairs and comply with new activity and funding restrictions with added obligations. On the other hand, domestic NGOs are governed by the Charity Law, also passed in 2016, which relaxed registration and fund-raising requirements for most domestic NGOs. This evolution of jurisdictions between Civil Affairs authorities and Public Security authorities indicates the differentiation of various types of CSOs. The evolution of the laws and regulations relating to this topic is discussed in detail in chapters 5, 6, and 7.

Public Security also has jurisdiction over the internet space when the content is not shared publicly.[29] For example, the private messaging between two individuals or a group of individuals is under the jurisdiction of Public Security authorities. If the content could be seen by the public and could be circulated, then it is under the jurisdiction of both Public Security and the Office of Cyberspace Affairs. In that case, Public Security authorities focus on security-related issues (counter-terrorism, drug control, hacking, extortion, prostitution, etc.) while Cyberspace Affairs is in charge of propaganda and ideological issues.

Cyberspace Affairs

The Central Cyberspace Affairs Commission is a ministry-level office directly led by the CCP's Central Committee, the political body that comprises the top leaders of the party. In order to have more legitimacy to participate in governance, the office also has a title under the State Council as the "State Internet Information Office." The office was first initiated on the state side in 2011 and formalized on the CCP side in 2014. The main functions of the office involve monitoring and managing content over the internet, including, but not limited to, text, pictures, audio recordings, and videos, as well as comments on such content. Much of the internet censorship is governed by Cyberspace Affairs authorities.

Even though the bureaucracy of Cyberspace Affairs may be small, a major city with multimillion people may have less than five staff members. Much of the work and responsibilities are assigned to individual internet companies. For example, one of the largest internet companies in China, Tencent, owns WeChat and the official account platforms. Tencent, therefore, has to maintain its own content censoring team, including a regular staff team and the automatic dynamic word bank that screens key sensitive words. Media outlets also have their own specialized censor teams to perform similar functions. *People's Daily*, the official newspaper of the CCP, tripled its stock price during the first four months of 2019 mainly because its income from "content review" grew by 166 percent.[30] This means that content creators on the internet who cannot afford their own content review teams can send their material to *People's Daily* for a fee so that they can have the material published. Only when those review teams are unsure about specific content do they pass along the content to the Office of Cyberspace Affairs for determination.

This chapter has discussed the historical roots of state-society interactions in China and captured key debates and conceptualizations of the Chinese civil society since the 1980s. Under this backdrop, important key players in the state-society relations in China from both society and state have been briefly introduced. The detailed processes of how these players would interact within the proposed three-staged interactive authoritarianism are discussed in the subsequent chapters.

PART II

The Three Stages of the Interactive Authoritarianism Model

CHAPTER 2

Stage I

Authoritarian Tolerance of Civil Society Activities

> Our activity is Taiwan- and Hong Kong–related, so we are supposed to declare ourselves to the local authority. But we haven't—the local authority here does not care.[1]

> When we organize local villagers to participate in our activities, the local government does not intervene—they only occasionally show interests in what we are doing.[2]

> We have hundreds of CSOs here, mostly not registered officially, but the local government continues to let us operate.[3]

Three different CSO leaders from three different provinces told me in separate interviews, reflecting a common theme, that civil society activities are tolerated by local governments, albeit working in different domains and under different circumstances. Later in this book, you will see cases that, along with social organizations, other types of civil society activities such as independent self-media publications and ride-share drivers' organized protests are also tolerated to a certain extent under authoritarian China. What explains authoritarian toleration and the degree and variations of it?

The existing literature points out that toleration usually happens when CSOs are nonthreatening, exploitable, or the government benefits from an unrestrained public sphere. Repression is costly, and even authoritarian countries avoid needing to rule by coercion alone, as long as there are minimal legitimacy threats regarding its capability to rule.[4] Based on this logic, smaller and local actors are more likely to be tolerated. Even collective actions, which are typically seen as regime-challenging and are contained at the national level,[5] can be tolerated at the local level, especially if such actions are targeted at actors outside of the government (such as corporations) and the grievance focus is narrow.[6] At the local level, personal connections, individual experiences, and differences in the degree and scale of law enforcement are all factors that can lead to toleration.[7]

CSOs are exploitable in many ways, and their usefulness can lead to toleration. The first type of exploitation is information collection. Proponents of consultative authoritarianism[8] and diversification of civil society[9] argue that authoritarian states benefit from their interactions and collaborations with CSOs. The toleration of certain CSOs and the active use of consultative and deliberative mechanisms can solicit information, advice, and support from the society and, therefore, contribute to the resilience of the authoritarian rule.

The second type of exploitation focuses on the state's need to acquire the necessary resources and expertise to increase its legitimacy. Many CSOs are specialized in terms of their expertise and resources and may not have the intention to make regime-challenging claims. Therefore, the state may take advantage of the resources of such innocuous CSOs[10] and choose to enter a "contingent symbiotic" relationship with them.[11] Similarly, if the performance of a CSO is proven to be efficient[12] and there is organizational effectiveness[13] in service provision, the state is likely to make a distinction toward those CSOs and prefer to create alliances with them.[14] There is evidence that the funding sufficiency of a foundation impacts the government's decision of whether to co-opt or restrict.[15] And sometimes the motivation to tolerate is mostly financial and apolitical—for example, giving media more autonomy in order to make them more profitable.[16] Of course, the resources can also be intangible. The state can use popular demands and public mobilization, such as anti-foreign protests, to signal[17] and provide additional legitimacy in its foreign policy demands.[18]

A third type of exploitation finds utility in non-regime-challenging CSOs—not necessarily because of their resources, expertise, or effectiveness in public goods provision but, rather, because of their potential to shield the state from criticism and blame. For example, when local governments want to see policy innovation but the actions could fall under the legal gray area, it might be less risky to let CSOs be policy pioneers.[19] The experiences in Guangdong reveal that the transfer of authority to CSOs allows for innovation in public administration.[20] The state might outsource public services to nongovernmental entities and, in doing so, not only avoid direct account-ability[21] but also shift its responsibilities to its citizens onto other sectors.[22] This type of exploitation has mainly focused on the state shifting responsi-bilities to the private sector and, therefore, is described by Carolyn Hsu as the "privatization perspective."[23]

Sometimes toleration toward one or a collective of CSOs has less to do with the CSOs themselves and more to do with the state's need to utilize the unconstrained space. For example, with the online space, the Chinese gov-ernment sees opportunities to use social media to guide public opinion in a direction that is beneficial to its rule.[24]

In the subsequent section, I first provide the empirical evidence of the varieties of toleration of civil society activities based on my fieldwork. Then I go on to explain how and why "toleration" consistently tends to be the first stage of the three-stage unifying model of interactive authoritari-anism, which captures the dynamic nature of the factors and processes mentioned above.

THE VARIETIES OF TOLERATION OF CIVIL SOCIETY ACTIVITIES

Toleration is the first stage of the evolving three-stage approach (toleration-differentiation-legalization) of interactive authoritarianism presented in this book. Various CSOs under different conditions are tolerated by the Chi-nese state. The most common cases from my sample satisfy at least one of the following key conditions: low risk, (foreseeable) high return, and being sub-jected to the right political and institutional environment.

Low Risk

Most organizations at their inception are considered by the state as low risk, for they usually lack the resources and power to pose a meaningful threat to the state. As a matter of fact, local governments are less concerned about threats than the potential competition because certain CSOs can do a better job than the local government in service and public goods provision, and the government does not want its legitimacy to be challenged. But small and nascent organizations are less likely to be competitive (or threatening) to the local government. This low-risk nature can lead to the initial toleration of many CSOs.

One CSO leader mentioned that his organization worked with an insignificant budget at its initial developmental stage, and because of that, the government did not think his organization could become an immediate threat. The same interviewee mentioned another CSO that does similar work but was significantly more resourceful and influential and was facing pressure from the local government to cut down its operational scope or move to other provinces.[25]

A provincial Civil Affairs leader commented that when organizations are small and new, like an infant, a typical approach is to keep/raise them and watch them (*yang zhe kan* 养着看):

> Controlling or blocking every organization is impossible and would be wasteful even if it is doable. Why not wait and see what their intentions and capabilities are? If they continue to be low risk, and sometimes helpful, to the government's agenda, we could even give them some milk (*gei dian nai* 给点奶)—give them some necessary resources.[26]

Another official who supervises civil affairs in a major city made the case that the Ministry of Civil Affairs' announcement of only four types of low-risk organizations was not ambitious enough:

> You pick only four out of thousands of types of CSOs without backing such a decision with systematic analyses. It's just meaningless. We need to classify all types of CSOs first—like how you classify species in biology—and then have specific guidelines about how to manage CSOs at each level, who we should administer, and who we should tolerate. It is necessary to adhere to Deng Xiaoping's analogy of "crossing the river by feeling the stones" (*mozhe shitou guohe* 摸着石头过河) and be open-minded when we manage CSOs, especially if they are harmless and have good intentions.[27]

Low risk is not only indicated by the developmental stage on the temporal dimension but also by the administrative level on which the CSO is operating. A village-level organization could easily be tolerated, while CSOs operating at higher administrative levels might face more scrutiny. One of the organizations I interviewed even borrowed an office room from the village committee (*cun wei hui* 村委会) for day-to-day operations. The leader of the organization (a farmers cooperative) said that the government mostly does not interfere with their activities and that the organization is independent and autonomous.[28]

The condition of being "low risk" is also relative. During a major institutional disruption such as an earthquake, activities that would be heavily scrutinized during normal times may be tolerated. An organization that entered the quake-stricken region after the 2013 Lushan earthquake was not only organizing community collective activities to mobilize the mass for self-help but was also collecting data through surveys and interviews. The institutional disruption changed the power structure in many villages in the region. Due to large sums of money made available through donations and government funding from the above, many township governments stripped the village governments of their autonomy, or even authority, so that they could decide directly who would get what in terms of resources. CSOs were thus able to form alliances with village governments and carry on with their missions. Even though the township governments did not trust the CSOs completely, the services that CSOs were providing were low risk in nature (caring for seniors, the young, and women in need). Therefore, most CSOs were still tolerated and allowed to operate.[29] After the quake-recovery period was over, many of the previously tolerated CSOs faced increased obstacles (such as being forced to go through the process of "getting on the record" or 备案), but still quite a few managed to continue with their operations. On the other hand, in other localities where local governments are confident about their capacity to repress when CSOs act out of bounds, toleration is also more likely to happen than in localities where bureaucratic capacity is limited.[30] Therefore, toleration happens when bureaucratic capacity is completely disrupted (unable to repress) and when bureaucratic capacity is high (do not need to repress, since there is a credible threat and the situation is under complete control).

Sometimes the lower risk has something to do with the individuals who are running the organization or the individuals being served. If the leader of an organization has previously worked with local leaders/authorities under other capacities, then the foreseeable risk of the organization in the eye of the local state is smaller.[31] At times it is based on personal ties,[32] other times it is because of business dealings,[33] and occasionally it is due to a retired military officer or government official leading the organization.[34] If an organization is serving children, the handicapped, or seniors, all of whom are less likely to organize and pursue regime-challenging agendas, it is also considered low risk.[35] In addition, student volunteer groups have applied for funding from the central government, so having the status of "being funded by the state" they can also provide additional incentives for toleration. If the higher-ups think they are all right, why should the local government resist their service?[36]

High Return

CSOs are not automatically considered the enemy of the state. Quite often it is their "usefulness" that catches the local officials' eyes. Such "usefulness" can be mutually recognized through interactive signaling. Immediately after the 2013 Lushan earthquake, a CSO went into a quake-stricken village to provide quake relief and, later, to initiate the rebuilding process. The leaders and volunteers from this organization consistently embraced a discourse that CSOs should complement the work of the government and shoulder the work the government does not do or could not do without causing trouble (butianluan 不添乱). Their work with the community—especially engaging women and children for environmental protection, helping each other, and caring for the elderly—was exceptionally effective. Their normal practice is to pull out after the quake response period, but the village officials and the villagers begged them to stay. The local government even recommended that the village serve as a model village due to their work with the community. The CSOs' work was recognized not only by the villagers they helped but also by the local government for the public goods and services they provided and the capacity building and individual empowerment.[37] This CSO conducted tasks that met the demands of the local people and government and filled the gaps in service provision that were nonexistent (disaster response). And the CSO was more effective than the local government in areas that the government covered (community development).

It is apparent that many CSOs were not officially registered when operating initially. But interviews revealed that local governments have a demand for the work they do; in particular, many of them provide the expertise and effectiveness that other organizations or local bureaucracies cannot provide.[38] To better acquire CSOs' productivities, the city of Ya'an created a mass organization center that provided office space, and sometimes funding, for dozens of CSOs. Officials from both the Sichuan and Guangdong provinces mentioned that quite often the government is not able to "get the point" (mo bu zhao dian 摸不着点), and they see huge benefits in bringing community social organizations to help with governing, because they are quite often better at such tasks.[39]

Specific subgroups of the population that many CSOs focus on can also generate high returns for the government. "Unstable groups," in the eyes of local officials, are often targets of service provision by CSOs. By helping the children of migrant workers, mothers (including those who lost their only child during the earthquake), and those with various grievances, the CSOs have the effect of providing regime stability (*weiwen* 维稳).

Besides political and social benefits, the economic gain created by tolerated CSOs can also be an important motive for tolerating them. A CSO turned many village houses into motels and incorporated them into their experiential tours. Such efforts brought tourists into places that rarely encountered visitors and thus played significant roles in stimulating the local economy. Unlike some other CSOs that received the majority of funding from large charitable foundations, this CSO largely sustained its own operations. Therefore, it was not competing with the local government for resources. In the meantime, the organization was creating new jobs and increasing local incomes. "We get the local government's full support," the leader of the CSO told me.[40]

The Right Political and Institutional Environment

A third essential condition that leads to toleration of CSOs is the right political and institutional environment. There are local, provincial, and sometimes national political environments that can facilitate the toleration of CSOs. For example, officials from one village I interviewed distrust CSOs and fear that CSOs are cult organizations that could potentially challenge the legitimacy of the local CCP's authority. Without the earthquake, the local government would probably not allow CSOs to enter their jurisdiction. Even after the CSOs started providing effective services that the local government might not be as good at, the officials frequently asked the members of the CSOs when they planned to leave. However, the local Communist Youth League was very supportive of the CSOs and reassured the local officials that specific CSOs were low risk and could bring high returns. Such reassurance led to a longer-term collaboration between the CSO and the local government and also extended the toleration period.[41]

At the provincial level, toleration has a lot to do with the leaders' personal beliefs. Multiple interviewees mentioned that when Wang Yang (汪洋)

was the governor of the Guangdong province, he encouraged CSOs to be more active and the government to be less intrusive in their activities. Wang wanted to mobilize societal forces, simplify politics, and empower the non-government sectors (*jianzheng fangquan* 简政放权). Therefore, CSOs and their activities were tolerated to a tremendous degree. Once Wang left Guangdong, the situation changed immediately and the space for CSOs was tightened.[42] Similar incidents also happened in many other provinces with different open-minded leaders at various levels of the bureaucracy. There are plenty of officials who intend not only to tolerate CSOs but also want them to be autonomous and sustainable.[43]

On the other hand, many officials believed that the existing institutional constraints were sufficient to deter malicious activities by CSOs so that they could focus on letting the regime-supporting CSOs better themselves and be more useful to local government. For example, since CSOs in general cannot publicly raise funds (unless going through an extremely challenging process), officials believed that as long as they could control the funding, they could also control the organization.[44] Some local governments even came up with their own rating systems, defining which types of CSOs are "good." Since higher-rated CSOs had better chances of receiving funding from foundations and from governments' service purchasing efforts, many CSOs would voluntarily adjust their behaviors to be "good." In order to be "good," some CSOs would put on a show when reviewed by officials or examiners. "They ask us, 'Are you clear?' And we just pretend to be their grandchildren (*Zhuang sunzi* 装孙子)." One interviewee mentioned that patience during such grading reviews could get them significantly enlarged space and flexibility to operate.[45] The local government officials were also confident that as long as they hold the leverages, CSOs would not be able to do too many damages.

This understanding leads to the toleration of many CSOs that the government is not sure of but has the patience to wait and see whether they could remain low risk and become useful in bringing high returns. For existing risky and especially politically sensitive groups, the government intentionally lured them into the domain surrounded by the current institutional constraints. For example, the government organized workshops to teach rights-claiming individuals how to protect their rights based on the laws (*yi fa wei quan* 依法维权). Many workers were asked to go to these training sessions on a regular basis so that they would then protest within the official channels rather than challenging the official channels.[46]

One interesting observation against conventional wisdom is about college students. College students are typically seen as dangerous to authoritarian regimes, for they are well-educated, have critical thinking skills, and can organize collective actions against the regime. The 1989 student movements (and the student movements in the 1980s in general) manifested this line of thinking. However, the interviews reflected that college students who regularly attend voluntary activities and participate in these activities under the existing institutional arrangements are more tolerated. The reason is that officials believe there are already so many institutional hurdles that these students have to jump over and so much scrutiny that they have to be under that no significant risk is foreseen. It is those who do not regularly participate in activities within the institutional constraints that could become surprises and be dangerous to the regime.[47]

TOLERATION AS THE INITIAL STAGE OF
INTERACTIVE AUTHORITARIANISM

Even though still being an authoritarian state, China in the twenty-first century is different from its totalitarian past under Mao. A space exists between the state and the private sphere, albeit heavily scrutinized and sometimes controlled. This space is where toleration happens.

Unlike many scholars' intuition that an authoritarian state would automatically and immediately assert complete control and crack down on all civil society activities that have emerged within this space, what I observed is quite the opposite. The de facto response is often toleration, as newly emerged CSOs are typically low risk, have high return potential, and are sometimes in the right political and institutional environment. The officials are confident that existing institutional constraints are sufficient to deter major and imminent risks so that toleration can potentially cultivate partners in government who can contribute to the regime stability that local governments are aiming for.

The word "toleration" may indicate that the government is already aware of all players and activities and chooses to permit their continued existence. However, toleration in the interactive authoritarianism model is not limited to the period of "knowing" but could extend to the period beforehand. When any new players and activities emerge, it is possible for them to stay under the radar for a while, despite the advanced technology of surveillance and bureaucratic capacities. The Chinese state does not preemptively and exhaustively mobilize resources to prevent new civil society activities. Thus, such an "ignorance" phase could also be seen as part of the toleration stage due to the intentionality to tolerate even when the players and activities are unknown to the government.

Toleration, as the initial stage of interactive authoritarianism, can often be expanded by an institutional disruption. During or immediately after the institutional disruption, new conditions and constraints may arise that would prevent the default state-society arrangements of the past from continuing to function. While new players and activities start to emerge, new rules and constraints have not come about or are not solidified. Newly emerged actors could also experience a brief period of "ignorance." Such a combination of factors leaves an administrative gray area where the state could choose various degrees and methods of control.

As a result, new CSOs moving from the state of being unknown to being known but are still not resourceful or capable enough to become useful in the eyes of the local governments eventually would be tolerated. Once the CSO is known, the government could immediately start its data collection process, trying to understand the nature and capability of the CSO. Thus, differentiation (stage two of the three-stage model) could already be happening on the government's books. However, the government may continue to tolerate the CSOs while accumulating data.

The state-society relationship during the toleration stage is also interactive. On the state side, the government is not passive or merely reactive to what happens but actively monitors and engages with newly emerged CSOs. Local officials often create opportunities to interact with CSOs, asking what they need[48] or even providing them with office space[49] or connecting them with volunteers.[50] While strengthening CSOs operations, the government can also monitor CSO activities closely. On the society side, CSOs also actively take initiatives to take advantage of this toleration period. Most CSOs try to speak the language of the officials, quoting provincial or central government leaders' speeches or other documents frequently,[51] signaling that they are not the enemy or that their goals align with those of the government. Some may secretly operate activities that are not in the interest of the government (especially the local government), but the performative legitimacy can usually get the CSOs through the toleration stage. Other CSOs may have nothing to hide and have goals aligned with the government, so they are willing to engage the government to the fullest extent, declaring themselves and their activities (*baobei* 报备) wherever they operate and creating Communist Party branches or Communist Youth League branches within their organizations without being asked to do so. Some CSOs within this group deliver results such as creating jobs and economic activities or assisting those in need or left behind. Such performance legitimacy almost certainly guarantees toleration from the local government, especially if the CSO is still small and new. CSOs also seek connections to the decision-makers within the jurisdictions they operate so that the initial trust can be established. Whether it is through the CSO's performative or performance legitimacy or by using personal connections to sustain the toleration, CSOs actively make adjustments to their actions and public narratives and constantly interact with the local government, presenting themselves as low risk, high return societal partners of the government and creating favorable political and institutional environments.

There is consistency between today's China and the imperial China in terms of the state's involvement in society and welfare provision. The bureaucracy is strong and powerful but still lacks sufficient personnel and resources to control and govern every aspect of society tightly at every administrative level. The state remains heavily involved in welfare provision but welcomes the contribution and participation of society to improve the effectiveness of welfare delivery and to increase social stability. The result is lightly governed local societies where many CSOs and their activities are tolerated, if not encouraged. It is definitely an atypical civil society model, for the toleration could be terminated at any time at the will of the state, but it is also not a typical corporatist system, as multiple competing and loosely controlled groups can operate at the same time. The logic for toleration is to cultivate potential helping hands rather than to shut down the social forces completely.

There are, of course, specific types of CSOs that are deemed risky and are, therefore, contained once their regime-challenging intentions (or appearances) are determined by the local state. This usually happens after the more ambiguous toleration period and is the subject of discussion in the next chapter. The state continues to cultivate those CSOs that they deem helpful with their governance while differentiating, and sometimes eliminating, the regime-challenging CSOs at the same time.

CHAPTER 3

Stage II

Differentiation—Outsourcing Responsibility for Governance

Given the multitude of activities and types of CSOs operating within the nascent civil society in China with various missions and under different political and institutional conditions discussed in the previous chapter, it is not surprising that toleration toward newer and smaller CSOs is a common approach by local governments. However, the intent to differentiate CSOs might exist as early as during the toleration stage, and when CSOs become mature and their capabilities and objectives become more apparent, they are no longer tolerated in a similar fashion and are likely to be differentiated.

The second stage of the interactive authoritarianism approach can be described as "deliberate differentiation," in which the local governments have a tendency to intentionally treat different types of CSOs—sensitive and non-sensitive—with varying policy responses.[1] However, scholars provide a multitude of reasons as to why deliberate differentiation exists. The dominant explanation appeals to the priority of cracking down regime-challenging CSOs while collaborating with those aiming to provide services. The graduated controls approach sees the CCP dividing CSOs into those that might become antagonistic and problematic versus those that can safely be allowed to enhance public goods provision,[2] with some arguing that the state's fear of the collective action potential may be the primary determinant.[3] Thus, social (rather than political),[4] small-scale,[5] and regime-supporting CSOs tend to be treated differently. Of course, there are scholars who see this differentiation behavior as non-intentional. The Chinese state is not monolithic,[6] has multiple agencies horizontally, and is decentralized vertically; therefore, the CSOs can be treated differently due to regional and administrative variations.[7] There are also variations in personal experiences, beliefs and expertise,[8] political ties,[9] and networks.[10] In some cases, it is simply because of insufficient epistemic awareness of CSO activities in certain places.[11]

What warrants further investigation is whether such differentiation exists systematically and, if so, which factors or motivations actually drive the state's deliberate differentiation. Some factors may be more important than others, whereas some may be irrelevant. In short, I see an opportunity to test falsifiable claims about the sources of variation in China's authoritarian responsiveness to CSOs.

Drawing evidence from an online field experiment and dozens of in-depth interviews with government officials and leaders of social organizations in the Sichuan province, this chapter first demonstrates that policy differentiation toward CSOs exists and, second, that at the local level differentiation aims primarily to increase productivity and outsource responsibility for public goods provision. While higher levels of government and more urban localities may be focused on collecting information from CSOs or disciplining potential regime opponents, local governments concentrate more on getting the most out of "good" CSOs than repressing "bad" ones. Under a decentralized system, grassroots county-level officials have the freedom and motivation to allow various CSOs to exist, particularly those that provide public goods and contribute to the stability of the regime. Local officials encourage and facilitate CSOs in sharing the workload and let the groups face public criticism if necessary. Furthermore, contrary to what Xueguang Zhou suggests,[12] self-organized grassroots CSOs are primarily seen not as sources of spontaneous collective action at the county level but as new sources of bureaucratic support. In sum, evidence reveals that the variation in the treatment of CSOs is common and is determined in ways that are different from what existing theories suggest.

The term "outsourcing responsibility" in this chapter has two dimensions: shouldering the burden of workload and being accountable in case of potential retribution. It is clear that local officials intend to not only solicit help from the "good" CSOs but to also ensure that the organizations take the blame when things go wrong. Therefore, what is outsourced to CSOs is both the responsibility to assist local governance and the responsibility to protect the reputation of the local state by shielding it from blame.

Thus, the deliberate differentiation approach by the local Chinese governments is not merely a tactic to collect information, to manage the society with a variety of tools (consultative authoritarianism), and to control and deter threats (graduated controls); rather, it is intended to have "good" CSOs be much more integrated into its local governance. The logic is similar to why township governments need to have village governments, even though the official five-level bureaucracy (central, provincial, municipality, county, and township) does not include the village level. "Good" CSOs are intended, just like village governments, to provide services, shoulder responsibilities, buffer criticism, and channel controls.

At the theoretical level, this chapter also serves as a response to the authoritarian responsiveness and authoritarian resilience literature. Responsiveness is a pivotal marker of the local state's treatment of a CSO, and regime resilience may be an outcome of how shrewdly it manages civil society. A growing body of literature exists that aims to explain authoritarian responsiveness, whether in terms of fearing collective action,[13] gaining support from loyal insiders,[14] pleasing higher-ups for better job prospects,[15] collecting information,[16] or setting up mere window-dressing channels to increase public satisfaction.[17] However, the cases selected by existing studies tend not to be systematic. Those more systematic studies using methods such as experiments are typically at the national level and assume that policy implementation is relatively centralized. Most field experiments on related topics, though pretested, also do not originate treatment conditions from what actual individuals (that is, the sender or the receiver of the information) in such scenarios would do.

Differentiation discussed in this book consists of two types: the intent to differentiate and the act of differentiating. As mentioned previously, the intent to differentiate can happen as early as the toleration stage. Even when a CSO is largely tolerated, the government may already be keeping score and accumulating impressions, positive and negative. The experiment in this chapter focuses on the intent to differentiate, as the treatment condition largely reflects a potential CSO that the government has not taken action upon yet. The language from pre-experiment interviews with real CSOs trying to get registered and newly registered CSOs was used directly to construct the treatment condition. The follow-up interviews with government officials and CSO leaders were conducted to investigate the underlying logic of the experimental results with a focus on the act of differentiating.

This chapter finds that the government is less responsive to politically sensitive CSOs, which receive slower and lower-quality responses to their requests for information, and is more responsive to those regime-supporting

CSOs that could increase the bureaucracy's productivity and shoulder the burden and responsibility of the local state. Getting help from regime-supporting CSOs would strengthen the state. Sometimes after interacting with a questionable CSO, government officials decide they would rather keep it close (perhaps by providing it with office space at the incubation centers) rather than risk setting it loose without supervision. This chapter confirms that such relations are not static, as both the government and civil society organizations interact with each other and adjust their policies and behaviors accordingly.[18] These learning experiences create a dynamic, interactive process for both the state and society.

With respect to authoritarian resilience, the contribution here is to suggest that an authoritarian regime might deliberately adopt some democratic institutions not because it is forced to by a contentious society or international actors, nor as baby steps toward more thoroughgoing political reform, but rather as tools to improve governance in the service of perpetuating control by the ruling elites. This chapter also makes a quantitative contribution to the vigorous debate among China scholars about the nature of the rights consciousness of Chinese citizens[19] by focusing specifically on the unacceptability of rights claims. The distinction demonstrated here is that while organizing is acceptable, demanding rights is not, although how rights claiming is framed still matters.[20]

RESEARCH DESIGN FOR THIS CHAPTER

To confirm whether such policy differentiation exists and to explore the motivations for it, I conducted in-depth interviews and a field experiment. The experiment assessed, via email inquiries, local governments' relationships with CSOs.[21] Rival hypotheses were tested in order to demonstrate whether the state's main motivations were collecting information and preventing collective action or increasing productivity and outsourcing responsibility.

Preliminary interviews revealed that organizations working with vulnerable populations (such as mothers who lost their only child) and with groups claiming rights (such as workers who were owed significant backpay) were politically sensitive.[22] The government dislikes such organizations due to their potential to organize collective action, challenge the state's legitimacy, and disturb the stability of the regime.[23] Such organizations are perceived as anti-government and tend to receive no support (if not hostile treatment) during registration within their jurisdictions. This was a consistent finding across all levels of government, though officials may frame the differentiation in slightly different ways, calling one kind of CSO the "rights claim and advocacy group" and the other the "service provision only group."[24]

Less sensitive, yet still eliciting caution, are religious organizations and international organizations. According to several officials, "Religious organizations are ideologically driven and provide an alternative to our socialist ideology."[25] Even when dealing with religious organizations, however, officials suggested that local and more peaceful religions (here mainly referring to Buddhism and Daoism) should be promoted in place of foreign religions with anti-state potential (such as Christianity and Islam).[26] Christian and Islamic groups are seen to have more current foreign connections and, therefore, have more subversive inclinations on both the ideological and security fronts.[27] Such differentiation based on political sensitivity informed the experimental design.

Methodologically, the approach used in this chapter resembles audit studies, which also measure discrimination directly with experimental fieldwork.[28] To assess the political logic of how different CSOs would be treated, I sent emails to county governors to inquire about new CSO registration. This strategy was chosen because it is realistic and convenient. In 2007 the State Council announced the "Open Government Information Ordinance" (OGI), which required governments at the county level and higher to increase transparency, leading many local governments to establish official websites.[29] Most counties have a "county governor's inbox" so that people can voice their complaints. By emailing county governors, I could conduct a randomized experiment aimed at revealing the underlying logic of the policy behaviors of the Chinese authoritarian state.[30] In addition, inquiring about starting a new CSO is something commonly done at the local level, according to the CSO interviews. At the county level, administrative heads are still directly involved with CSOs. By looking at the creation of CSOs, this research also offers a unique perspective on how a nascent civil society is perceived and dealt with in China.

The internet in China is an important platform for public debate, problem articulation, and new kinds of protests.[31] The government is not promoting the internet to build participatory democracy. Rather, it sees the web as a useful tool for promoting development, setting policy agendas, supervising its bureaucracy, and increasing public legitimacy.[32]

The CCP supports the internet as a legitimate yet controlled channel for communication between China's government and its people. There are many reasons for this, including the rising cost of stability maintenance[33] and the need to acquire reliable information about the populace without face-to-face confrontation.[34] The cadre responsibility system motivates local officials to collect accurate information in the form of public feedback to improve their job prospects.[35] Therefore, the county governor's inbox takes not just complaints but also policy suggestions. A recent study found that officials are similarly receptive to citizens' suggestions submitted through traditional channels and the internet, provided there is no perception of hostile intent.[36]

During the randomization process, each of the 114 county governor's inboxes had a 50 percent chance of being assigned to the treatment group. In order to include a robust and less ambiguous treatment in the experiment, I included in the treatment email the phrase from the interviews "organization[s] . . . protect vulnerable groups' (*ruoshi qunti* 弱势群体) individual interest and citizen rights (*gongmin quanyi* 公民权益)." The control group received an email inquiring about the process of potentially starting a social organization within the county's jurisdiction and asked the county governor to point the sender to the right resources. All of these words were meant to be politically sensitive and to indicate a misalignment of the government's and the CSO's interests and goals. Below is the full text sent in Chinese and the translation in English (the underlined text showed up only in the treatment emails but not the control emails):

尊敬的领导：

您好！

　　学习了《党的三中全会关于深化改革的若干决定》里提到的"社会组织在农村兴办各类事业"、"激发社会组织活力"、以及"交由社会组织提供公共服务"等词条我深受鼓舞。特别想请教一下咱们这组建社会组织的流程是怎么样的，可以找谁来办理此事，需要哪些材料？已经有哪几个组织可以学习、借鉴的？我特别希望了解如何办一个社会组织来维护弱势群体的个体利益，保障公民的权益。
　　非常感谢您百忙之中为我答疑。
　　请回复我邮箱：xxx@xxx.com
　　谢谢！

Dear Mr. County governor,

Greetings!

After studying the "Chinese Communist Party's Third Plenum decision about deepening reform" and reading "to ask social organizations
to set up various enterprises in villages," "motivate the vitality of social
organizations," and "let social organizations provide public service" and
other quotes, I am greatly encouraged. I want to inquire about the procedure of how to set up a social organization in the county, whom I
should contact, and what materials I should prepare? Are there any
existing social organizations that you can refer me to? *I particularly wish
to inquire about how to start an organization to protect vulnerable groups'
individual interest and citizens' rights.*
Thank you very much for answering my questions.
Please reply to my email: xxx@xxx.com
Thank you!

CSO leaders have reported that officials tend to be more responsive and
supportive when the leaders are speaking the same "language."[37] Preliminary interviews suggested that most CSOs (whether officially registered or
not) have some connections with local governments, and such connections
can be personal (shared experiences or strong ties) or institutional. CSOs
actively learn about government documents and "key phrases" when interacting with the government. Therefore, the first few sentences of the emails
reflected sender awareness of ongoing political developments and familiarity with newly issued government documents. This tactic made officials
more likely to take the email seriously and gave a better approximation of
what a CSO leader looking to register an organization would say. By convey-
ing political sensitivity in a context-appropriate way, the treatment avoided
being provocative in a way that might lead officials to doubt that the requests
came from their localities.

The randomized assignment of treatment was done before the emails
were sent, so it is assumed that the variation in the response time, rate, and
content can be attributed directly to the treatment rather than other potential confounders related to the experiment. Because in China, officials of the
same bureaucratic rank generally avoid speaking to one another for fear of
being accused of conspiring[38] and no major official meetings were ongoing

during the period of the study, one can also safely assume that there was minimal interference between the control and the treatment groups. The task was designed to be minimally burdensome for the officials (or their offices), as it only marginally increased their workload. Such a minor request also ensures that future researchers' ability to utilize similar approaches will not be infringed.[39]

Doing the experiment at the county level allowed me to see policy variation more clearly and make sufficient observations. Preliminary interviews with local officials revealed that policies related to civil affairs are mainly decided at or above the county level. Below the county level, officials are primarily involved in implementing policies. Policies sometimes vary at the township level, but the differences are mostly in implementation.

Sichuan province was chosen as the site for the experiment and the interviews because the massive 2008 earthquake, an institutional disruption, triggered CSO development in the region, potentially increasing incentives for government responsiveness to CSOs. Since "not replying" in this experiment is treated as "one type of response" rather than missing data, the assumption is more valid in a region where the local government is generally expected to respond to emails of this kind. Therefore, a "non-reply" is more a deviation from the expectation. Previous studies of authoritarian responsiveness in China suggest the national response rate is around 30–40 percent, with the baseline group response rate being around 30 percent.[40] Various treatments, such as the threat of collective action or reporting to superiors, can increase the response rate. The response rate in the control group from Sichuan province in this study was 60 percent, a figure much higher than that of existing studies. This could be because of the treatment condition being directly from interviews with leaders of CSOs. Government responses may be in the form of policy outcome, direct action, or information provided.[41] As a standard practice in this literature for ethical and practical reasons, this study requested only information for the benefit of the sender.

There are 165 county-level administrative regions in Sichuan province. Seventeen of their website inboxes required a personal identification number to send an email (which the government can trace to the sender). Another 26 had pages where the email function did not work properly or the link did not exist. There were eight websites that selectively posted responses from past emails, but the emails had not been updated within the previous six months. In this study, for obvious reasons, I chose to leave out those websites that required a personal identification number.[42] I also discarded the non-updated websites, as well as those without functional email inboxes. With the remaining 114 counties, it is reasonable to assume that, ceteris paribus, we could expect similar potential responses from them. The above exclusion process may affect the study's external validity, as those offices that require an identification to send an email or do not have a properly functioning email mechanism may be different in their bureaucratic capacity or local conditions.

Because the sample size was not extremely large, it was worth checking the assignment outcome to see whether the procedure, ex-post, produced treatment groups correlated with county characteristics. Table 3.1 reports the results of logistic regression of each county being randomized into the treatment group on eight different county characteristics, including area, number of families, number of townships, number of communities, the population in 10,000s, work population, agricultural population, and number of firms.[43] These geographic, demographic, and socioeconomic covariates were also included in various models during analysis when assessing the duration of response and quality of response, as such indicators may reflect governance capacity, request frequency, and other confounders that should be controlled.

As expected, the results indicate that the county characteristics were not predictors of the treatments assigned, individually and jointly. The standardized differences for stratified comparisons would show the similarly balanced assignment of treatment having fewer assumptions.[44] For the 114 counties, 55 were assigned to the control group, and 59 were assigned to the treatment group. The emails were sent during the weekend of August 17, 2014.

RESULTS AND ANALYSIS

As table 3.2 shows, among the 55 counties in the control group, 33 responded, and 22 did not. Among the 59 counties in the treatment group, 22 responded, and 37 did not. The total response rate by officials was not very different from the results of similar designs utilized by other scholars.[45] Of the 55 total responses received, the majority were received during the first ten days. As we can see from figure 3.1 (response frequency by the number of days), the number of responses also diminished as time went on.

TABLE 3.1. Logistic regression of the treatment assignment

Treatment	
Area	−4.61e-11
	(−0.54)
Families	0.00000469
	(0.54)
Towns	0.0134
	(0.67)
Communities	−0.000874
	(−0.23)
Population in 10,000s	0.000000147
	(0.36)
Worker population	−0.0000230
	(−0.69)
Agriculture population	−0.00000379
	(−0.58)
Firms	0.00973
	(0.61)
Constant	0.227
	(0.44)
N	114

t statistics in parentheses
* $p < .10$, ** $p < .05$, *** $p < .01$

The estimated treatment effect (difference in means) is -0.23, while the p-value for the t-test result is 0.0151. The reply rates from the control group and the treatment group are statistically different from political sensitivity, leading to a lower response rate from the county governors.[46] The effect can also be estimated through permutations. With statistical packages developed by Jake Bowers, Mark Fredrickson, and Ben Hansen, and with one million permutations, a confidence interval was constructed with the upper bound of -0.05 and the lower bound of -0.40 for the effect.[47] This means that when the treatment is included, the probability of getting a response from government officials will be reduced by 5 to 40 percentage points.

The duration of the reply time also varied among the responses (see table 3.3). It took the treatment group longer to respond than the control group. Here the response duration variable is an ordinal variable based on reply

TABLE 3.2. Response table by treatment assignment

Condition	Replied		Total	Replied
	No	Yes		
Control	22	33	55	60%
Treatment	37	22	59	37.3%
Total	59	55	114	48.2%

time. "No response" technically means it took an infinite number of days for a response, but on a continuous scale, disproportionate influence will be created from these observations. Therefore, an ordinal variable was created to convert the number of days into seven ordered categories. Grouping by week also reflects the typical work cycle, as the expectation of response during the weekend can be different from that during the weekdays. The variable, therefore, is coded from 0 to 6. Response within 1 day is coded as 6; 2–7 days is coded as 5; 8–14 days is coded as 4; 15–21 days is coded as 3; 22–28 days is coded as 2; 29 and above is coded as 1; no response is coded as 0. Since the latest response was received on the 35th day, each category covers one week. A smaller number indicates a longer response time.

The response speed models suggest that when sensitive CSO requests were made, the negative treatment effect was present regardless of model specification. Therefore, politically sensitive CSOs had to wait longer for a reply. When a reply was received, there were several different kinds. The quality of the responses was incorporated into the study, as some responses were less meaningful than others. It is important to note that non-response in this study has meaning and should not be treated as "data missing." Simply responding by seeking more information from the sender has less quality (and potentially different intention) than detailed answers. Referring the question to another person also has less quality than directly answering the question. Therefore, the response quality variable is coded with the instructions described in table 3.4.

Such coding is ordinal because each higher number satisfies and improves upon the conditions of the previous number. The basic ordinal logistic regression indicates that the treatment email negatively and significantly affected the quality of the response. In other words, responses were received from both the control and treatment groups, but the quality of response differed between the two groups. All but one detailed personalized response was from the control group. A research assistant who was not aware of the

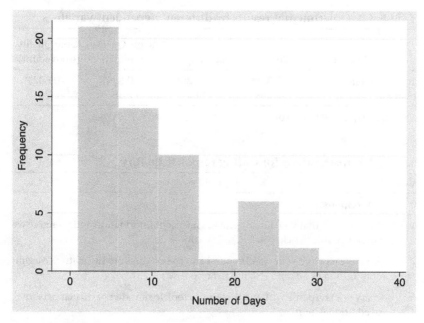

Figure 3.1. Response frequency by number of days

details of the research performed an inter-coder reliability check. The result had a Cohen's Kappa inter-coder agreement of 99.24 percent.

Estimates of the treatment effects controlling for other covariates, such as county area; population size; worker population; agricultural population; and the number of townships, families, communities, and firms, would produce similar outcomes. The treatment effect of lower response quality is significant across different model specifications. This result indicates that replies to requests from sensitive CSOs tend to be less meaningful. The population size of the county is positively correlated with responsiveness. This point may require further investigation, as the size of the population might be directly related to the size of the staff and, therefore, the capacity to govern.

A simple word count was also used as a more direct way of approximating the quality of response. Since "no response" has meaning in this study, the word count was turned into an ordinal variable in which "no response" was coded as 0 with successive categories covering a range of 500 words (that is, 1–500 was coded as 1; 501–1000 was coded as 2; etc.). The quality of response

TABLE 3.3. Experimental results by different dependent variables

Dependent Variables	Replied	Reply Speed	Reply Quality (ordinal)	Reply Quality (word count)
Treatment Effect	–0.23**	–0.725**	–0.850**	–0.807**
t statistic	–2.468	–2.04	–2.36	–2.22

* $p < 0.10$, ** $p < 0.05$, *** $p < 0.01$

TABLE 3.4. Instructions for coding response quality

Value	Type of Response
0	Non-response.
1	"We are sorry that you did not provide sufficient information and therefore we will not be able to help you."
2	"We have received your email/request and are looking into the matter. We will reply as soon as we can." (No further response.)
3	A very brief response with instructions to look for another particular person for additional help.
4	A very brief response with a list of questions to answer.
5	A brief response, including a phone number or a particular location (e.g. the Bureau of Civil Affairs' service window), inviting the sender to speak directly or face-to-face.
6	A very detailed response with procedures and relevant regulations about starting the social organization.
7	A personalized response that provides everything in the previous response and addresses particular questions in the email to better assist the sender.

was consistently lower when more sensitive CSOs made requests. As in the coded model, the word count model also indicates the negative treatment effect (see table 3.3).

The effects, if the experiment can reveal any, may be underestimated because the government has incentives to allow some politically sensitive organizations to operate. The option of being able to crush such organizations would not only set an example for others but would also be seen by officials as a routine exercise of their authority (discussed in chapter 2). One government official, describing hostile actions against religious organizations (such as taking down crosses from the top of churches in Zhejiang province), said that the government's actions are sometimes purely for the purpose of testing the effectiveness of its policy commands. Similarly, officials may test their authority and power using the CSOs they do not like.[48] The literature also suggests that authoritarian governments tend to want to collect information about their bureaucracies and identify potential threats.[49] Therefore, even a small treatment effect is worth examining because it is likely to be underestimated, which supports the argument made in this chapter—differentiation exists.

These experimental results differ from and are complementary to the national study in China by Jidong Chen, Jennifer Pan, and Yiqing Xu, albeit with different treatments.[50] The key difference is that the study by Chen and his colleagues introduced an "immediate" threat, while the potential threat the treatment condition in this research may pose to the government would occur in the long run (social organizations might form and, in the future, organize collective action). This contrast provides potential evidence, which may need further exploration in future research, for a temporal dimension in authoritarian response to political threats (whether it is collective action, bureaucratic competitiveness, insufficient loyal support, or lack of information). The response rate would be lower when the potential threat is not imminent.

In addition, it has been assumed in the existing literature that authoritarian responsiveness attenuates or eliminates potential threats. The treatment condition in this research is unique because responsiveness by the government might enlarge the threat by assisting the regime-challenging CSOs. The treatment can also tease out whether officials are more interested in avoiding potential threats or collecting information. If they are more interested in collecting information, then the response rate should be higher in the treatment group; if they are more concerned about the potential for collective action, then the response rate should be lower in the treatment group. The results accord with Gary King, Jennifer Pan, and Margaret E. Roberts's finding that the Chinese government is more concerned about potential collective actions even at the expense of losing information.[51]

A DYNAMIC PROCESS OF DELIBERATE DIFFERENTIATION AS THE SECOND STAGE OF INTERACTIVE AUTHORITARIANISM

The preliminary interviews with government officials in Sichuan province revealed the common theme that they are not worried about sensitive organizations, especially for newer and smaller CSOs that have low risk, high potential return and are situated in the right political and institutional conditions (see the detailed discussions in chapter 2.) From the experimental results, we have also observed that deliberate differentiation of regime-challenging and regime-supporting CSOs exists, and the intent to differentiate can be present as early as when CSOs are still nascent.

The follow-up interviews, in combination with the experiment, revealed that the policy focus of the act of differentiating was not eliminating regime-challenging groups but, rather, cultivating potential partners among regime-supporting groups to extract productivity while outsourcing responsibility to those partners. In other words, the primary concern for many officials was not the fear of lack of information and the control of politically sensitive groups but the lack of sufficient support from service-provision groups that could ease the burden of local governments.[52] As a city-level official told me:

> Local governments face many social governance challenges, and we hope social organizations can play a role. Recognizing the limitations of local governments, especially their inability to deal with the mismatch between policies from the top and implementations at the grass roots, we need to cultivate social organizations and make them step up. We can help them find the right people, and most importantly, we can also purchase services when necessary.[53]

Another city-level government official praised the work that CSOs typically do:

> Most social organizations are good. For organizations that are into advocacy, we are strict whenever necessary. However, if you are providing service, restrictions should be as loose as possible—they are helping you to do good work.[54]

In order to share the responsibility of the local government, groups that are seen as politically non-sensitive and have the potential to provide services needed by the locality would likely be invited into a mass organizations center (*quntuan zhongxin* 群团中心) or an incubation center. In these types of centers, the actual productivity of the groups is monitored and assessed. Through this process, the local governments are able to identify the regime-supporting groups through the differentiating strategy first and then cultivate the groups with higher productivity to form partnerships and outsource responsibilities.

Of course, groups' behaviors are not either black or white. Sometimes the differentiation stage takes a while as the local officials see elements of both "good" and "bad" in certain organizations. Their attitude toward such organizations can thus fluctuate, and the impression might be changed from "regime-challenging" to "regime-supporting," back and forth. However, initial impressions are more important, as one CSO leader reflected:

> We work on various issues from youth empowerment, housekeeping, senior care, and community medical service—most CSOs only choose to work on one of those issues, but we have comprehensive operations. Local officials were not sure exactly what we do or what our focuses were initially. They are typically nicer to certain helpful organizations and harsh towards those they see as trouble makers. They couldn't figure us out first. It took them two years to finally understand us and believe we are helpful to them.[55]

Such policy differentiation was not always the case; before 2008 there were limited CSOs operating in China, which were more commonly referred to as "NGOs" by officials. The translation in Chinese—非政府组织—often led government officials to misunderstand them as "anti-government organizations." Local governments often had an antagonistic attitude toward the CSO sector as a whole.[56] There was not much differentiation at the time, and all of the organizations faced similar control, manipulation, and penetration from the government. To reduce the interference from local governments, CSOs often registered as private companies or kept a low profile by not registering at all.[57]

Since the 2008 Wenchuan earthquake, many local governments have had the opportunity to witness closely the work done by CSOs during quake relief efforts; some CSOs did an impressive job providing social stability and local governance. Many local governments have since realized how valuable these "good" social organizations can be, especially if CSOs do not take resources (money, time, staff, etc.) away from the government.[58] Such effects were not limited to Sichuan, as government officials and CSO leaders from multiple provinces all point out the spillover effect—in other words, what happened in Sichuan made governments and CSOs adjust their behaviors in their own localities.[59]

Why would local governments not profess concern about regime-challenging CSOs and the need to actively and heavily monitor them? Officials interviewed typically pointed to existing institutional constraints. Before the 2016 Charity Law, domestic organizations needed to have a "sponsor organization," either a government department or government-organized nongovernmental organization (GONGO), in order to be registered.[60] Such sponsor organizations usually could threaten to shut down the operations of the CSO by rejecting its annual budget should the CSO cross any lines.

Even after the 2016 Charity Law, CSOs still need to submit annual reports. A local government might keep an "abnormal list" to identify individual organizations with bad records. The 2016 Charity Law further shows that the Chinese government intends to provide the necessary leeway but also retain constraints within which "good" social associations need to operate.[61]

Another powerful constraint on CSOs is financial support. The 2016 Charity Law did not grant public fund-raising rights to social service organizations or CSOs in general. This means that CSOs mainly get money from foundations (usually government-affiliated) or through the governmental purchase of services.[62] Because the 2016 Foreign NGO Law has cut off foreign support for local CSOs, the government has even stronger control over CSO funding.

Besides legal status and funding, the government has also reshaped people's behaviors. Members of CSOs (whether regime-supporting or potentially regime-challenging) said in interviews that they intentionally put on a cooperative face when interacting with the government. Such behavior change was evident from the 2008 Wenchuan earthquake to the 2013 Lushan earthquake. Many of the CSO leaders have since formed the habit of reporting to local governments and putting themselves on the record (bei'an 备案) before starting their operations.[63] For example, scholars have documented positive changes happening in environmental protests across China, capturing how the anti-PX campaign (an environmental movement by citizens of Xiamen protesting the establishment of a PX factory in the city) might be changing the landscape of state-society relations in China.[64] However, in interviews, almost all environmental groups mentioned that they had made the conscious decision to pick their fights and no longer want to be involved in anti-PX campaigns, since the government is sensitive to those specific protests.[65] Such adaptation is consistent with Timothy Hildebrandt's argument that CSO emergence in China may not weaken the state but could effectively strengthen it.[66] CSO leaders reported such practices as beneficial because they made local governments less suspicious of CSO activity.

But the Chinese government is warier when it is less able to verify what CSOs are doing and aim to introduce more regulations and constraints to uncover where CSO funding comes from, who is operating what projects, and what the actual objectives of a group might be. The Foreign NGO Law[67] is one example. Within the legal domain, there is a difference between how domestic and foreign CSOs are treated. Control over domestic organizations seems to be loosening while control over foreign NGOs is tightening (to be discussed in chapter 4).[68] That being said, there are exceptions to these trends, and the situation is a dynamic one. For example, there were 221 foreign NGOs officially registered in China during the first nine months of 2017, and 291 events operated by foreign NGOs were officially documented.[69] We could potentially see an increase in the number of "good" CSOs helping out governance in China despite the concern of foreign influence.

Differentiating CSOs is a dynamic process, proceeding in three overlapping phases: an ambiguous first encounter (usually accompanied by the intent to differentiate immediately), initial differentiation (the act to differentiate), and the decision whether or not to outsource responsibility (to reap utilities from differentiation). In phase one the government is exposed to a new CSO. The intent to differentiate can already exist even though the organization is still completely tolerated and uninterrupted.[70] After some initial observations and when officials are unsure of an organization, they like to keep it close by, perhaps by providing the group with office space at incubation centers. Several cities in China have piloted social service organization incubation centers that nurture and assist newly organized grassroots organizations, providing resources that the groups desperately need but also making sure the government gets to know them. The government, the party, or other entities trusted by the government may organize the incubation centers. It is clear that as long as an organization is not clearly antagonistic toward the local government, they are assumed to be "keepers" during the first encounter.

Institutional disruptions can also provide opportunities for groups to demonstrate their usefulness during this first phase of the differentiation stage. During normal times, many individuals in the society who have the potential to create new CSOs or initiate relevant activities may fear repression from the authoritarian state and choose not to organize. Because institutional disruptions like an earthquake could be viewed as a consensus crisis,[71] in which different parties are motivated by a common goal to undertake practical tasks, the toleration of civic engagement activities is more expected. Once CSOs are operating, they stand a chance to be viewed favorably by the local government. CSOs also actively seek to be viewed favorably during this interactive process. Institutional disruptions could shorten the length of the "undecided" period, as the number of opportunities to observe and differentiate CSOs could increase significantly and intentions and behaviors during special circumstances are also more convincing. If when local governments are incapacitated, the CSO is still helping maintaining stability, providing the needed services, and listening (at least pretending to be listening) to local officials, then when normal times return (or the institutional disruption is normalized), there is less reason to doubt that the organization would pursue regime-challenging goals.

Once the local governments know more about a CSO, the officials start to take actions to differentiate based on the logic and actions described above, thus entering phase two of the differentiation stage. However, differentiation does not necessarily mean repressing all regime-challenging organizations instantly. A leader of one rights-claiming group mentioned that he is very clear about the type of reactions he will face due to previous interactions with the local authorities. The strength of repression he would face in his locality is based on the number of people he organizes when holding a meeting or protesting. As long as the number of people is less than two hundred, and no major political event (such as a CCP plenum or a visit by an important head of state) is ongoing, the government does not care too much. Of course, this measure varies by locality, but it indicates that even with anti-government collective actions, participation needs to be large enough, or the timing has to be sensitive enough, before the government takes action.[72] Such experiences and expectations are gained through repeated interactions between the local government and CSOs, so small-scale protests are still occasionally allowed, while local officials, knowing CSO leaders are aware of the boundaries, can prolong and expand toleration of certain regime-challenging CSOs.

CSOs can also utilize phase one and phase two of the differentiation process to create a good relationship with local governments and adjust their operations so that they can actively establish their image of being regime-supporting rather than regime-challenging. Natural disasters, a typical institutional disruption, can be catalytic for increasing trust and building relationships between CSOs and local governments. Both CSOs and government officials see such institutional disruptions as opportunities to potentially cultivate win-win relationships.

The gradual adaptation of CSOs to state preferences is also apparent when comparing interviews between 2011 and 2017. In 2008, CSOs were not as organized and sent people directly to the quake-stricken region to provide services instead of first coordinating with other CSOs or with the government. After the government regained control of the localities in the immediate aftermath of the disasters, some CSOs faced severe scrutiny and interference while others started to build trust and a working relationship with the local government. By 2013 many CSOs had adjusted their working procedures and voluntarily registered with local governments to report about their intended activities before entering a jurisdiction. This comforted many government officials and built trust between the government and the organizations.[73] The CSOs reported that by voluntarily becoming subordinate (or at least appearing to be subordinate), they enjoyed a much larger space to conduct their projects, and fewer suspicions and confrontations arose.

Voluntary subordination leads CSOs to adjust both their goals and the ways they conduct their projects. In interviews, several religious organizations emphasized that during the quake relief period, they entered the quake-stricken region by abandoning or downplaying the religious aspects of their organizations.[74] For example, a Christian organization involved in relief focused on helping the local people, not spreading the gospel. Adjusting one's goals to align with those of the government and eliminating disaligned projects might help a CSO survive in an authoritarian regime like China's but, unfortunately, makes CSOs less diverse.

Local governments also realize that maintaining a bureaucracy is very costly. Since the tax and fees reform, local governments' sources of income have been reduced tremendously. For tasks such as quake relief, it may not be realistic to utilize a government-run team. For other tasks, such as mental health assistance, the government lacks expertise. Therefore, it is better to let the CSOs take care of such tasks, and the government can provide money to support the CSOs.[75] Thus, one of the main purposes of the differentiation stage is so that regime-supporting CSOs' productivity can be used to help achieve the government's goals.

During the third phase of the differentiation stage, the local government routinizes the process of outsourcing responsibilities to the regime-supporting CSOs while maintaining checks on the regime-challenging ones. "Widely integrate social forces" (*guangfan naru shehuililiang* 广泛纳入社会力

量) is a phrase mentioned by several government officials interviewed, and some even complained about not having enough active organizations in their jurisdiction. Through the intent to differentiate and the act of differentiating phases, the interactions between CSOs and local governments have generated enough trust. During the third phase, officials are focused on getting enough help from those trusted social forces. The government has invested in building relationships with CSOs, and they would like to see concrete returns—after all, avoided risks are not usually showable achievements. But the progress made in economic development, poverty alleviation, and more social safety nets covering the vulnerable population could get officials promoted. CSOs also would like to maintain long-term relationships with local governments by demonstrating their high productivity so that potential boundary-spanning activities (intended or unintended) down the road may not trigger irreversible repressions and crackdowns. High productivity is often a combination of strong capabilities and the choice to work on the right issue areas (discussed further in chapter 5's case study). Through this process, CSOs increase their chances of survival, and local governments can get additional help and even additional responsible parties to shoulder the blame when things go wrong.

The differentiation of CSOs may not solely depend on the issues the CSO is promoting or the capability of the CSO, as CSO leaders' personal backgrounds and past government-CSO interactions can have a significant impact. For example, one CSO in the study is led by a married couple, and the husband is a retired military officer. In interviews with his counterparts in the government, officials mentioned that such organizations run by former government officials or retired military officers are more trustworthy and easier to work with than other organizations. The authoritarian government sees democratic activities facilitated by this CSO (such as community deliberation, freely elected autonomous governance groups, etc.) as promoting the stability of local communities and therefore condones the efforts, even if the activity is creating an alternative source of power and decision-making mechanism. The organization now trains government officials routinely on facilitation and deliberation skills. This CSO passes on expertise to government officials, thereby gaining more government trust along the way.[76]

It is worth pointing out that only the CSO leader's personal expertise and reputation, not the CSO's role in society, has been legitimized in the eyes of the local government. This phenomenon explains why, during the county governor's email experiment, several responses sought to learn more about the individual behind the request and the details of the project before making any decisions regarding the organization.

During an institutional disruption, new constraints and realities come about, and they facilitate the occurrence of the toleration and deliberate differentiation stages. However, once the business is back to normal and there has been a routinization of interactions between certain CSOs and local governments, lessons learned from such interactions are formalized, and the third stage of the interactive authoritarianism model, legalization without institutionalization, emerges. The following chapter discusses this process in detail.

CHAPTER 4

Stage III

Legalization without Institutionalization

The interactive authoritarian governance process moving from toleration to differentiation is neither stable nor final. The third stage, in which the state makes an attempt to set boundaries and make new rules to normalize behaviors and relationships, is referred to in this book as "legalization without institutionalization." This means that new rules and laws are proposed, deliberated, and even passed. Yet, they are only intended to be used to govern and contain the social forces rather than subjecting the state and the ruling elites to the same set of rules—therefore, no institutionalization. Different rules and laws, following the differentiation stage, can target specified CSOs and can also be altered when deemed necessary by the state.

The legalization stage is an important component of the Chinese state's policy experimentation and diffusion, which temporarily solidify incremental achievements and store newly learned experiences in institutional memories. Policy experimentation has been well documented by the scholarly community, often seen as evidence of "Chinese exceptionalism." Central policy makers recognize, and sometimes encourage, specific policy innovations at the local level to tackle challenges faced not just by the local community alone, then transmit the innovative methods, if proven to be effective, to other localities, eventually leading to the formulation of national policies, usually in the form of new laws, regulations, and guidelines. The "point to surface" (*youdian daomian* 由点到面) policy experimentation processes have led to rapid economic growth and transformation but have so far restricted meaningful political reforms.[1]

Some scholars, although being disputed, have noted that the history of policy experimentation of the Chinese Communist Party can be traced back to the early days of the CCP in the 1920s in situations where the Marxist-Leninist prescriptions would not offer details about how to lead a peasant revolution in rural China. Therefore, improvising and gaining experience from successes became a strategy that was often used to defeat both the Japanese and the Nationalists.[2] The "experimentation under hierarchy" approach continued and evolved after the PRC came to power, and particularly in the post-Mao era, as risky policies were tested at the local level and then enacted nationwide as laws or regulations if proven to be successful.[3]

There are several unsolved questions about policy experimentation in China. First there are disputes about the source of such experimentation. Gerard Roland gives credit to the township and village enterprises (TVE), for TVEs successfully developed within the non-state sector and became the main source of economic growth and transition.[4] Hongbin Cai and Daniel Treisman, on the other hand, assert that the appearance of experimentation is the outcome of factional competition at the top level. Top leaders belonging to different ideological factions used local experiments to demonstrate the effectiveness of their chosen policies.[5] The criticisms of the experimental zones during the reform and opening era by the conservatives, particularly the accusations of such experiments as capitalist practices, have also been documented.[6] While some see these experiments as genuine scientific methods to test the effectiveness of policies, others argue that sometimes policy experimentation is manipulated as a political symbol to create performative legitimacy.[7] Jinghan Zeng observes that the Wenzhou financial reforms in 2012 were means to maintain socioeconomic stability during the power succession at the 18th Party Congress rather than to produce meaningful policy efficiency.[8]

The process of policy experimentation is also disputed among scholars. Some scholars see it as center-led first and then followed by the local implementation process; others argue that the central government does not have predetermined goals and targets before the experimentation and utilizes selective control and adjusts preferences throughout the experimentation.[9] Scholars like Shaoguang Wang see the adaptation of innovative policy by both the decision-makers and advocates as crucial to the experimentation process.[10]

Experimentation involves promoting and enacting policies that are not yet stipulated by the legal system or, sometimes, even directly in conflict with the legal system. Therefore, experimentation in China is also associated with the discussion of the "benign violation of the constitution."[11] Sebastian

Heilmann points out that such a process to implement policies before law-making is in direct conflict with the "rule of law" concept that many Western countries have.[12]

While much of the policy experimentation literature talks about experimentation's role and significance in China's economic development, not much has been written on how similar processes would work outside of the economic domain, when the goal is not clearly growth and economic development—with the exception of very few studies, such as Wen-Hsuan Tsai and Nicola Dean's "experimentation under hierarchy" model.[13] Both coherent logic and unique aspects exist as to how the Chinese state governs the society with experimentation and how the "legalization without institutionalization" stage of the interactive authoritarianism model I propose brings out the intrinsic mechanisms of policy experimentation when the Chinese state governs the society. The rapid increase of civil associational behaviors and the development of CSOs in the past two decades, especially after the 2008 Wenchuan earthquake, also provides a good opportunity for us to study policy experimentation in society. Such research may help us to clarify the questions and disputes mentioned above in the literature.

Taking advantage of the institutional disruptions that could accelerate the process of policy experimentation, this chapter demonstrates how legalization is an essential component and a natural third stage of the interactive authoritarianism model. Following the differentiation stage discussed in the previous chapter, I use process tracing and in-depth interviews to illustrate how different CSO activities—particularly domestic charitable activities versus foreign NGO operations—are legalized. The evidence I have gathered suggests that policy experimentation in the society combines a top-down and a bottom-up process that is initiated by individual citizens, CSOs, and local governments—what I call "interactive experimentation." Such a process would happen in a legally gray area, in what Tang Tsou calls the "zone of indifference."[14] The linkage between the three stages in the interactive authoritarian model is also addressed in order to show how the state initially tolerates the relevant CSO activities (discussed in chapter 2), and then mid- or top-level governments intervene once certain practices reach a scale and use resources and mandates to provide guidance and boundaries so that the experimented activities gradually align with the goals of the government. The reactions toward actions with potentially regime-challenging (or mis-aligned) goals and regime-supporting (or aligned) goals can lead to deliberate differentiation (discussed in chapter 3). Eventually, as boundaries of activities become more evident and new rules are proposed to govern the relevant actors and their behaviors, state-organized legalization occurs.

DIVIDE AND RULE: EXPERIMENTING WITH CHINESE SOCIETY

This section demonstrates the interactive experimentation and the transition from toleration and differentiation leading to the state-organized legalization process by the Chinese government toward civil society actors. As illustrated in table 4.1, I compare and contrast the process of how charitable CSOs and foreign NGOs are governed. These two types of CSOs faced similar conditions and treatments after their initial emergence in China. The various institutional disruptions accelerated their growth, and as experiments moved forward, these organizations and their activities were tolerated, interacted—with initiatives from both the state and society—and replicated. It was only the differentiation from the top that put the two types of CSOs on separate trajectories of legalization, eventually leading to the Charity Law and the Foreign NGO Law that would govern them, respectively.

INITIAL CONDITIONS AND INSTITUTIONAL DISRUPTIONS

For a long time, the totalitarian Chinese state penetrated every corner of the society that no formally codified documents were in place to stipulate how society, and the actors within, should be governed. The first law relating to CSOs in China since the establishment of the People's Republic in 1949 was the 1989 "Provisional Regulations for the Administration of Foreign Chambers of Commerce in China" (*waiguoshanghui guanlizanxingguiding* 外国商会管理暂行规定, hereafter referred to as the "1989 Regulations of Foreign Chambers of Commerce").[15] In the same year, the "Regulation on Registration and Administration of Social Organizations" (*shehuituanti dengjiguanlitiaoli* 社会团体登记管理条例)[16] was announced. Both regulations were products of previous legalizations consistent with features of an interactive authoritarian state. This indicates that legalization, even though being the third stage of the interactive authoritarianism model, is still an impermanent arrangement in a continuously evolving process. For illustration pur-

TABLE 4.1. The process of state-organized legalization in China

Subject of analysis	Initial conditions	Intentional Legal Gray Zone (zone of indifference)		Outcome of legalization
		Institutional disruptions	Interactive experimentations	
Domestic CSOs	Inadequate law; incremental regulation patches when necessary	Reform and opening, 1995 UN Women's Conference, 1998 flood, 2008 earthquake etc.	Chengdu (tolerate) → Mianzhu (participate) → Ya'an (take initiatives) → Sichuan (promote) → Nationwide (further replication)	Charity Law
Foreign NGOs			Chengdu (tolerate) → File documentation (participate) → Yunnan (take initiatives) → Xiamen, Beijing, Shanghai, Zhejiang (further replication) → *intervention from the top* → Civil Affairs to Public Security	Foreign NGO Law

poses, this chapter uses the 1980s as the initial condition for process tracing, which is a time when the laws were inadequate and required incremental regulation patches when necessary.

Institutional disruptions could create new motives to change or update procedures of governing the society by the state and to provide societal actors with windows of opportunities to enlarge their presence. The Chinese state realized that economic development could benefit from foreign NGOs. Therefore, in 1987, alongside the Ministry of Civil Affairs, the Ministry of Foreign Trade and Economic Cooperation, the Ministry of Foreign Affairs, and the Ministry of Finance requested approval from the State Council to set up the China International Economic and Technical Exchange Center to facilitate foreign NGOs' support (mainly monetary) for economic development in rural areas. In about six years, more than one hundred foreign NGOs contributed over 50 million RMB (renminbi) to China through the center.[17] In 1988 the Ford Foundation, having observed an opportunity, became the first foreign NGO to acquire formal status in China, after negotiating with the State Council and eventually having the China Academy of Social Sciences as its Professional Supervisory Unit (PSU).[18] During most of the 1980s, foreign NGOs were seen as friendly forces that could be utilized for China's economic development.

Even though the 1989 Tiananmen incident alerted the government about the potential "ulterior motives" of foreign NGOs, Deng's 1992 southern tour, which changed China's priority back to economic liberalization, and the 1995 UN Women's Conference in Beijing further stimulated development of foreign NGOs in China, disrupting existing institutional constraints as perceptions about foreign NGOs and their activities continued to evolve. In 2004 the phrase "foreign foundations" first appeared in the 2004 "Regulation on Foundation Administration." Anticipating being welcomed, more and more foreign NGOs started to set up offices and operate in China, following the precedent set up by the Ford Foundation. However, there were no standards set regarding the procedures or rules about the application process, as they were mostly done on a case-by-case basis.

On the domestic side, the 1998 flood in the Yangtze River led to an outpouring of societal donations. The cash and goods donated by the public were reported to be at least 7.2 billion RMB (about 1 billion USD),[19] not including donations from Taiwan, Hong Kong, Macau, and foreign countries. Although this is not comparable to the 76.2 billion RMB worth of cash and goods received after the 2008 Wenchuan earthquake,[20] it was already a significant amount at that time. Back then, China had no regulations about managing these donations or maintaining accountability for the usage of the donations. These new developments could also be viewed as institutional disruptions. While the emergency response was mainly made by the government and military, individuals started to organize donations to help those in need. In the meantime, the making of both the 1998 "Interim Regulations on Registration Administration of Private Non-Enterprise Units" (民办非企业单位登记管理暂行条例, hereafter referred to as the "1998 Regulations")[21] and the "Law of the People's Republic of China on Donations for Public Welfare" (*zhonghuarenmingongheguo gongyishiyejuanzengfa* 中华人民共和国公益事业捐赠法, hereafter referred to as the "Donations Law")[22] were sped up.

The 1998 regulations were seen as a milestone in the legal development of the CSO sector. The concept of "non-enterprise unit" in the regulation mainly refers to CSOs that are privately run by individual citizens. The rules state that they are not allowed to have ownership, no regional branch offices, no tax breaks, nor can they get loans from banks. Such an incentive structure pushed many social entrepreneurs to register their CSOs as commercial companies rather than "non-enterprise units," because commercial companies pay no more taxes yet are less politically sensitive. While the state continued to be cautious and heavily involved in controlling activities in the society, the 1998 regulation did formally grant some space for CSOs. It recognizes CSOs' legal status and stipulates the detailed process of how to register and operate a CSO in China, therefore providing legitimacy to organizations that were previously operating in the shadow.

The 2004 "Regulation on Foundation Administration" (*jijinhui guanlitiaoli* 基金会管理条例, hereafter referred to as the "2004 Foundation Regulations")[23] was another major step forward, providing new space for CSOs. Before 2004 all CSOs were under a "dual management system." CSOs needed to find a PSU as a sponsor, usually a government agency in a similar field, and then register with the Ministry of Civil Affairs. Thus, CSOs could only be "state-run" or "state-affiliated" before 2004. The "2004 Foundation Regulations" allow private individuals to organize private foundations. These foundations, not allowed to raise funds publicly, could then directly register at the Ministry of Civil Affairs without the PSU. This symbolic break away from state affiliation was a step toward more autonomy for some CSOs.

The 2008 Wenchuan earthquake was another critical moment for CSOs operating in China, whether the CSOs were locally --grown or foreign-born.

Immediately after the earthquake, there was an explosion in the number of new CSOs, mainly informal, non-registered community associations. Seeing this new development in society, the Ministry of Civil Affairs started to research and prepare the drafting of the Charity Law to improve its governance of the new players in the society.[24] However, because the state knew little about the prospects of the development of the CSO sector, the condition was not yet mature enough to make laws. Thus, the initiation of drafting the Charity Law was abandoned in 2009. With such a background in mind, I now describe how seemingly similar trajectories of interactive experimentations led to very different outcomes of legalization of domestic and foreign CSOs' activities.

INTERACTIVE EXPERIMENTATION: DOMESTIC CSOS' ACTIVITIES

Step I: Tolerate

As discussed in chapter 1, the Chinese government has five official administrative levels: national, provincial, municipality, county, and township. The village level (which is below the township level) is semi-formal because cadre wages are paid out of local funds, while the township (and higher) level cadres' wages are from state funds. Individual village cadres also do not need to pass the civil service exam (公务员资格考试) to take office. As a result, many of the operations are open to creativity and adjustments based on local conditions. This is also why it was acceptable for competitive elections to happen at the village level while those moving up toward the township or county level faced tremendous hurdles.

To a certain extent, there are many similarities between village governments and government-run social organizations. With the government mandate and the party secretary sent down from above, village governments have government sponsors (township governments) above them while maintaining some autonomy and flexibility at the local level. This is also why there are many variations of relationship types between local governments and CSOs (described in chapter 5). CSOs and local governments can share or compete for the same resources. They can also share or differ in their mission and goals. Based on the existing capacities of the local government, there are also variations in government effectiveness. Therefore, cases can be found in almost every category when a few of these main variables differ.

When CSOs are dealing with governments at the county level and above, the power dynamic is much more clear-cut. The governments at these levels are much more dominant. They can wield their power over CSOs. On the other hand, they are also relatively more confident in dealing with CSOs, thus more willing to explore different options.

The 2008 earthquake was a critical juncture for CSOs in China. Most regions struck by the 2008 Wenchuan earthquake had volunteers and CSOs flooding in after the quake. These CSOs--whether self-organized or organized by other, more established CSOs, whether developed organically from within or supported by outside resources--started to bond with local community members. Local governments saw both opportunities and risks with this new development within society.[25] To any authoritarian regime, abrupt changes in society's structure, especially with increased associational behaviors, may enlarge the risk of organized opposition. Furthermore, there were no adequate legal constraints to contain the actions and behaviors of those newly created CSOs. Yet, with the experiences of interactions between the state and these CSOs, the state would gain more knowledge about who these CSOs were and what their intentions might be. The officials also saw how these CSOs could potentially do a good job in delivering public goods and services--maybe even with a much lower (or zero) cost. Therefore, instead of crushing all CSOs at once, the local governments looked for ways to manage both the risks and opportunities and maximize the benefits. The local governments also noticed what was already happening with the CSOs.[26]

Chengdu, the capital of Sichuan province, was within the quake zone during the 2008 earthquake, although the infrastructure in Chengdu was not severely affected. The toleration of domestic CSO activities and even the coordinated actions by CSOs were visible immediately after the earthquake. Unlike in rural areas, where formally established CSOs were rare back then, and where most associational behaviors were informal and based on lineage and temple, in major cities like Chengdu, CSOs were already flourishing, registered or not. The 2008 Wenchuan earthquake had several significant effects on these CSOs:

1. CSOs started to coordinate actions and specialize tasks using their competitive (or comparative) advantage after the earthquake.
2. Volunteers, especially those formerly working for another CSO, became a key source to produce leaders of new CSOs.
3. Local governments noticed the networking behaviors of the CSOs

and allowed (sometimes illegal) experimentations while providing an enlarged space for CSOs. Such experimentations of local governance are imitated by governments from other localities once experimentation proves to be successful.

4. CSOs formerly not registered sought legitimization, and the state also tried various ways to accommodate the rise of CSOs, including putting together a new law to regulate the sector.

The networking and coordination between different CSOs started immediately. There were two major platforms that were established for CSO coordination in Chengdu: the Sichuan Joint Disaster Relief Office (四川联合救灾办公室, hereafter referred to as "Joint Relief Office") and the 512 NGO Services Center (四川512民间救助服务中心, hereafter referred to as "512 Center").[27] The former is mainly in charge of goods and service delivery, while the latter is in charge of information verification and the planning of resource allocation. In other words, the latter is responsible for thinking and the former is responsible for execution. The leaders of the two platforms are also good friends.

GZ[28] was both a government official and the leader of a GONGO in the city of Panzhihua in southern Sichuan before the earthquake happened. He was nominated as the coordinator of local CSOs to start the Joint Relief Office right after the earthquake. He hesitated mainly because of the potential pressure he could face from the government but eventually agreed to take the role.[29]

The Joint Relief Office was in charge of the delivery of essential goods and services to the quake-stricken region during the first week after the earthquake. Government vehicles are usually trucks that would not be able to enter the mountainous regions after the earthquake, while the Joint Relief Office was able to organize a fleet of SUVs owned by CSOs and individual volunteers that were able to enter the quake-stricken regions. As a result, the Joint Relief Office was an effective complement to the government and military; it was also a time to utilize the specialties of different CSOs. Individual CSOs might not have the capacity to carry such complex tasks, but once they are coordinated, certain organizations that excel at inventories are in charge of inventories. Others are in charge of organizing volunteers, goods purchasing, and fund-raising, respectively. The individual leaders and volunteers built a strong trust and a tight network through this effort.[30]

In Sichuan, CSOs were not seen by the government and their peers as organizations but as "a leader plus a group of staff or volunteers." People usually identify CSOs by their leaders' names rather than the name of the organization. For example, the name "Joint Relief Office" is usually replaced with "GZ's team." Such practices not only indicate the organizational dynamics for CSOs (less about the brand name, more about personal reputation) but also have significant consequences. Local governments tend to collaborate with those organizations led by leaders they trust more (whether based on past interactions or the individual's background). Donors also tend to contribute more resources to organizations led by leaders they know better. Therefore, if an organization changes leadership, the organization usually needs to reconfigure its relationships with the local government and the donors. Organizational relationships are the extension of personal relationships.

The individual-based approach directly led GZ into trouble. The major donors wanted to transfer funding directly to GZ, indicating that they did not trust anyone else but him. They also did not want to wire the money to GZ's GONGO, as the bureaucracy would slow down the process and the money would not be used in time to save the people in the quake-stricken region. They wanted the money to follow GZ because he was the one they trusted. On the other hand, putting donations directly into an individual's private account violates the law. Even GZ's GONGO did not have the credentials to receive donations directly. Donations have to be wired to foundations having credentials first, then given to CSOs that are registered, and eventually used for projects. GZ thought that being a government official himself, he could take the responsibility later and that the punishment would not be that severe. He was later investigated by multiple departments, including being taken away for a month by people from the National Security department. Yet, because they did not find any evidence of GZ's embezzlement of the money—he had spent all the money on individuals who were in need in the quake-stricken region and had followed good record keeping—no case was brought against him. What brought GZ down was not the legal system but a factional fight within the political system. There were conservatives and progressives within the Panzhihua government, and GZ was one of those progressives. Given that GZ had received donations directly and put the money into his personal bank account, the conservative faction attacked him vehemently, and he was forced to resign less than three weeks after the earthquake.

Because GZ was under investigation and entangled with this factional fight, those CSOs that had already registered were quite reluctant to participate in the Joint Relief Office platform, fearing their license would be revoked. Instead, those unregistered CSOs played a vital role in this networking and coordinating endeavor. The Joint Relief Office lasted only about two weeks before it was dissolved. GZ argued that its only mission was emergency rescues, and they planned to exist for only about seven to ten days to begin with. Some people have speculated that GZ's investigation and factional fight might have had something to do with the dissolution of the office.

GZ mentioned during an interview later that he was touched by the volunteers' compassion and motivation even after the office had been dissolved. Since he had already quit his job three weeks after the earthquake, he and his friend WZ initiated the NGO Disaster Preparedness Center, or NGODPC (NGO 备灾中心). NGODPC continued the work of the Joint Relief Office in the city of Mianzhu (at the epicenter) in post-disaster reconstruction. Some of the volunteers previously working for GZ also started their own CSOs after the dissolution of the Joint Relief Office. By the time of my interview in 2013, GZ had registered NGODPC in the city of Dujiangyan and had branch offices in counties including Shifang and Mianzhu. GZ was aware that if the 1998 Regulation on Registration and Administration of Social Organizations is strictly enforced, he might be under investigation again. So far, the local government is comfortable with its power, knowing that whenever they want to shut down NGODPC, they can; it is experimenting with NGODPC by not enforcing the law.

The 512 Center led by HG, a social scientist from Sichuan Academy of Social Sciences, was the second major platform that was initiated because of the 2008 Wenchuan earthquake.[31] HG believes that many people with small actions, if coordinated, can create a major impact. HG is well respected in the CSO community in Sichuan. When she facilitated the initiation of the 512 Center, many existing CSOs joined. The 512 Center has several teams, including information, volunteer, material supply, and finance. They played a supportive role in all CSOs during the quake relief period. The idea was mainly to keep a list of all volunteers, money, and goods so that energy and time would not be wasted for duplicated work by different CSOs. Suppose a CSO at the front line of rescue wanted specific goods and resources. In that case, they looked up the information from the 512 Center's list, and then another CSO in charge of goods delivery was dispatched to deliver the goods or resources. The 512 Center also facilitated meeting spaces, communication support, and logistical support. After the earthquake, the 512 Center continued to facilitate the betterment of resource allocation among CSOs for post-quake reconstruction and economic development. Thirty-seven CSOs have signed a memorandum of understanding (MOU) with the 512 Center, and over eighty CSOs maintain more extended collaboration and information sharing with the 512 Center.

The 512 Center realized that it would be a mismatch if it continued to operate as a post-disaster platform while the main work it does is less and less disaster-related but supports CSOs in general. It also operated without formal registration, so it was, in fact, an illegal organization. The government was aware of that and allowed the center to be temporarily affiliated with the Chengdu River Research Association for accounting and legal purposes, but that was not going to be a permanent solution. Therefore, the center registered under the Sichuan Department of Civil Affairs, using the Sichuan Society Scientific Community Federation as its PSU in March 2012.[32] They continue to focus on public welfare information sharing and service and play a key role in creating a network to connect CSOs in Sichuan.

Step 2: Governments Participate and Then Take Initiatives

Besides the toleration of the 512 Center and the Joint Relief Office, both of which played vital roles immediately after the earthquake, other localities developed social innovations that would coordinate not only the CSOs but also the government and businesses during the recovery period. On June 21, 2008, forty days after the Wenchuan earthquake, the government of Mianzhu was invited to participate in a forum organized by the China Social Entrepreneur Foundation (友成企业家扶贫基金会) and McKinsey and Company to discuss post-disaster reconstruction in Mianzhu. A month later, the Mianzhu post-disaster social resources coordination platform (hereafter referred to as the "Mianzhu platform") was created.

The Mianzhu platform relies on resources from the government, businesses, and a private foundation to coordinate and support CSOs for post-disaster reconstruction. The platform has four main teams: project and emergency response, organization and public relations, integration and management, and development and outreach. Such a structure provides human capital, technological support, capacity building, volunteer training, and coordination to CSOs. The project and emergency response team plans sustainable development projects, evaluates projects during different phases, and formulates plans when an emergency happens. The organization and public relations team conducts event planning (such as group dances or choirs), media relations, and volunteer recruitment. The integration and management team conducts research on social demand, organizes data collected, monitors ongoing projects, and keeps records of meeting minutes and relevant documents. The development and outreach team focuses on capacity building, social innovation, social collaboration, and CSO support.[33]

The Mianzhu platform was seen as a great success. It optimized resource allocation, promoted the development of CSOs, increased the efficiency of the government, and, of course, enhanced the positive image of the government. Initially, the government was invited to join the forum only to deliberate solutions for post-disaster reconstructions, but it ended up being one of the key participants in the Mianzhu platform. China had no rules or precedents of the government, businesses, foundations, and CSOs, in general, collaborating to achieve a common goal together under such integrated mechanisms before the Mianhzu platform, and it was an experiment that largely succeeded.

Other local governments learned lessons from the Mianzhu platform experiment, and adjustments were made in the experiments that followed. On April 20, 2013, there was another major earthquake in Sichuan province in Lushan County, less than one hundred miles south of Wenchuan. The CSOs immediately followed previous examples of the Joint Relief Office and the 512 Center and formed a network of CSOs for emergency response. The city of Ya'an (where Lushan County is located) imitated the Mianzhu platform and initiated the Ya'an Mass Organizations Social Service Center (hereafter referred to as the "Ya'an Mass-Org Center").

A few changes were made. Instead of directly involving the local government (and therefore being responsible), the Communist Youth League was designated to coordinate government affairs. During an interview, the leader at the Ya'an Mass-Org Center emphasized that they did not want to leave the image that the government or the Communist Party are heavily involved, so they decided to let the Communist Youth League take the lead. They also involved the many mass organizations that are mainly GONGOs, including the Federation of Trade Unions, Women's Federation, and China's Disabled Persons' Federation, among others. Such actions ensured that the government was present and could be reached yet also prevented (at least the image of) the heavy and direct involvement of the local government.[34]

The Ya'an Mass-Org Center set up a permanent office and not only facilitated the post-disaster reconstruction efforts and coordinated the CSOs to provide goods and public services to villagers in the quake-stricken region but also, after the disaster, provided office space and some funding for CSOs to continue their developmental work, as some of the CSOs have expertise in farming and raising animals.

Step 3: Promote Successful Models and Further Replication

The Ya'an Mass-Org Center, learning from the experiences from the Mianzhu platform, was a great success. Therefore, from 2013 to 2017 the Sichuan provincial government decided to set up such a center at the provincial level and let other county-level governments set up their own mass-org centers. The provincial-level mass-org center had by then registered as a social organization called Xieli Gongyi (协力公益),[35] while at least eighteen cities and county-level mass-org centers are up and running.[36] In 2015 the central government organized a Mass Organizations Conference in Beijing to promote the Sichuan experiences so that other provinces could also set up mass-org centers to coordinate work between the government, businesses, and CSOs.[37]

Experimentation with CSOs was not only going on in the quake-stricken region in Sichuan. Guangdong province also started to experiment with more straightforward and accessible ways to get CSOs registered. Guangdong disconnected industry and business associations from local governments, increased the transparency of CSOs, and developed new types of CSOs that would be able to tackle new challenges in society. Of course, the initiation of party structure within CSOs was also experimented with and later adopted.[38] Other cities, such as Ningbo, Shanghai, Tai'an, Tianjin, Shantou, and a dozen provinces, also had various experiments with CSOs.[39] Some experiments were replicated, such as the evolution from Mianzhu Center, to Ya'an Mass-Org Center, to mass-org centers all over Sichuan, and, eventually, nation-wide; other experiments were only tested locally. This was a clear strategy of "from point to surface," just like what happened in the economic domain in the 1980s–1990s.

While the experiments were going on, the state used this opportunity to adapt and learn and eventually use innovative strategies to control and govern society. The earthquakes led to the sudden increase of CSO activities in the quake-stricken zone. The government, on the other hand, was incapacitated. So how could the government check and monitor the large number of

CSOs within their jurisdictions? The Sichuan provincial government decided to recruit a few hundred social supervisors (社会监督员) about ten days after the earthquake. They accepted applications from the public and selected 308 social supervisors from over 2,600 applicants.[40] If the government did not have the capacity to check on society, it could co-opt parts of society and use them to monitor other parts of society. These social supervisors were hired for three months and monitored the whole process of purchasing, stocking, delivering, and distributing goods. They reported directly to the provincial government and were well received by both citizens and local governments.[41]

Chapter 3 discussed the deliberate differentiation strategy adopted by the government. Letting society check society and report suspicious activities to the provincial government also made CSOs less likely to organize regime-challenging activities. The bureaucracy's size is limited, but once the state has parts of the society working for the bureaucratic apparatus, it becomes more effective in deterring regime-challenging activities. Based on the study done by Huimin Bian, Zhenyao Wang, Puqu Wang, and Yan Feng, even though the over three hundred CSOs had various themes and emphases, almost all organizations limited their functions to disaster response and post-disaster reconstruction, regardless of the original mission of the organization.[42] The government was also happy to facilitate the operations of these CSOs, including providing office and activity spaces; helping their communication with upper-level governments; arranging room and board for volunteers and staff; and providing consultation, transportation, and financial support.

It is worth noting that some of the CSOs built relationships and trust with the government due to their interactions during the quake relief periods. A few of these CSOs would be able to lobby effectively, resulting in policy change. For example, XR, a CSO leader who provides support to farmers about rabbit-raising techniques and resources, noticed that the design for rebuilding had turned farmers' homes into apartment buildings or townhouses. Some people in Sichuan like to raise chickens, ducks, or pigs in their backyards. Backyards are also an excellent place to store farming tools. Therefore, XR wrote a letter to the government to petition to leave at least 45–60 square meters of backyard for each household in the design. He also framed the issue as "protecting Sichuan's culture," a strategy proven to be quite effective in China.[43] As a result, the new homes in Mianyang, Deyang, and Shifang all had backyards for about 65 square meters.

Step 4: Legalization

While the experiments and state-CSO interactions were happening in the field, the central government was also starting to reconsider drafting the Charity Law to govern the newly evolved better and replicated interactive experimentations. Previously, researching and drafting were initiated by the Ministry of Civil Affairs in 2009, but the efforts were paused due to a lack of familiarity with the CSO developments. In 2010 the Interior Judicial Committee of the National People's Congress (全国人大内务司法委员会) again made attempts to research the Charity Law, hoping to accompany it with the Social Assistance Act (社会救助法), which was also being considered at the time. However, not much meaningful progress was made, and the Charity Law was put on hold again. In 2012 the CCP's 18th Party Congress decided to make social development a key national development component. Social organizations, providing an opportunity for citizens to participate in public affairs, became a critical domain for societal governance. The third plenum of the 18th Party Congress also announced the decision about deepening reform--specifically, to ask social organizations to set up various enterprises in villages, to motivate the vitality of social organizations, and to let social organizations provide public service.[44]

Based on the experiences and development at the local level, especially the benefits the government saw with CSOs providing public goods and services cheaper and often better[45] than the local government or GONGOs, the State Council announced the "Plan for the Institutional Restructuring of the State Council and Transformation of Functions Thereof" (国务院机构改革和职能转变方案),[46] which suggested emphasizing the development of four types of social organizations: industry and business associations, science and technology associations, public welfare and charitable associations, and urban and rural community service organizations. This indicates that there are specific public goods and services the government would want to extract from the productivities of specific CSOs but not necessarily others.

The utilization of local CSO resources and productivities also started to appear in government agendas. For example, in 2014 the Ministry of Civil Affairs and the Ministry of Finance jointly announced the "Notice on the Support and Normalize the Service Purchasing from Social Organizations by the Government" (关于支持和规范社会组织承接政府购买服务的通知)[47] as well as the "Selections from the Policy Documents of Government Purchasing Services" (政府购买服务政策文件选编), which was used to train 136 budgetary units of the central and local government Civil Affairs officers.[48] The government was apparently preparing to persuade specific regime-support CSOs to be more involved in local governance.

In November 2014 the State Council released the instructions about "Promoting the Healthy Development of the Charity Industry," which was the first time the central government released a policy document specifically targeting the charity industry. As a result, the Charity Law drafting team was formed, an effort directly led by the Interior Judicial Committee of the NPC. After about twenty months, on October 30, 2015, the draft law was discussed in the NPC for the first time. The law was then immediately released to the public for additional input. Two months later, the revised draft law was discussed and released again to the public for the second time. During the NPC and CPPCC meetings (两会 or two sessions) in March 2016, the draft law was discussed again and was passed on March 16. President Xi Jinping immediately signed the law so that it could be put into effect on September 1, 2016.

The legalization of domestic CSO activities was seen as a positive step to provide guidance and support for individuals and CSOs to participate in public goods provision. For example, people and organizations that do not have the qualifications to raise money publicly (公开募捐) can now do it legally through collaborations with organizations that do have those qualifications or use directional fund-raising and target a specific group to raise money independently (定向募捐). The new Charity Law also replaced the concept of "people-run non-enterprises" (民办非企业) with "social service groups" (社会服务机构) so that charitable organizations could be in the forms of foundations, social groups, and social service groups. However, charitable activities are not limited to charitable organizations. It is now legal for individuals and organizations that are not charitable organizations to organize charitable activities. Besides the narrow definition of charitable activities (such as poverty alleviation, disaster response, and senior or weak care), the law also allows activities that fall under a more extensive umbrella of social welfare (such as education, science and technology, culture, sports, and health.)

The control over charitable organizations has also been loosened to allow more flexibility and wiggle room. For example, organizations used to be required to get an annual inspection from their PSU, which was an essential mechanism for the government to control the CSOs, since the threat of "not approving" is credible and could be used to shape the actions of CSOs. In the Charity Law, the annual inspection was replaced with an annual report describing their activities to "inform" the government without having to request approval from their PSU beforehand.

The people who were involved in drafting the law had expressed the core idea behind the provisions: the government should not take the lead role or be the only player in charitable activities but should step back and provide guidance and information. Individuals and organizations should be encouraged to organize charitable activities and provide public goods and welfare.[49] It is clear that more doors have been opened for domestic CSOs and individuals to organize activities in society, as long as the goal is to provide welfare to the society.

INTERACTIVE EXPERIMENTATION: FOREIGN NGOS' ACTIVITIES

Step 1: Tolerate

The 2008 Wenchuan earthquake, again, was a significant moment for foreign NGOs in China. Donations from foreign sources increased by 83 percent between 2007 and 2008. However, the trend of rising donations has stopped and reversed since 2009.[50] The year 2008 was an excellent opportunity for domestic CSOs, but it also foreshadowed the tightening of space for foreign NGOs. Domestic CSOs, as mentioned previously, face multiple constraints, and the rules prevented them from operating freely across provincial borders. On the other hand, foreign NGOs had no such constraints, simply because no specific rules regarding their activities have yet been made.

For a long time, the vast majority of foreign NGOs in China operated in a legal gray area, and the government tolerated them because they posed no credible threats and were bringing resources into their jurisdictions. Some foreign NGOs had local partners, and some were registered as commercial enterprises. The quake relief effort in 2008 to some extent was a wake-up call for the Chinese government. The state suddenly realized the urgency of having to put together a set of comprehensive and coherent rules to regulate the foreign NGOs, since there are so many of them operating in the gray area, and any possibility of a potential color revolution in China is not going to be tolerated by the state.[51]

Step 2: Governments Participate and Then Take Initiatives

Experiments started in Yunnan in 2009 when the provincial government released the "Interim Provisions on the Regulations of Overseas Non-Governmental Organizations in Yunnan Province" (云南省规范境外非政府组织活动暂行规定, hereafter referred to as the "Yunnan provisions").[52] Yunnan province has a significant foreign NGO presence mainly due to the anti-HIV/AIDS efforts and the environmental movements to protect the last undammed river (Nu River) in China.[53] The local government previously tolerated the existence of foreign NGOs within its jurisdictions. Some foreign NGOs voluntarily filed documentation (备案) with the government before starting their projects, hoping to reduce potential tension between the state and CSOs.

The interviews in Sichuan province conducted in this research also revealed similar behaviors. In 2008 after the Wenchuan earthquake, those CSOs that filed documentation with the government before taking action were usually better received by local governments, so by the time of the 2013 Lushan earthquake, most CSOs filed documentation first and then took action. Therefore, the key idea in the Yunnan provisions was to spell out how, when, and with whom to file the documentation. Through documentation filing and PSU clarification, foreign NGOs could register and enjoy their legitimacy to operate in Yunnan. It was clear that the Yunnan provisions were not intended to discourage operations of foreign NGOs but to make foreign NGOs more transparent so that the government would be able to monitor and control their activities.

Step 3: Promote Successful Models, Further Replication, and Top-Down Disruption

The experiments in Yunnan were then copied (and slightly modified) in Xiamen to document economic and trade associations from Taiwan setting up representative offices in Xiamen[54] and other places such as Beijing, Shanghai, and Zhejiang.[55] The replications of the original pilot case were used to test whether the same method would be effective when governing different types of foreign NGOs with variations in local bureaucratic conditions. All of these regulations had significant portions that were similar to Yunnan's stipulation about how to encourage foreign NGOs to file documentation.

The interactive experimentations between the local governments and foreign NGOs almost looked like they were going to follow a similar path of the interactions between the state and domestic CSOs, until a significant turning point occurred in 2013 when Xi Jinping took office. The new central leadership initiated a major crackdown on foreign NGOs in China for national security purposes. In 2014, one month after the first National Security Commission meeting, investigations of foreign NGOs in China began. Around the same time, the Chinese state started drafting the new Foreign NGO Law. Before that, the Ministry of Civil Affairs was drafting regulations based on the Yunnan experience and subsequent experiments. In 2014 this process was interrupted by a different priority, and the Ministry of Public Security, an office that was much less accommodating toward CSOs, took over.

Step 4: Legalization

Legalization would still happen, although it was clear that drafting the new Foreign NGO Law had a different motivation once the Politburo Standing Committee deliberated the first draft of the law in 2014.[56] Getting the resources from these foreign NGOs to support economic development was still a possible motivation. Nevertheless, it was overshadowed by the more critical motivation: preventing foreign forces from initiating color revolutions and Western infiltrations in China. From that point, the bottom-up process of experimentation had been forcefully halted with a top-down agenda.

When the final version of the Foreign NGO Law was passed in April 2016, there were a few significant and notable differences between the Charity Law and the Foreign NGO Law in terms of governing domestic and international CSOs. Domestic CSOs have already moved beyond the dual management system and no longer need the PSUs. The "supervisory unit" is not a "guidance unit." The dual management system remained for foreign NGOs, and the PSUs are still necessary. Foreign NGOs have two ways to operate legally in China: register as a representative office or register for a temporary activities permit lasting one year. Using the term "representative office" means that the offices do not have a legal person's qualification. Their foreign organization, therefore, could be pursued for legal responsibility and liability. With burdensome procedures, the temporary activities permit is extremely difficult to get. This is also why there were zero cases of permit requests in the first three months after the law had taken effect.[57] Foreign NGOs are also directly under the Ministry of Public Security's jurisdiction, unlike domestic CSOs, which remain under the Ministry of Civil Affairs.[58]

Other restrictions are applied to foreign NGOs but not necessarily to domestic CSOs. For example, foreign NGOs are not allowed to fund-raise in China (rules that have been loosened for domestic CSOs) nor recruit members (the function of domestic social groups). Foreign NGOs are expected to register at the provincial level with PSUs as national government agencies, while domestic CSOs can register at different levels of the government.

Such stipulations do not mean the Chinese government wants to drive all foreign NGOs away. The government still encourages some foreign NGOs to provide expertise and spend their money on clearly defined fields such as rural education, poverty alleviation, and water conservation. Activities in rights protection, advocacy, religion, and other areas are generally prohibited. This is to recognize that even among the foreign NGOs, there might still be regime-supporting groups with resources that the government needs or with goals that are similar to those of the government. The deliberate differentiation strategy also works at this level targeting foreign NGOs.

INTERACTIVE EXPERIMENTATION AND STATE-ORGANIZED LEGALIZATION

If we compare the process of legalizing actions by domestic CSOs and foreign NGOs, we see striking similarities. The government allowed a period of an intentional legal gray zone for CSOs to operate while it became more familiar with the CSOs. The government's method of dealing with CSOs growing in society was also consistent until the central government intervened with foreign NGOs. Therefore, the legalization process started to diverge when the bottom-up process was quashed by the more determined top-down process. Thus, the outcome is that we have a relatively friendly Charity Law, which mainly governs domestic CSOs, and the somewhat constraining Foreign NGO Law, which mainly contains foreign NGOs.

At the initial step, when the number of CSOs started to grow after institutional disruptions, the government was open-minded about such a new phenomenon. With confidence in managing the CSOs and expectations to take advantage of the resources and opportunities some of the CSOs might bring, the government did not make that many rules to stipulate their actions. The regulations made were mainly incremental rules that became necessary but still minimal, and they governed only a specific aspect of the society, whether it was the chamber of commerce, non-enterprise units, or foundations.

Institutional disruptions, particularly natural disasters, would stimulate the development of CSOs and therefore speed up the legalization process. The 1998 floods and 2008 earthquake were significant times for the development of both domestic and international CSOs, and so were major international events such as the 1995 UN Women's Conference. Natural disasters could increase trust, networking, the norms of reciprocity between community members, and the rise of voluntarism. Such organic developments within the society also led to natural bottom-up experiments.

The interactive experimentation process also happens in the "legal gray zone." The making of both the Charity Law and the Foreign NGO Law started with a similar process when experimentation began. The government allowed the 512 Center and Joint Relief Office to play their roles without too much intervention, even though such coordination between CSOs was unprecedented. In addition, the government tolerated the new developments of CSOs, even though there were no specific laws to regulate them and their status was mainly illegal. The government understands that it would be easier to comprehend their behavior and assess their consequences by allowing their activities and space. Since the scope was initially minimal, the government had the confidence to manage the risks. Furthermore, the leaders of those experiments all had some past government background or affiliation. So toleration was the norm at the initial step.

Once it was clear that certain benefits would arise, the government started to participate and become a player in the experiments. The state's presence in such experimentation can sometimes further improve the outcome of the experiments. For example, the government participated in the Mianzhu platform and provided resources and some legitimacy to the networking of CSOs as well as cross-sector collaboration for quake relief and reconstruction efforts. The government not only witnessed the more efficient resource allocation and the speedy recovery after the 2008 earthquake, but it also realized that participating in such efforts would increase the government's positive image.

The next step of state participation is mainly an opportunity for the government to better understand the new developments from within and along with their respective pros and cons. During this step, the foreign NGOs started the filing documentation practices voluntarily. Multiple organizations, during the interviews, mentioned that they realized reporting to the local government voluntarily and that documenting their activities usually is quite rewarding. This does not mean they will give in to the local government, but transparency would bring trust and goodwill, making their work more effective. After the 2008 Wenchuan earthquake, and especially during the subsequent major earthquakes in western China, CSOs overwhelmingly learned this technique. It was also rewarding for local governments, as they were able to have an excellent grasp of the activities without having to invest too many resources.

The state gradually changed from being a participant to taking initiative by starting experiments during the third step. The state, learning from past experiences, adjusted the experiments to reflect its preferences. The Ya'an Mass-Org Center was set up in the name of "mass organizations" and led by the Communist Youth League because the government wanted to be involved but not too much. Therefore, using the mass organizations and Communist Youth League as liaisons would be a good solution to achieve goals without exposing the government to too much liability should the experiment fail. On the governance of foreign NGOs, the government relied on the experiences of voluntary documentation filing and used Yunnan as a pilot case to further test the effectiveness of this process. The specific stipulation of government documentation included in the Yunnan experiment is an effort on the part of the government to get to know more about foreign NGOs' operations in Yunnan province in order to inform further coping mechanisms.

The subsequent step involves replicating the successful experiences, whether it is promoting the Ya'an experience to the entire Sichuan province, and eventually to the entire nation, or the imitation of the Yunnan provisions in other regions such as Beijing, Shanghai, and Zhejiang. The replications were not significantly different from the original version. At this step, the government was already quite comfortable with the experiment and confident that the practice would be effective nationwide. Therefore, the stipulation of formal laws based on such experiences was put on the agenda after this step.

The main differentiation happened when the central government, especially the CCP top leadership, intervened with the Foreign NGO Law development, turning it from a civil affairs matter into a public and national security matter. It was also clear that before the top-down intervention, the Ministry of Civil Affairs was already working on the Foreign NGO Law based on the Yunnan template. After the intervention, the Ministry of Public Security took over. So the experimentation initiated at the grassroots level did not run its entire course as it had with the Charity Law.

This does not suggest that the Foreign NGO Law is an outlier while the Charity Law is the norm. Differentiation points exist throughout the process. This chapter has presented the legalization strategy by the state, which follows differentiation based on goal alignment and government effectiveness toward domestic CSOs. Even though foreign NGOs are under much stricter scrutiny, there are still differentiations and legalization of their specific behaviors, as some of the foreign NGOs are still able to bring resources without too many additional risks. For example, foreign NGOs working in rural education, poverty alleviation, and water conservancy–related fields are still encouraged to operate in China, especially if they work closely with a domestic partner.

It is also important to point out that allowing the experiments to play out their courses does not mean the state has minimal involvement during the early steps. In fact, the state is constantly sensitive about how effective policy tools could be used to intervene when necessary. Therefore, incidents similar to the one of taking crosses off the top of churches in Zhejiang province could happen. The government would gain no utility from such actions other than testing the power of its authority. This way, the government would know that it is still in control even during the most creative period of social innovations and experiments.

The strategy the Chinese state utilized has been quite effective so far in managing risks and opportunities. The initial zone of indifference exists so that not all unfamiliar and illegal activities are quashed. To some extent, this tolerates (if not encourages) creativity in society. If no major risks are foreseen, the government could gradually transition from observer to participant and eventually implement the experimentations. Laws will be made once this whole process runs its entire course. If, at any point, there are issues that raise concerns, it would alert the particular level of the government, and then the government would become more cautious during the next phase. Such alerts would not completely shut down the process but would serve as differentiation points for the government to target (and tightly control) the regime-challenging factors while allowing the regime-supporting players to continue with the experimentation. The development would be more limited but not stopped. This also means that formal lawmaking does not indicate the end of the experimentation process but serves as a critical differentiation point in a continually evolving process.

LEGALIZATION AS THE THIRD STAGE OF INTERACTIVE AUTHORITARIANISM

This chapter has connected the dots of the previous two chapters and captured how the toleration-differentiation-legalization process would occur in terms of the authoritarian governance of society. Such a process would enable the state to be more adaptive and tackle its governance challenges more effectively when facing a new phenomenon in society. The chapter has also depicted the fundamental challenges the Chinese society is facing on its way to creating an autonomous mature civil society.

The government tolerates and observes new CSOs and their activities (often stimulated by institutional disruptions) that are not covered by existing rules and laws. Instead of using repression or issuing new rules and laws immediately, the government patiently waits and interacts with these societal actors, allowing information to flow between the state and society in order to better inform decision-making while soliciting help from society for better service provision. New CSOs also utilize the new windows of opportunities to adapt while remaining innovative in their struggle to survive and make meaningful impacts. Thus, toleration is often the status quo strategy by local governments when new players or procedures emerge (for example, new ways of running activities, delivering services, or making decisions).

Then the government deliberately differentiates different types of CSOs to more efficiently and effectively manage the risks and opportunities and take advantage of the potential resources and benefits CSOs could bring, in preparation for legalization, as different new practices and tactics by CSOs are documented and studied. It is worth noting that many existing CSOs may already be at the differentiation stage when new interactive experimentations start—due to the emergence of other new CSOs—so in the eyes of a specific organization, the lengths of the three stages could vary. It is also possible that certain CSOs could be tolerated for a long time before differentiation and legalization occurred.

Once the successful pilot cases are replicated and tested in different regions and domains, new laws would be drafted to temporarily solidify the successes from the interactive experimentations. Yet, those rules and laws are not permanent, as a new round of toleration-differentiation-legalization could be triggered at any moment in a dynamic interactive authoritarian state. As a result, the interactive experimentation process could lead to a significant amount of social innovation and policy optimization regarding better delivery of public goods and services and could constantly renew itself to better adapt to new circumstances and challenges.

However, the bottom-up force is vulnerable in the face of the top-down will of the party-state. Any major intervention could create differentiation points and change the course and consequences for certain actors in society. Therefore, even though the major disasters have opened up space and given us the possibility of creating a nascent civil society from the accumulation of social capital and the sudden space opened up for CSOs, we still don't have a clear path to a mature civil society, given the likelihood of strong top-down power intervening in the process. In the following chapters, I use three distinct case studies—in different spaces, from various regions, with specific key actors—to demonstrate how such a three-stage approach is used in various conditions and to reveal the logic of how the Chinese state governs the nascent civil society and the approaches it might take to meet future challenges.

PART III

Three "Most-Different Cases" Illustrating the Interactive Authoritarianism Model

CHAPTER 5

Case I

The Sichuan Earthquakes and the Governance of the Rising CSOs

At 2:28 p.m. on May 12, 2008, an 8.0 magnitude earthquake struck the Wenchuan region of Sichuan province. An estimated 4.5 million people were affected in some way, including 69,229 mortalities and 17,923 missing persons. Over 15 million residents had to be relocated due to one of the most destructive earthquakes in China's recorded history.[1]

Earthquakes of such magnitude posed severe challenges to the capacity of local governments. CSOs, in the meantime, were able to provide services and support while the local governments were incapacitated. Forty days after the earthquake, the Xinhua News Agency reported that over a million volunteers had already poured into the region and mobilized their resources to support the quake relief efforts.[2] Some of the volunteers turned into organizers. Many CSOs, whether formally registered or not, were created as a result.

Although highly tragic for the people affected, this moment provides an ideal opportunity for researchers to investigate how the Chinese state reacts to a new societal phenomenon during an institutional disruption. This chapter uses the 2008 Wenchuan earthquake and the subsequent Lushan earthquake (2013) and Ludian earthquake (2014) to demonstrate the evolution of the state's governance strategy following the toleration-differentiation-legalization stages discussed in the previous chapters. In this case, the institutional disruptions were earthquakes, and the space occupied by actors was the physical space in localities in rural areas. With a focus on CSOs, I demonstrate how unregistered "illegal" associations were allowed to exist first while the local governments observed; then, during the differentiation stage, there were crackdowns of specific CSOs and assistance provided to other CSOs to ease their registration and help them get funding. Rules and mechanisms tested at the local level are then briefly discussed, eventually leading to the making of the Charity Law and the Foreign NGO Law as a part of legalization. In the end, after the three stages interactive process, the authoritarian state was able to get more local public goods and service provision.

More specifically, individual citizens' attitudes toward CSOs throughout the process are presented. Then a dynamic typology of the state-CSO relationship framework is provided to illustrate how the state and CSOs interact with each other and adjust their policies and behaviors accordingly. Such a typology results from the dynamic differentiation of CSOs based on the relative *effectiveness of service provision* by the local government and the *degree of goal alignment* between the state and CSO. Both the short-term outcomes and long-term evolving trajectories are present under each combination when these key variables take different values. Thus, even though immediately after institutional disruptions, we see state-CSO relationships in the forms of competition, complementarity, cooperation, and confrontation (or no interaction due to ignorance), the long-run outcomes after extensive interactions can lead to co-optation, cooperation, confrontation, and even destruction. However, as the government adapts to the changing circumstances and becomes more effective in service provision, co-optation and destruction are likely to be the more prevalent relationships. Therefore, this chapter asserts that the state-society relationship is not static and provides the depiction of how seemingly stable power relations between the state and CSOs in an authoritarian state came about.

METHODS AND DATA

This chapter draws data from over 1,220 surveys of villagers, interviews with more than a dozen government officials and more than sixty CSO leaders, and employs tools such as natural experiments and process tracing.

First, the difference-in-difference approach has been utilized for the southern Sichuan region (see fig. 1.4 from chapter 1). Participants from thirty-six villages (about five people per village) were randomly selected to complete a survey interview. The first round of data was collected from May to June 2014. In August of the same year, Ludian, a county in the northern Yunnan province bordering southern Sichuan, was hit by a magnitude 6.1

earthquake. Twelve out of those thirty-six villages were severely affected by the earthquake. Therefore, another round of surveys and interviews was conducted from December 2014 to January 2015 to capture the post-treatment condition. The central question of interest in the survey for this study was whether the interviewee preferred the local government or a social organization to provide the public goods and services that the community was lacking. In other words, the participant had to choose between the government and the CSOs. In reality, some participants refused to give a clear answer and sometimes wanted to pick both or neither, but that was only a tiny portion of the sample. What I used, therefore, was a binary variable that was coded "1" if the participant preferred a social organization and "0" for all other choices, mostly favoring the government. Since prior to the Ludian earthquake, the development of CSOs in southern Sichuan was minimal, many of the CSO activities came about during or immediately after the earthquake. This means that the CSOs were usually small and new with little human and physical capital. As discussed in previous chapters, toleration was the primary strategy by the government during this stage, and the government wanted CSOs to shoulder more blames. Did the local citizens prefer the government over CSOs or vice versa?

Second, in order to investigate the more mature and professional CSOs, data from the original natural experiment design were examined. As discussed in chapter 1, the original design was to see whether individuals had different attitudes about CSOs from the region hit by the 2008 Wenchuan earthquake as opposed to the region that was not in southern Sichuan. There was a rise of voluntarism and a wave of new CSO activities immediately after the 2008 earthquake, and many of them developed, evolved, and professionalized during the next several years. In 2013 another major quake hit almost the same region, and many of those CSOs were able to test their capacities and further hone their disaster response and community development skills during and after the earthquake. Surveys and interviews of 1,220 villagers from forty-three counties were conducted from May to June 2014.[3]

Participants were selected using the following procedure for the above two approaches. The research team traveled on the major highway (in such remote regions, it was most often a provincial level highway or lower). After randomly selecting three not-so-close entries to three villages, the team first exited the highway, drove a few miles, and then took another random turn and interviewed five individuals randomly selected in each of those villages. Therefore, about fifteen people were randomly selected from each county and answered the questions in the survey. Basic demographic questions such as age, gender, years of education starting from elementary school, monthly income estimates, and the number of dependents were also asked.

Third, more than sixty CSO leaders were interviewed, plus about a dozen officials. Although the CSO leaders and officials were not randomly selected and were largely accessible based on referrals, many of them agreed on vital ideas while still having diverse perspectives on other issues. What I was interested in was mainly their individual and organizational stories.

To measure the earthquake's intensity, I distinguished between counties in Sichuan province that were strongly affected (where the intensity of the Wenchuan earthquake was greater than 4.0 on the Modified Mercalli Intensity Scale, or MMI) and counties far away from the epicenters that were minimally affected. (Unless otherwise noted, MMI data are from the US Geological Survey.) According to the USGS:

> The Modified Mercalli Intensity value assigned to a specific site after an earthquake has a more meaningful measure of severity to the nonscientist than the magnitude because intensity refers to the effects actually experienced at that place.[4]

The abbreviated description of the levels of MMI provided by the USGS says that at Intensity III, "many people do not recognize it as an earthquake." Only at Intensity IV, when shaking intensifies from "weak" to "light," would real damages start to occur: "Dishes, windows, doors disturbed; walls make cracking sound. Sensation like heavy truck striking building."[5] Therefore, we decided to use MMI 4.0 as the cutoff point. The intervention is thus dichotomized into a binary variable.[6]

However, during a severe disaster, different regions experience various sizes of unmet demand for public goods. What is theoretically relevant here is that this condition of institutional disruption would be created (a binary variable of 0 or 1) whether the size of the disruption was small or large.

"BLAME THE CSOS": EVIDENCE FROM THE 2014 LUDIAN EARTHQUAKE

Descriptive data by village indicates the changes of preferences for service provision before and after the Ludian earthquake for villages inside versus

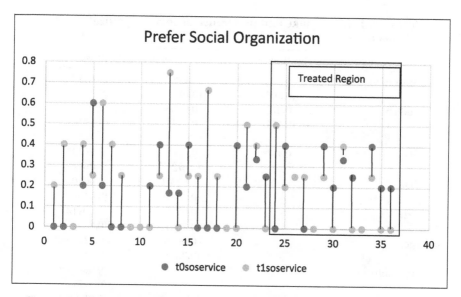

Figure 5.1. Changes of preferences for service provision before and after the Ludian earthquake

outside the quake zone. As figure 5.1 indicates, for the unaffected region, the preference for social organizations to provide services varied, but for the quake-stricken region (shaded), such a preference was overwhelmingly reduced.

Using the difference-in-difference regression analysis produces results that are statistically similar to those of the initial descriptive visualization. The estimator for this study could be expressed as the following:

$$PRSO = B + date + ludian + treatment[7]$$

"PRSO" (preference of social organization) is the dependent variable, "B" is a series of control variables, "date" is a time dummy variable (date = 0 for the pre-quake, date = 1 for the post-quake), "ludian" is the indicator for earthquake impact (ludian = 0 for the control region, ludian = 1 for the treatment region exposed to the Ludian earthquake), and the product of the two, date*ludian, is the "DD" (treatment), the quantity of interest. The observations are clustered at the county level, as some county features may influence the outcome. The regression results presented in table 5.1 indicate that the Ludian earthquake led villagers in the earthquake region to reduce their

TABLE 5.1. Earthquake and preference of social organization at village level

	Benchmark ~1	BM with co~s	Full Model
treatment	−0.203***	−0.215**	−0.224**
	(0.009)	(0.013)	(0.034)
ludian	0.0729	0.0808	0.105
	(0.154)	(0.218)	(0.130)
date	0.117*	0.115*	0.0923*
	(0.055)	(0.072)	(0.069)
age		−0.00311	−0.00307
		(0.403)	(0.444)
edu		0.00184	−0.00412
		(0.880)	(0.779)
gender		−0.0825	−0.122
		(0.382)	(0.358)
monthincome			0.0000385
			(0.477)
religious			0.0929
			(0.554)
clan			0.194
			(0.120)
Constant	0.147***	0.313	0.205
	(0.007)	(0.107)	(0.334)
Observations	72	72	72

Source: Taiyi Sun
p-values in parentheses
* $p < 0.10$, ** $p < 0.05$, *** $p < 0.01$

preferences of social organizations more often than villagers in the control region.

If we are using 95 percent confidence intervals to express the variables in the model, we can see that the result holds across different models.

But why?

Follow-up interviews with villagers, CSOs, and local government officials in the quake-stricken region provided some explanations. Immediately after the earthquake hit, local governments were incapacitated for a short period. CSOs, whether temporarily self-organized or preexisting, came to help. Given their good intentions, the preoccupied local governments tolerated the CSOs' activities. "The local government doesn't have the capacity to do it, so we got our chance to do some work," a CSO leader said in an interview.[8]

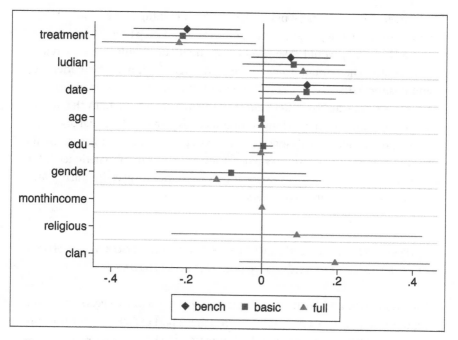

Figure 5.2. Confidence interval of variables based on different models

Many CSOs felt that civil society's power increased and that the space for nongovernmental activities was enlarged.[9]

Yet, some local villagers saw unprofessional CSOs and volunteers. Quarrels and fights sometimes happened between volunteers, the reselling of donated goods was observed, and the distribution of supplies was sometimes disorganized, giving villagers terrible first impressions. One villager said during an interview, "Some of them are here not to help us, but to make themselves feel good."[10]

Once the local governments recovered, they realized that they could potentially use the CSOs, even if some local villagers were not happy with them. Some of the villagers blamed the CSOs for standing between them and donations and speculated that the CSOs were taking a cut from the donations: "Why are they getting some of the money that was donated to us? Aren't they volunteers?" Others thought CSOs were not fair, for their neighbors received more help than they did. Usually, the CSOs in this situation were focusing on spending money and resources effectively rather than distributing them equally. Yet, CSOs provide public goods and services (although some are pretty new at what they are doing and are not doing a good job). Therefore, local governments wanted to keep them there as a buffer so that CSOs would take the blame under those unfortunate circumstances after the natural disasters. Being disorganized, new/inexperienced, and misunderstood, CSOs drew criticism from villagers. This explains why there is a significant treatment effect in the quantitative data in the quake-stricken region: citizens no longer want services provided by social organizations. Understanding this logic, we can extrapolate that local governments tend to tolerate CSO activities when they are new and inexperienced, for they serve as shields for unsatisfactory governance, especially during and immediately after natural disasters.

"OUTSOURCE TO CSOS": EVIDENCE FROM THE 2008 WENCHUAN EARTHQUAKE AND THE 2013 LUSHAN EARTHQUAKE

The Wenchuan and Lushan earthquakes, even though five years apart, hit regions that largely overlapped in the northern part of Sichuan. For the purpose of clarity and for methodological reasons, when I talk about both of them at the same time, I use the term "northern earthquakes." I collected data in rural areas from 2014 to 2015, a time period after both of the northern earthquakes. Therefore, what I observed could be the outcome of either or both of the earthquakes, and it was, to a large extent, difficult to parse out their unique effects on CSO development and, subsequently, attitude changes toward CSOs by citizens and government officials. However, it is apparent that the time period between the northern earthquakes and when data were collected for this research was longer than the time between the Ludian earthquake and its data collections. Therefore, for theory-building purposes, I treat the data point of the observations for the northern earthquakes as being qualitatively different from that after the Ludian earthquake; there was a significantly longer time for the CSOs involved to develop and evolve professionally. Therefore, this was also an opportunity to observe individual attitudes, CSO activities, and state-society relations at a different developmental stage.

Methodologically, the natural experiment setting for the northern earthquakes was weaker than that of the Ludian earthquake. The assumption that northern and southern Sichuan were similar at the county level might be less valid due to the lack of pre-treatment data for practical and

TABLE 5.2. Background comparison at the county level (2007)

Category	Variable	Units	Control Region	Treatment Region	Difference	t-test p-value
Demographic	Total population	in 10,000s, mean	25.65385	30.07586	4.42201	0.5265
	Agriculture population percentage	%	81.5	72.27586	-9.22414	0.1237
Financial	GDP per capita	in Chinese RMB	12828.75	15607.83	2779.08	0.2707
	Local gov. revenue	in 10,000 RMB	17293.92	32815.69	15521.77	0.2955
	Local gov. expenditure	in 10,000 RMB	45687.46	60267.52	14580.06	0.342
Public goods provision	Hospitals per 10,000 people	#	1.45508	1.407238	-0.047842	0.8834
	Primary schools per 10,000 people	#	4.148126	3.292701	-0.855425	0.3983

ethical reasons. Yet, we can compare the background of the treatment region (the quake-stricken region) and the control region based on their demographics, financial conditions, and public goods provision conditions. Even though there are numerical differences, the differences are not statistically significant. Comparing the counties in the control region and the treatment region, the population mean, percentage of agricultural people, GDP per capita, local government revenue and expenditure, and hospitals and schools per ten thousand people are not significantly different from each other.

By looking at the data I collected, particularly the pre-treatment variables (that earthquakes would not influence the outcome of those variables with the concern that the data were collected only after treatment), the age difference is significant through a t-test. Logistic regression with treatment assignment (the earthquake) as the dependent variable also reveals that gender and education may not be balanced. However, such differences do not prevent us from drawing exploratory evidence, and subsequent models in my analysis control these key variables (using less of the natural experiment setting but treating it as typical observational evidence).

Unlike the result from the short-term post-quake data from the Ludian earthquake, the longer period of interactions between CSOs and citizens leads to different outcomes. There is no significant difference between the control and treatment regions in terms of preferences of social organizations for service provision, although the mean difference is positive. This means that in the sample I collected, more people preferred social organizations for service provision in the quake-stricken region.

The 95 percent confidence intervals shown in figure 5.3 provide a visualization of the three models in table 5.4. In this case, older people significantly preferred social organizations less for service provisions.

This result, compared to that of the Ludian earthquake, suggests that individuals preferred social organizations significantly less immediately after the earthquake, but once they got to know more about these organizations, and as social organizations become more developed and professionalized, such negative preferences disappeared.

Interestingly, when asked if the respondent knew the name of their local leader, there was a significant difference between the quake-stricken and non-affected regions. People in the quake-stricken region knew their leader significantly more, even when controlling for gender, age, and education, among other variables.

TABLE 5.3. Balance of self-collected data on pre-treatment variables

	Unit	Control Region	Treatment Region	Difference	t-test p-value
Age	Year, mean	43.40566	49.62814	6.22248	0***
Gender	Male (1), Female (0)	0.5377358	0.4785894	–0.0591464	0.16
Education	Year since 1st grade	6.457547	6.596977	0.13943	0.71

TABLE 5.4. Earthquake and preference of social organization (the northern earthquakes)

	Benchmark ~1	BM with co~s	Full Model
soservice			
quakelevelbi	0.161	0.262	0.268
	(0.313)	(0.107)	(0.104)
gender		0.115	0.109
		(0.456)	(0.495)
age		–0.0173***	–0.0164***
		(0.001)	(0.003)
edu		–0.000882	–0.000895
		(0.583)	(0.607)
monthincome			0.0000430
			(0.192)
dependents			–0.00701
			(0.935)
Constant	–1.435***	–0.761***	–0.875***
	(0.000)	(0.003)	(0.003)
Observations	1,049	1,046	1,030

Source: Taiyi Sun
p-values in parentheses
* p < 0.10, ** p < 0.05, *** p < 0.01

Interviews revealed that many of the surviving CSOs had developed close ties with local government officials six years after the Wenchuan earthquake. When providing public goods and services in local communities, many were working on behalf of the local government, and they made that clear to the people. This, on the one hand, improved the legitimacy of CSOs in the eyes of the people but, on the other hand, also helped the propaganda of the local officials. The actual image of the local officials may or may not be improved, depending on the real work done by the CSO and the govern-

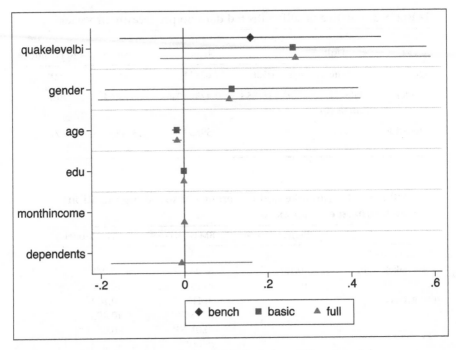

Figure 5.3. Confidence interval of variables based on different models

ment. But one thing is clear: the government intentionally outsourced responsibilities to the maturing CSOs so that those CSOs' productivities could be utilized in local governance in the medium to long run.

FROM TOLERATION TO DIFFERENTIATION:
THE DYNAMIC TYPOLOGY OF STATE-CSO RELATIONSHIPS
AFTER THE EARTHQUAKES

Now that we have captured the state-CSO relationship and the logic of the state strategies from the side of citizen attitudes, I provide a model based on the sampled CSOs that directly captures the dynamic relationship and the path of its evolution. Although the existing models of CSO-government relations are mainly static, they are helpful starting points to illustrate typical relationships. Borrowing from their core ideas, the starting point of the model here (extremely simplified for illustrative purposes only) is a two-by-two table (table 5.6). The relationships are decided by whether the govern-

TABLE 5.5. Earthquake and awareness of leader name

	Benchmark ~1	BM with co~s	Full Model
leadername			
quakelevelbi	0.579***	0.454***	0.443***
	(0.000)	(0.001)	(0.001)
gender		0.253*	0.328**
		(0.051)	(0.015)
age		0.0359***	0.0335***
		(0.000)	(0.000)
edu		–0.0291*	–0.0258
		(0.075)	(0.133)
monthincome			–0.0000697**
			(0.030)
dependents			–0.0744
			(0.237)
Constant	0.262***	–1.216***	–0.977***
	(0.007)	(0.000)	(0.002)
Observations	1,220	1,217	1,195

Source: Taiyi Sun
p-values in parentheses
* $p < 0.10$, ** $p < 0.05$, *** $p < 0.01$

ment is effective in providing a particular service and whether the goals of the civil society organization are aligned with the government. The combination of the two variables leads to four different types of relationships: competition, complementarity, confrontation, and cooperation. Note that the starting point of differentiation is toward the end of the toleration stage discussed in previous chapters.

Initially, supposing that the government is effective in an issue area and that a CSO's goal aligns with that of the government, the relationship would tend to be competitive in the sense that both parties are effective in the issue area, and they would compete for a similar set of resources. Six CSOs would fall into this category within the sample. CSOs in this category would report that government officials are unhappy about CSOs taking the spotlight or taking control of specific vital resources. In the long run, this relationship would gradually turn into co-optation or even result in the dissolving of the civil society organization.

When the government realizes that the CSO's goal clearly diverges from that of the government, then the relationship is confrontational because they are both effective in an issue area, and the government would try not to let the

TABLE 5.6. Simple illustration of the starting point of the
conceptual framework (short term)

	Effective Government	Ineffective Government
Convergent goals	Competition	Complementarity
Divergent goals	Confrontation	Cooperation

CSO operate. One example could be the field of ideology. Providing spiritual
food for the individual citizens is something both the local government and
religious organizations could do well, while the ideas they want to promote
are somewhat different. This would lead to direct confrontation unless the
government were not yet aware or not sure of the existence of such activities
within their jurisdiction. Such cases are challenging for researchers to encounter, since they risk the underground operations being exposed and subsequently facing harsh treatment from the state. Only two cases in my sample
fall into this category, but there are probably many more similar cases that
prefer not to be exposed. Once such activities are aboveground, it almost
always leads to the destruction of the CSO in the long run. Although the government is quite conscious about when to take out a CSO, sometimes it keeps
specific organizations in this category longer than usual so that when it needs
to test the effectiveness of its authority, it uses the organization as a target.[11] At
other times, the government places informants inside these organizations
and keeps observing them rather than pushing their operations underground
to risk their being outside the government's reach.

The more complicated relationships exist when the government is ineffective or when existing services are lacking in the domain. Now suppose the
government is ineffective in an issue area when the CSO's goal converges
with the government's. The relationship is then complementary in the sense
that the government relies on the CSO to solve the problem or provide the
necessary service with its expertise. This type of relationship is quite common, and the majority of the CSOs interviewed (and therefore have survived
so far) belong to this category—forty out of the sixty-one cases. In the long
run, what happens depends on whether the government feels the threat. If
the government thinks there is no threat from an organization, and if the
organization provides some unique resource to the locality, the complementary relationship may remain (twelve cases). If the organization is providing

basic services that the government is not effective at delivering, then cooperation might happen (twenty-four cases). The government collaborates with the CSO through service purchasing and usually allows some degree of freedom and independence. If the government feels a threat, then the relationship is likely to be confrontational simply because of a perception that individual citizens no longer give credit to the local government and that the CSOs are there to take the government's place and power (four cases).

When the CSO's goal diverges from the government's and the government is not effective, especially during an institutional disruption, the initial relationship is usually temporarily cooperative because the government does not have the capacity to counter the efforts made by the CSO. This relationship might be possible for only a very short period after the institutional disruption, when the local government is incapacitated and service is delivered by some of the organizations that it refers to as politically sensitive. Gradually, the government seeks to use legitimized forces to confront and eliminate such CSOs, even when facing the danger of losing credibility, thus leading to a confrontational relationship (eight cases). However, CSOs were acutely aware of such potential outcomes, and some adjusted their actions and behaviors so that they could survive. Some abandoned their mission entirely by providing only the services the government wanted them to provide. Such realignment of goals happened in several CSOs, especially multiple religious organizations, which abandoned their religious mission so as to provide quake relief service without the government eliminating them (five cases). For those organizations moving from a temporary cooperative relationship to a more stable complementary relationship, it was almost impossible for them to get back to work that reflected their initial missions once those missions were abandoned. As a result, they stuck with doing something that was not part of their original missions. The above-mentioned descriptions of relationships and their evolutions are captured in table 5.7.

In this categorization, this chapter assumes the CSOs are effective,[12] because if they are not, they might not exist at all, and even if they do, the government would not have much interaction with such CSOs. If the government sees no use for the CSO, then there is no potential threat. Thus, they are tolerated until there is a change in the CSO's capacity. All of these descriptions can be visualized in a dynamic figure indicating how state-CSO relations evolve (see fig. 5.4). Below I provide a more detailed description of this process.

TABLE 5.7. Illustration of the evolution of state-society relations from the sample

Government	Goals	Initial type	Frequency in the sample	Evolved type	Frequency	Notes and descriptions
Effective	Aligned	Competition	6	Co-optation	6	Government took over or made the CSO a branch of the gov.
Not effective	Aligned	Complementarity	40	Complementarity	12	CSO has independent financial, logistical, human resources
				Cooperation	24	Gov. purchase service from CSO; CSO leaders have personal ties with gov.; CSO strategic subordination
				Confrontation	4	Foreign personnel involved; gov. feels threatened or out of control
Effective	Not aligned	Confrontation	2	Destruction	2	INGO, rights claim groups
Not effective	Not aligned	Cooperation	13	Complementarity	5	Abandon original core missions, avoid sensitive projects
				Confrontation	8	Rights claim groups, collective action potentials

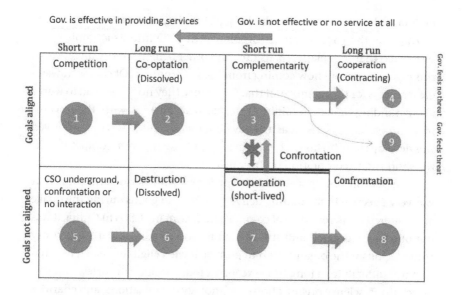

Figure 5.4. The dynamic conceptual framework of state-CSO relations in China. *Note:* Numbers here indicate specific scenarios in this dynamic framework to which the following discussions will refer.

Goals Aligned and Government Effective: We Can Take Over

In this domain (scenarios one to two in fig. 5.4), I encountered several cases that transitioned from a competitive relationship to a more co-optative relationship in the long run (here, eight years after the earthquake). One interviewee who is the head of a CSO reported that their partnering organization established a relationship with the government during the immediate response period, but they knew they were in competition. "The local government's and our service provision are overlapping so that we, unfortunately, got into a competition,"[13] the CSO leader mentioned. That organization contributed a considerable number of volunteers to help the effort of quake relief. The particular region in which they operated was not hit severely, so the government did not lose its functionality entirely in terms of human resource management. Therefore, their goals were aligned and the government was still effective in providing its service. However, with the existence of that CSO, the government felt the organization might potentially do a better job, at least in the eyes of the people. After the earthquake, the CSO maintained a relationship with the government, and one year after the earthquake, the government incorporated the CSO into its administrative systems so that the salaries, pensions, and other benefits of the members of this organization are now coming from the government. Of course, it was a great success for the members of that CSO, since they no longer had to worry about funding and maintaining external relationships with the government. However, it was seen as a betrayal for many other CSOs that observed this development.[14] This is a typical example of moving from competition in the short run to co-optation in the long run.

Co-optation can appear in different forms. Another organization that was very effective in facilitating delivery of first-aid goods during the quake encountered a different type of co-optation. Like many CSOs in China, it was not officially registered and still needed to find a Professional Supervisory Unit to sponsor the organization to provide it with eligibility (such registration was difficult for a long time except for four specific categories: industry associations, science organizations, technology organizations, and charities and entities providing community social services). This sponsorship also meant giving up financial and administrative autonomy. Since the PSU needed to approve the budget and other plans for the organization annually, the threat of disapproval was an effective interference to challenge the organization's autonomy. In one particular case, the PSU was bluntly assertive and constantly utilized the tool of potentially "not approving budget" for actions they did not approve of.[15] For the same reason, many CSOs choose not to register officially.

When CSOs are not registered, the government sometimes is unsure of their intentions; nevertheless, it is usually aware of the many unregistered CSOs in its jurisdictions. Local governments do not want to ban unregistered CSOs entirely. In particular, based on their interactions with some of the organizations during the earthquakes and other disasters, they have had favorable impressions of some organizations and enjoyed the "free service" the organizations provide that they otherwise had to offer themselves. Therefore, in the short run, the government allows the existence of such organizations but keeps an eye on them. Organizations in this situation usually transitioned from doing quake relief work to community development projects after the earthquake and helped to alleviate poverty in many communities. About four years after the 2008 Wenchuan earthquake, one day the leader of one organization received a phone call from the local head of

Civil Affairs asking them to get registered. The local leader said the government would provide resources to support their work. In this case, the local government happened to be initiating an incubation center for those "unregistered" or "nascent" CSOs. And the government promised to provide free office space with the potential to purchase services from them.[16] As one local official told me, "If we have decided not to kick them out, it will be better to have them directly work with and work for us so that we know what they are doing." Many CSOs also welcomed this proposal by the government, as funding was difficult to obtain.[17]

CSOs in China are not able to raise money publicly (unless they are government-initiated public foundations). Even though the 2016 Charity Law provided some new fund-raising channels, such channels are still heavily scrutinized. Therefore, CSOs either rely on private support or have an operation that generates revenue. Otherwise, they have to depend on the government. There are exceptions to that generalized depiction, as, informally, many CSOs secretly raised money and asked those eligible foundations to receive the money on their behalf. Then the foundation purchased services from the CSO to transfer the money to the original organization. Those foundations charge at least a 5 percent fee for this process. Financial sources also quickly dried up several months after the Wenchuan earthquake. During the 2012 round of interviews, most of the CSOs I interviewed complained that they were facing challenging financial situations. If nothing changed, they would be forced to shut down their operations.

While facing legal, financial, and operational challenges, many CSOs were compelled to transition from being in a competitive relationship with the government to being co-opted by it. The degree of the co-optation varied, ranging from operating under the government umbrella as a semi-independent organization to dissolving entirely so that the individuals in effect became government employees.

Goals Not Aligned and Government Effective: We Do Not Need You

CSOs in this situation are most difficult to get access to (scenarios five and six in fig. 5.4). Since the CSOs' goals do not align with those of the government, even when providing services to the local people, they are generally not tolerated once their intentions and capacities are known. The underground CSOs, particularly family/underground churches, belong to this category.

However, because they tend not to have interactions with the government (if they do, they are probably forced to shut down), I do not discuss them extensively here.

One typical example that belongs to this category is an environmental organization. After the earthquake, it entered a village with the mission to build an "eco-village." The local government first thought it would bring resources and allowed it to operate. Then the government realized that the CSO was competing for resources such as labor and money. The local government also did not care much for the environmental mission, mainly because they had a coal mine project planned to generate some additional income and suddenly realized that the CSO was opposed to it and was organizing an effective opposition to prevent the mine from being built. The tension gradually became more conflictual as both sides tried to mobilize support while competing for the same resources, including intangible resources, like ideological support from the public, and tangible resources, like financial and human resources. Several months later, the government said "enough is enough" and kicked the organization out from its jurisdiction and banned it from operating. The transition from confrontation to destruction is typical in this category. Unlike CSOs in liberal democracies, in China they are not allowed to monitor and check the power of the government, let alone challenge it.[18]

Some exceptions might make the toleration stage longer for this relationship. One example mentioned previously is that the government may want to save a few opportunities to test its authority in the future. Such CSOs are like "lambs waiting to be butchered" for a future occasion of "killing the chicken to scare the monkey" (*sha ji jing hou* 杀鸡儆猴.) Another exception is that the government may fear losing track of the activities because shutting down the CSO may mean pushing the people underground. The government may choose to place an undercover agent into the CSO to observe and keep track of its actions rather than pushing the organization entirely underground and having them out of reach.

Goals Aligned and Government Not Effective: We Can Buy You

The more dynamic relations exist when the government is ineffective in certain areas, and such relations are frequently not fixed (scenarios three, four, and nine in fig. 5.4). Most CSOs that reacted to the earthquakes and provided services in regions where the government was temporarily but totally incapacitated belong to this category. After the 2013 Lushan earthquake, some organizations had already created a collaborative mechanism for first aid. The head of one CSO was designated by this collective group of CSOs to gather more information about the quake-stricken region first before they organized quake relief efforts together. When that person was on the way to his destination, passing a village, the villagers all came to him complaining about how incapable and corrupt the local government was. He then started to mediate between the local government and the villagers. This village ended up being the CSO's targeted village for operation later on. The local government realized that when a CSO is between the government and the people, it can serve as a cushion to absorb some tensions. There is an old saying in China: "People are not worried as much about poverty as unfairness." This is particularly the case in rural China. When the government distributes goods to the villagers, the government may be seen as corrupt and practicing favoritism if there is any unfairness. With the arrival of CSOs, the local government found a solution. If goods were to be distributed, it asked the CSOs to handle the task on behalf of the government so that if unfairness occurred, it would not be the government's fault. Such CSOs helped to fill the vacuum that the local government created immediately after the earthquake and continued to provide services the government was not good at or did not want to do itself. This is a typical complementary relationship.

Another example is an organization that started eco-tourism among some impoverished villages. The CSO helped to turn villagers' homes into motels so that tourists who want to experience the rural lifestyle can come and stay with their families. This has brought a new source of revenue to the local government, and the government does not have enough resources to facilitate the projects itself. The government, therefore, started to cooperate with the CSO in additional domains, seeing the potential benefits the CSOs can bring.[19]

Scenario number four in figure 5.4 is ideal for many CSOs because they enjoy some government support (at least no confrontation) but remain autonomous. The government occasionally purchases services from those CSOs, and the CSOs sometimes do need the resources from the government to better achieve their goals. This cooperation is sometimes referred to as a symbiotic relationship.

I You She is an organization that moved into areas where the government is not so effective and seeks cooperation. Originally, their operation was making films to promote the donation of blood in Sichuan (the leader works at the donation center). During the earthquake, the organization was very helpful in supporting the disaster relief effort and, thus, gained the government's trust. They then initiated a few community development projects in which the government did not intervene at all. The government even asked them to do more once they had shown their capabilities and expertise. I You She, therefore, was asked by the government to conduct and replicate their work in various communities in Chengdu. The government knew that I You She does a better job than the bureaucracy, so it purchased services from the organization on an ongoing basis.

During several interviews with government officials, the interviewee used metaphors to describe the people-CSO-government relationship:

> [The] government is tired of being the player and referee at the same time, and the people are not stupid. After witnessing how helpful and effective certain social organizations can be, we want to let them be the players so that the government can focus on being the referee.[20]

It is also worth noting that most of the organizations I interviewed have at least one important staff member who is either an ex–military member or an ex–government official. It is rare to have a current official leading a CSO, since the government is making an effort to separate itself from CSOs due to a mandate from the higher-level officials and a desire to reduce conflicts of interest.[21] Those retired military officers and officials are well connected within the government and have trust in the local government. Therefore, it is common for the government to leave such CSOs alone and remain in a cooperative relationship.

Not all complementary relationships end up transitioning to the cooperative, symbiotic relations. Sometimes such a relationship ends up in a confrontation state (moving from scenario three to nine in fig. 5.4). The macro-environment facilitates a different outcome. For example, about two years after the Wenchuan earthquake, many interviewees recalled a government crackdown of those "unregistered" CSOs, many of which had previously been in a complementary relationship with the government. There were just too many CSOs for the government to deal with (of course, some might have ulterior motives other than helping the local people and providing services), so in the process of regulating the status of CSOs, many were pushed out, especially those CSOs that had potential foreign connections.

Goals Not Aligned and Government Not Effective:
We May Need You but Not That Much

This is a very special scenario because it is common that the organizations, supposedly operating under this domain in the short run, shifted to a different domain in the long run (scenarios seven, eight, and three in fig. 5.4). For example, several religious organizations I interviewed emphasized that they entered the quake-stricken region during the quake relief period, mainly abandoning the religious nature of their organizations.[22] If it was a Christian organization, it did not spread the gospel but only helped the local people with quake recovery. They were acutely aware of how the government would react if they included a religious mission during the quake relief operations. Therefore, even though their goals did not align with the government to begin with, the CSOs would initiate a realignment process that abandoned the functions that did not align with the government and kept the part of their operation that did align for their survival. Figure 5.4 shows a shift from scenario seven to scenario three. It is no longer possible when they want to reenter scenario seven to pick up their conflicting goals with the government. The institutional hurdles and the existing arrangements prevent them from moving away from that equilibrium. This is why, in the illustration, the line between scenario seven and scenario three is a one-way street. One can exit scenario seven, but it is very difficult to reenter. There were cases when suddenly an organization started to pass out Bible verses or spread the gospel, and the government immediately banned their operation in the locality even when the government still could not adequately provide services themselves.

Another environmental organization depicted a similar situation. Protests were going on against a chemical factory being built in the locality. The environmental organization was fully aware of how destructive the factory could be to the local environment. However, they chose not to pick up this fight against the government, knowing that if they did so, they would not even be able to operate the other environmental projects they had. It was a conscious decision to move away from scenario seven and not reenter again.[23] Those CSOs that choose to reenter would mostly disappear or have to provide tremendous resources (particularly money and expertise) that could boost the government's ineffectiveness at the locality.

Heifer's case in China is particularly worth mentioning. Before the earthquake, the organization was doing only one kind of work: animal husbandry.

Since the earthquake, the leaders of Heifer felt a vivid distinction that the government had more trust in them. They played an active role when the government lacked capacity, and they have been working in a way so that their goal aligns with the government. Now they have entered into various areas such as capacity building, empowerment of women, environmental protection, and so forth. They have also made use of the space created and attempted to maximize their productivity in areas where space is still limited. For example, CSOs (let alone an international organization) are typically not allowed to operate in the Xinjiang region, as it is politically sensitive. However, the city of Shanghai has a governmental relationship with the government in Xinjiang, whose projects Shanghai funds and supports. Heifer excels at helping local farmers, and the Shanghai government immediately thought about them when such work was needed. Therefore, even though Heifer might not be able to get into Xinjiang by itself, through the Shanghai government's demand or ineffectiveness in a certain area, Heifer can enter Xinjiang and conduct projects they are good at.[24]

THE INTERACTIVE AUTHORITARIAN GOVERNANCE OF CSOS POST DISASTERS: LEGALIZATION AND BEYOND

It is essential to point out that both CSOs and governments make choices and adjustments, and it is an interactive process. Local governments can learn and improve, especially recovering from the incapacitated state after major disasters such as earthquakes. The long arrow at the top pointing toward the left in figure 5.4 indicates that when the government starts to learn and improve, especially as it gains adequate resources and sees the cost of taking over to be minimal, relationships tend to move toward scenarios in which the government is more capable and effective. Therefore, the eventual equilibria are more likely to remain at either co-optative or destructive relationships. Only when the CSOs have competitive advantages and are willing to share a great number of risks and responsibilities (as suggested in chapter 3) does the government hesitate to co-opt or destruct them in the long run.

One CSO interviewee mentioned that when they first arrived at a village after the earthquake, the local government allowed it to operate without disruptions. However, after about a month, the local government suddenly announced that the CSO should leave and the government would take over. This surprised many volunteers on the ground, as they had made plans that would last for at least several months. However, the local government realized that it had recovered sufficiently and, therefore, had moved from an ineffective state to an effective state.[25]

Michael Foley and Bob Edwards distinguish two different types of "civil society." "Civil Society I," the neo-Tocquevillian approach, focuses on the importance of association for governance, which is the "habitat for the hearts," while "Civil Society II" emphasizes the importance of civil association as a counterweight to the state.[26] These two forms are fundamentally different and lead to different outcomes. Such a dichotomy can serve as a reference to my argument regarding the case of China today. The opening up of the space has created some complementary, cooperative, or even symbiotic relationships, with the CSOs sometimes being autonomous. Still, it remains at the level of "habits of the hearts." The government has the capacity and willpower to differentiate and regulate the work CSOs do and can effectively respond with policies in order to maintain the type of relationships it wants.

There is minimal evidence that the possibilities of relationships would stabilize at a competitive or confrontational relationship, which would be closer to the "Civil Society II" type that Foley and Edwards describe. There are cases where CSOs attempt to break through (such as the rights protection movement), but the results remain unsuccessful so far. Some CSOs exist within these domains, but they are mainly underground and face the risk of elimination.

Relationships are not stable in this dynamic interactive authoritarian framework presented above, since factors—particularly the learning behaviors of CSOs (such as adaptation) and local governments (recovering from incapacity, adopting innovative policies and institutions)—may shift the relationship into different outcomes. Some CSOs may also be trapped in doing complementary work that does not reflect their organizations' goals/missions. Most organizations are driven by their funding and have to deprioritize the "mission-driven" focus, and therefore would be vulnerable to be lured into the complementary domain.

What's more important is that the government is also actively learning and can shift their relations so that complementary relationships turn into co-optations (besides the rest of the relationships that are still moving toward cooperation in the long run when the government remains ineffective in specific domains). After getting a concrete sense of specific CSOs' operations and resources, the government might want to make rules to solidify benefits and minimize risks. They do so by creating new rules and laws.

Immediately after the earthquake, the local governments were unsure about how to deal with the upsurge of voluntary activities within their jurisdictions, so they tolerated activities and observed in order to better understand the players and the activities. After a few years of interactions with CSOs, the utilities and risks of specific CSOs are clearer, and the camps of regime-challenging and regime-supporting CSOs are more apparent based on the relative *effectiveness of service provision* by the local government and the *degree of goal alignment* between the state and CSO. New rules and mechanisms of governance were tested at the district level in urban areas, and the rules and mechanisms point directly to the experiences and lessons learned from the toleration and differentiation stages.

In 2010 the Jinniu district in the city of Chengdu asked a citizen-organized deliberative council and CSOs to serve as a bridge between the CCP and the people and cultivate self-governance in local communities.[27] Two years later, in 2012, the Chengdu Bureau of Civil Affairs published the "Guiding Opinions on Strengthening the Self-Governance of Community Residents," promoting successful experiences throughout residential communities in the city. Some districts in the city, such as the Chenghua district, made unique plans to implement such rules and guidance[28] and indicated specific and separate responsibilities for local governments and CSOs.[29] In 2014 other cities in Sichuan province started to publish rules and guidelines about incorporating CSOs into their governance structure. For example, the city of Suining published the "Guidelines for the Participation of Social Organizations in the Declaration and Evaluation of Social Service Projects."[30] Complementary rules such as the "Guidelines and Standards for the Government to Purchase Social Organizations' Home Care Services" have also been published to further stipulate the legal instructions of state-CSO interactions.[31] Then in 2015, legalization moved from the city level to the provincial level. The provincial government of Sichuan published the "Opinions of Sichuan People's Government Regarding Promoting the Healthy Development of Philanthropy (Draft for Comments)."[32] Then in 2016, the Charity Law and the Foreign NGO Law were passed at the national level (discussed in chapter 4). Such a process of legalization--from experiments at the local level, to making rules at the district level, then city level, and then promoting successful models for other cities to refine the rules and laws and eventually make laws at the provincial and national level—

happened with many issues concerning different types of CSOs. The legalization sets boundaries for CSOs to better contribute to governance and, of
course, shoulder the blame when needed.

In this chapter, I have used the earthquake as an example of institutional
disruption and demonstrated the toleration-differentiation-legalization
process for the case of CSOs in Sichuan. After the Ludian earthquake, when
CSOs were newly developed and not fully professionalized, they were tolerated mostly by the local government and served as an effective shield for the
local officials. A few years after the northern earthquakes of Wenchuan and
Lushan, we see the more capable and professionalized CSOs being the target
of state-initiated outsourcing, for they were sometimes more effective in governance. The dynamic process from toleration to differentiation based on
the evolution of state-CSO relations was also captured in a typology. Then,
the process of legalization was presented. Such a process, which reveals the
logic of governing society by the Chinese state, does not exist only in the
CSO domain. In chapter 6 I discuss how similar processes happened over the
internet, and then, in chapter 7, I address the case of guerilla protests that
occupy both physical and virtual domains.

CHAPTER 6

Case II

Dynamic, Decentralized, and Multilayered Internet Censorship

On March 26, 2018, a train arrived from North Korea in Beijing with a big entourage. Netizens on social media immediately started speculating as to who had arrived. There was no official reporting on this topic, and information control was tight. In the meantime, as the executive editor of *Global China*, a self-media political commentary publication in Mandarin, I was pretty sure that it was indeed Kim Jong Un who had arrived in Beijing. Why? The keyword "金正恩" (Kim Jong Un) suddenly became sensitive and was censored on that day, indicating that discussions of Kim had been temporarily banned in China. Unsurprisingly, since the day after Kim arrived and Xinhua News Agency, a Chinese state-run media outlet, reported on Kim's visit to China, Kim's name can again be mentioned in published articles and is no longer censored.

Censorship, just like many other tools the Chinese authoritarian government uses, is not only a way for the state to exercise its power over the society, but it also provides a channel for the society to collect information about the state, assess the political environment, and even influence the decision-makers through an interactive process. Therefore, the interactive authoritarianism model is applicable not only to CSOs operating in physical spaces in local communities after earthquakes but also applicable to online communities operating in virtual spaces. This chapter uses the three-stage model to examine virtual associations and speeches as a form of civil society activity and to provide an analysis of the state's interactions with self-media publishers after institutional disruptions such as technological innovations.

New self-media players (also a type of CSO, according to the definition pro-vided in the introduction) and their publications are likely to be tolerated initially until it has been determined that the players and their publications are either useful or risky. During the interactions, the state learns more about the CSOs' tactics and skills—whether it is about getting the audience's atten-tion to influence public opinion or evading control from the state—and then makes rules and laws to legalize what has been learned. The CSOs also utilize the tolerated space to maintain their survival and provide informa-tion and consultation to the government in order to improve their gover-nance and better utilize the resources that the online civil society can provide.

The practice of controlling information is not unique to China. Russia passed a law in May 2019 to legally cut its web connections with the rest of the world but stay online internally, and 97 percent of the Ethiopian popula-tion was cut off from internet service following a failed coup in June 2019.[1] Based on a study from January 2016 to May 2018, India—a democracy, although with growing authoritarian tendencies—shuts down its internet most frequently out of all countries in the world.[2] After facing Russian influ-ences during the 2016 presidential election and the subsequent elections in the United States, Facebook, among a few other influential social media companies, also started deleting accounts and web pages[3] and banned a series of incendiary political figures.[4] What's unique about Chinese interac-tive authoritarianism in dealing with activities in the virtual space is the more nuanced strategic interventions with differentiated and dynamic treatments.

It is worth noting that Chinese censorship today is quite different from that of the totalitarian period under Mao Zedong. Rather than having virtu-ally all political discourses unified and centralized, the authoritarian state still controls the flow of information but allows a certain degree of free expression. Some words and topics are banned at certain times, by particular authors and on specific platforms, at some locations, with various methods, and at different stages of the publication process.

Drawing evidence from the editorial experiences and interviews with rel-evant government officials and other self-media publishers, I have compared the editorial and publishing experiences from multiple platforms, including WeChat public account (微信公众号), Sina Weibo (新浪微博), and Toutiao (今日头条), and revealed the complex logic of governing the society through interactive authoritarianism. Chinese censorship reacts, differentiates, and adapts to different players, at various stages of the censorship, under specific macro environments, using a multitude of methods and tactics. Such an approach is neither a reversal of the totalitarian period under Mao nor a continuation of the controlled liberalization since Deng. Still, it is a discriminative approach that limits the costs of repression by targeting specific individuals under different circumstances through frequent interactions. At the same time, it continues to facilitate the opportunities of free expression for the vast majority of the nonthreatening public.

THE GAP IN THE LITERATURE ON CENSORSHIP IN CHINA

There is a vast literature about how an authoritarian state governs the virtual space—an essential component of the modern civil society—especially about its decisions about censorship. One can see clear evidence and logic of toleration, differentiation, and legalization.

The first set of researches focuses on toleration. It is convenient to think that an authoritarian state should control information tightly and allow only state-run media to dominate the public discourses. However, there are many reasons why voices from society are tolerated. When the state completely shuts down the virtual space, a valuable domain to gain regime support might be lost. For example, the state could promote positive propaganda by using astroturfing[5] or microblogs to interact and negotiate with society.[6] Even online grievances could be valuable. The online petition could be used as a vital information-gathering channel to identify and address public discontent so that concerns about certain issues would not lead to irreversible damages to legitimacy.[7] The frequency of such information, for example, on pollution complaints, could be a good measure of the actual level of pollution.[8] Similarly, this channel could provide information and would be a suitable venue for predicting future protests and corruption charges.[9] Furthermore, tolerating political expression (through nationalism)[10] and investigative reporting (at the lower level)[11] could potentially enhance regime support and help regime stability.

Toleration is sometimes adopted because the costs of the alternatives are too high. When states censor, there are bureaucratic costs and political consequences. Therefore, states sometimes delegate tasks to non-state and subnational actors.[12] Doing so may not only reduce the bureaucratic costs, as the subsidies provided are often cheaper, but political costs also can be lowered of the non-state actors take the blame when things go wrong.[13]

The state may also have more effective alternatives to censoring. For example, if the state co-opts the actors, there is no longer a need to silence their voices.[14] Some authoritarian states also continuously adapt to institutional disruptions and have survived without having to gain absolute control.[15] Of course, there are also governments whose state capacity is so low that they cannot control the virtual space. When the government fails to shut down all open debates completely,[16] the more they increase in censorship, the more curious the citizenry becomes, ultimately resulting in expanded access to information for a substantial subset of the population (using services such as the Virtual Private Network, or VPN).[17] Furthermore, internet users use parodic satire,[18] homophones and puns,[19] and even algorithms in order to circumvent censorship.[20]

The second set of researches focuses on differentiation. Even when the state chooses not to tolerate online activities completely, the virtual space is often differentiated. King, Pan, and Roberts have used quantitative evidence from big data to prove that censorship is specifically aimed toward preventing collective actions.[21] Indeed, avoiding collective actions and maintaining stability are prioritized when the Chinese state interacts with society.[22] The censorship can also target foreign actors to prevent Western influences, as alternative framing of public discourses might undermine the support basis.[23]

Since the Chinese state apparatus is often fragmented, differentiation could happen based on the level of the government. There are officials at the top who are more concerned with direct threats and those at the local level who are more interested in hiding negative news within their jurisdictions. The treatment toward material from traditional media as opposed to new media is also different.[24] Due to delegated censorship, this differentiation may also be caused by differences between individual internet service providers.[25] Counterintuitively, the state may specifically focus censorship on certain platforms or venues to garner support. There is intrinsic support of censorship from those who are high on authoritarian personality measures, so the act of censorship per se could improve regime legitimacy.[26] Similar to the logic of toleration, some scholars assert that completely shutting down the internet is unfeasible and ineffective, if not counterproductive, so differentiation has become the natural choice.[27]

The third set of researches focuses on the legalization of censorship. There are many pieces of research that directly analyze internet regulations, and some of them provide causal arguments as to why and how they are created. It could be aiming to provide a "healthy" environment for both political and economic development,[28] although others argue that censoring porn is sometimes used as a way to legitimize political censorship.[29] Legalization is often seen in the tight control of licensing news websites so that the state can control sources of news feeds, preventing others from conducting their own reporting.[30] Alternatively, the legalization of censorship could be used to solidify economic benefits as an exercise of protectionism as foreign internet companies are shut out from the Chinese market.[31] Some research specifically focuses on legalizing behaviors of surveillance, especially toward civil society groups and independent media.[32] Furthermore, even before laws are made, setting up work procedures in media has been used to turn staff members into self-initiated censors.[33]

Several weaknesses are apparent when using censorship to understand authoritarian governance and state-society relations. First of all, a key element that is commonly ignored—probably due to methodological reasons—is that the strength and method of censorship are different throughout the life of a publication and depending on the influence of the publisher. However, most studies on this topic tackle only a specific point or a short period of time. Therefore, they are unable to capture the dynamic nature of censorship, thus underestimating the often complex interactive relationship between the state and society. Some of the discrepancies that scholars have observed in the above-mentioned literature are likely due to different observation choices, similar to the old story of multiple blind people touching various parts of an elephant's body.

Another common limitation of the existing literature is that the materials utilized are often published by others. Censorship works not only in terms of deletion of published content, but frequently, prior to that stage, it blocks content from being published in the first place. Furthermore, before the state gets to do anything, self-censorship can occur before state censorship, and sometimes the two interact. If studying only materials published by others, one cannot capture the initial processes of "not allowing publication" and "self-censorship."

A third challenge related to the second is that quite often the testings are probabilistic in nature. One might be able to provide statistical significance but could rarely be certain. Therefore, it is still possible that the patterns observed are due to coincidence or stochastic factors.

A fourth problem with the existing literature is the type of material being studied. A preferred choice for the study is Weibo, for it is automatically public with short content (with character limits.) There is an advantage for quantitative analysis for the study subjects that are similar in length, and a large sample could be collected easily. However, as reverse engineering of the code of censorship has shown, there is little overlap between different companies regarding their censored word bank.[34] Also, there lacks an article-length study of political commentaries by actual scholars.

The fifth constraint scholars have faced on this topic is the narrow angle allowed for each study. Much of the testing starts with a limited number of specific hypotheses. Consequently, only a set of keywords—sometimes arbitrary and mostly non-exhaustive—are selected. Therefore, the holistic view of the censorship process might not be captured.

A sixth issue with the study of censorship, in general, is its politically sensitive nature. It is very difficult to get access to officials and staff members on the censorship team and inquire about their work. Therefore, the vast majority of studies focus on the outcome of censorship rather than the motivation or the process. The rest of the studies that are not aimed at the outcomes of censorship usually look at internal documents and archival materials.

Overall, the existing literature does not capture the variation and complexity of how censorship happens, missing an essential domain where society meets and interacts with the state. Censorship varies across time, place, and method in ways this study seeks to capture. This is not to say the existing literature is not valuable. On the contrary, the key phenomena observed in the existing literature concerning toleration, differentiation, and legalization—as I have organized them that way—are all present. What separates this study from most others is that I was on a real editorial team covering complete cycles of publications. Thus, I was able to examine the different levels of strength and censorship methods throughout the articles' life, including using the deterministic AB tests to identify actual triggers of censorship. I am not only able to look at the state's censorship more holistically, since I did not predetermine a keyword list, but I can also compare the censorship practices across different platforms. This chapter also documents the descriptions of the censorship practices directly from those individuals who censor through face-to-face interviews.

INSTITUTIONAL DISRUPTIONS IN THE VIRTUAL SPACE

Before the age of the internet, the Chinese state dominated political discourses through its effective propaganda apparatuses. In the past few decades, technological innovations have brought institutional disruptions to the way information is generated and disseminated. The pluralization of content generation is primarily driven by the shift from relying solely on traditional media toward greater use of internet-based media. Content for traditional media is typically produced by organizations through TV, radio, newspapers, and magazines. "New media" involve more advanced technologies, such as digital content, mobile platforms, satellites, and the internet.[35] Nevertheless, content producers of new media are still essentially organizations. That is not the case with other emerging media central to this chapter: self-media. As shown in table 6.1, self-media, sometimes referred to as "we-media" in other countries,[36] refers to independently operated media accounts that publish texts, audio, and video on various platforms. Self-media is a subcategory of new media in which content producers are typically individuals (rather than organizations) and operate independently and unofficially, making content generation swift but sometimes inaccurate. Self-media also differs from social media in that the audience is the public as a whole rather than only those in one's social network.

The rise of self-media in China poses new challenges to the censorship regime. Whereas traditional and new media are generated on platforms that are relatively easy to regulate, self-media lets every individual speak directly to the entire internet audience. Individuals do not have to follow the party line, and they sometimes cover events and issues and provide commentaries that are quite different from the official discourse. Since information control is a vital part of Chinese Communist Party governance, self-media poses unprecedented regime challenges. WeChat, Sina Weibo, and Toutiao, among many others, are examples of self-media platforms where individuals can register their accounts and publish content. The most popular platform in China initially was Sina Weibo because it allowed average citizens to follow or even interact with celebrities directly. Since the early 2010s, attention has shifted to WeChat because it combines features of WhatsApp, Facebook, Instagram, Twitter, and PayPal with additional functions in just one platform. Entering the 2020s, Toutiao is also taking shape to be the dominant platform for information dissemination, as its algorithms recommends content to users who are most likely be interested in increased user engagement and

TABLE 6.1. Key differences between media types

	Information Producer	Media Type	Audience
Traditional Media	Organizations	Traditional: TV, Radio, Newspaper, Magazine, etc.	Public as a whole
New Media	Organizations	Internet-based	Public as a whole
Self-Media	Individuals	Internet-based	Public as a whole
Social Media	Individuals	Internet-based	People in one's social network

in better allocating the supply and demand of information. The institutional disruptions created a window of opportunity for societal actors to produce and promote self-generated content and provide researchers a chance to look at how the state interacts with new actors and content in the virtual space.

METHODS AND DATA

The research in this chapter relies on two separate sets of publishable content in three different self-media platforms. *Global China* (海外看世界), a self-media online publication primarily operating on WeChat (but also has a website that's not subject to censorship), was co-founded by Professor Quansheng Zhao[37] and me. The authors of articles published in *Global China* are scholars of social sciences, mainly political scientists and economists, who can write political commentaries in Mandarin. Data were collected from January 23, 2017, to August 4, 2019, on 413 attempted publications, as within this period authors were exclusively from outside of mainland China (with a majority of authors based in the United States, Japan, and Taiwan), whom I assume would be less likely to self-censor. Authors either voluntarily submitted articles or participated in what we call a "quick comments series" (海看快评) reacting directly to a current event with a set of guiding questions provided by the editorial team. By August 2019, *Global China* had over eighty-one hundred subscribers from fifty-seven countries and regions from every continent—although subscribers were overwhelmingly from mainland China—and the highest-viewed article had over fifty-seven thousand views.

While *Global China* publishes political commentaries of scholars from all over the world, *Inside the Beltway* (华府圈内) is another self-media I set up. It provides succinct summaries of key developments of US politics that are relevant to China and news related to Sino-US relations. Each topic is covered using only a few sentences, and multiple topics are covered each day. Attempts were made to get the same material published on three different platforms—WeChat, Sina Weibo, and TouTiao—for cross-platform comparisons. In WeChat, all summaries were sent out in one batch, as WeChat allows publication only once every day, although up to eight separate articles are allowed each time. In Sina Weibo (Weibo, hereafter) and Toutiao, each summary is sent out separately in lengths similar to that of a tweet. Therefore, from June 7, 2020, to December 16, 2021, a total of 558 attempted articles were tried on WeChat, while 2,094 individual summaries were attempted on both Weibo and Toutiao—for convenience, I refer to each of those summaries as an "article" as well. By December 2021, *Inside the Beltway* on WeChat had over 9,400 subscribers from sixty-nine countries and regions from every continent, and the highest-viewed article had over 142,690 views. The Weibo and Toutiao publications also reached a large audience, with more than 40,000 followers on Toutiao, for example, and the highest-viewed article had over 13 million views.

The unit of analysis is the individual article published (or attempted to publish) on each platform. The key dependent variable is whether an article is censored or not. Any interference with a direct clean publication satisfies the condition as being censored. The survival rate (including articles being censored but still published) is also analyzed. Incidents of censorship at various stages of the life of the articles and in different forms are analyzed and discussed. Different parties could do the act of censoring, and the censorship process varied at different stages. I discuss censorship at each stage in the following section.

Key independent variables I paid attention to include sensitive keywords, the current events associated with political sensitivity, the parties conducting censorship, viewer locations, warning messages, as well as the size and age of the account. Multiple AB tests were utilized at various stages to localize targets of censoring and reveal the dynamic nature of those keywords. To be more specific, articles censored initially can become publishable with the tweaking of one word/picture or changing the publication time. Furthermore, crucial points shared by government officials and the staff members of censorship from in-depth interviews are presented.

Below, I first discuss the life of an article and the various interactions between the censors and censored throughout that life, using *Global China* on WeChat as an example. Then I provide a cross-platform comparison of *Inside the Beltway* in a separate section. After that, I provide an analysis of the entire set of empirical evidence collected and present the three-stage process of interactive authoritarianism in virtual space.

GLOBAL CHINA ON WECHAT

The life of an article is arduous. It can be eliminated at multiple points. First, a message announcing the topic for the "quick comments series" can be censored in the authors' WeChat group. This WeChat group is a private messaging group that includes only participating authors of *Global China*. Group announcements can be censored, and as a result, scholars might not be able to receive the notice. The service provider, Tencent, does this process of blocking or deleting messages within a WeChat group, and the direct supervising agency is Public Security rather than Cyberspace Affairs.[38] There is a clear division of labor between the two agencies. The former is in charge of censorship in the private sphere, while the latter is in charge of the public sphere.[39] The officials consider the space inside the WeChat group as part of the private sphere, and therefore, Public Security is in charge.

What is worth noting is that Tencent and Public Security agencies do not intend to completely shut down group chats, at least most of the time. The interventions are often temporary with various degrees. For a specific period, messages including certain words or by certain individuals can be banned, or scholars who use a Chinese cell phone number to register their WeChat accounts cannot see messages from those who have registered using international cell phone numbers. The state and the service providers do not want users to choose alternative ways to communicate, as being able to monitor what has been said might be valuable to the state, and users are financial assets to internet service companies. The one-on-one private messages are usually not banned, so if we want to send the notice to all of our authors, we can choose the tedious way and send it individually. This indicates that the interventions are mainly used to slow down communication that is deemed questionable.

The second point of intervention in an article's life involves saving an already written article on the editing page. The system often produces an error message automatically warning the editor not to proceed. The message might vaguely mention that the content could potentially violate the law, or it might be more specific, as the content might contain inappropriate use of the names or images of staff members of the state agency. The message sometimes can indicate that sensitivity comes from mentioning "an important state conference or activity" or "names and abbreviations." The editor may still choose to proceed and save the article, but the warning message might indicate a more extended wait period (such as three to four hours rather than the usual one to two minutes) and a higher potential for deletion. After seeing this message, the editors can ignore the message or conduct self-censorship. The error message might go away the next time if the editor correctly identifies the sensitive keywords. Our editorial team tried to avoid self-censorship as much as possible, but for this study I documented the incidents where the editorial team tweaked words to see which specific keywords triggered the error message and, once deleted, made the article publishable.

It is also possible that if some sensitive keywords are not changed, the system does not allow the editors to save the article to the system. In that case, our editorial team replaces the keyword with a different word that still expresses the same meaning. For example, the name of the Chinese president, "Xi Jinping" (习近平), is sometimes censored, but using only his last name, "Xi" (习), does not trigger the automatic censorship's detection. We later also found out that mentioning the word "Xi" too many times in an article can still trigger automatic censorship, and in those cases we would say "the Chinese head of the state" instead of mentioning his name directly.

Third, once an article is saved on the account editing page, it can be deleted without notice. This mechanism first appeared on June 26, 2019, about two and half years after our account was created. During an interview, an official with experience in censorship work emphasized that they were undergoing a campaign to move censorship work upstream: "It will be too late to disperse the crowd once protesters are already on the streets—like what often happens in the United States."[40] Therefore, the work has moved from simply deleting articles after they appear to occasionally deleting them even before they are edited.

The fourth stage is the actual publishing of the articles. Similar to, but more complicated than, the second stage, the fourth stage can result in the following outcomes for an article. It can fail to publish with an error message; it can get an error message indicating a more extended period of censorship time; it can be published (regardless of wait time) and then deleted;

or it can be published and stay published. The publishing process is interactive, as the editorial team uses a procedure to identify specific keywords triggering the "automatic keywords bank" that prevents articles from being published. This is made possible because WeChat allows a maximum of eight articles to be attempted as a group at once (even though only one successful attempt is allowed per day). Such an arrangement means that if the article cannot be published, it can be kept as the first of several articles in a group attempt (so that any given attempt will surely fail, providing another chance to try later), and the original article is broken down into smaller sections and attached as individual articles alongside the original article during the same group attempt. The specific section containing unpublishable keywords or phrases can be identified through this procedure. This procedure can be repeated to localize the exact keyword that's triggering the "automatic keywords bank."

The life of a published article is still not certain. A publishable article on the WeChat public account may not be allowed in Weibo and Toutiao and vice versa. The article itself may no longer be censored, but if the discussions posted by readers becomes questionable to the authorities, that can also trigger the deletion.[41] Whenever the international environment shifts, there might be campaigns to revisit published articles by censorship. For example, an article discussing Taiwan under Tsai Ing-wen was published on July 13, 2017, and was not censored at that time. However, when the relationship between the mainland and Taiwan changed and the discussion of Tsai Ing-wen and Taiwan politics became sensitive, the article was deleted on July 14, 2019, exactly two years after its original publication.

From January 2017 to August 2019, 413 articles were attempted during the 924 days—about 1 article every 2.24 days, or about 3.13 articles per week. Among the 413 articles, 44 (10.65%) were forced to be desensitized; otherwise, they would not be allowed to be either saved or published. Then 397 articles were published; 16 of these (or 3.87%; 7 were previously indicated as being sensitive, and 9 had no such indications) did not pass the initial censorship and were never allowed to be published (see table 6.2). Among the 397 articles that were published, 27 were deleted (6.80%). Therefore, 370 articles remain published as of August 2019, an 89.59 percent survival rate (or 10.41% deleted rate).[42] "Deleted rate" in other studies is the same as the "censored rate," but in this study the "censored rate" captures the rate of articles that faced any challenges throughout their lives of publication. The deleted rate is lower than what scholars have indicated in other studies on

TABLE 6.2. Articles going through censorship on Global China

(From January 2017 to August 2019)

Starting total	Sign of sensitivity	Stopped from publication (3.87%)	Published	Deleted after publication (6.80%)	Survived	Survived Total
413	44 sensitive and with keyword adjustments (10.65%)	7	37	7	30	370 (89.59%)
	369 no sign	9	360	20	340	
Total		16	397	27		

Weibo, a more public platform. On Weibo, King, Pan, and Roberts found the deleted rate to be 13 percent, and David Bamman, Brendan O'Connor, and Noah Smith found it to be 16.25 percent. Because information on WeChat spreads more slowly than on Weibo, it is seen as less intimidating to the regime, and therefore scholars have found WeChat content to undergo less strict censorship.[43] Another reason this deleted rate could be underestimated would be due to the initial 44 forced desensitizations, during which sensitive keywords were replaced, making some censored articles not deleted at the end. Even among the 44 desensitized articles, 7 were prevented from publication, and another 7 were deleted after publication, with 30 remaining published.

Based on the interviews and the data analysis, the process of censorship and the parties involved throughout an article's life has also become more apparent. Before an article is edited on the WeChat public account platform, many activities happen within the private domain. The Cyberspace Affairs Office has nothing to do with the censorship at this stage. On the other hand, Public Security has its own keyword banks to censor WeChat conversations or posts made by circles of friends. The keywords list and the strength of censorship varies by province, city, and, of course, the individual officials' personal judgments at those levels in different regions. Thus, the decisions are highly situational and are often based on feedback from or interactions with societal players.

Once an article is uploaded to the WeChat public account platform, Cyberspace Affairs takes over. The service provider (here Tencent) has its censorship team and a dynamic keyword bank that updates its list of words at least once a day, sometimes more frequently.[44] The triggering of the keyword bank may not be an immediate "death sentence" but likely makes the life of the article much more difficult down the road. Some of the articles that trigger the keyword bank are blocked from publication, and others are viewed by staff members to determine whether an article is publishable. Some articles fail to get published after the human review. Since each service provider (such as Tencent, WeChat, and Sina Weibo) has its own keyword banks and censorship staff, the same article that is not publishable on one platform may be published successfully on other platforms. There is also a built-in appeal mechanism, but the limited few appeal attempts we have made were never successful.

An article can be published if it is deemed "safe" or can be passed to the local Cyberspace Affairs Office for further review. This is the first time in the process that government officials are actually involved in censorship. The staff size for a typical first-tier city's Cyberspace Affairs Office (excluding Beijing, Shanghai, and Guangzhou, which are slightly different) is extremely small, usually fewer than ten people.[45] Thus, the vast majority of censorship has already been done by self-censorship or the service provider's censorship. An article sent up from the service provider is reviewed and discussed. If a determination cannot be made, the article is sent to the next level up— the provincial Cyberspace Affairs Office.

The keyword bank is automatic and usually sparks decisions within minutes. Once human censorship is involved, the decision can take hours, sometimes days. This is why an article can be deleted hours or days after it has already been published. The bottom line has changed within the Cyberspace Affairs Office from "blocking" to "dredging," and even the former deputy director of the Cyberspace Affairs Office of China, Ren Xianliang, has repeatedly encouraged officials not to have a "blocking" mentality, because that does not work.[46] This means that, quite often, while waiting for a decision to be made, the article is out to be published rather than waiting in the pipeline. The Cyberspace Affairs Office can also initiate major cleaning campaigns to delete articles published online, even if the article has been published for a long time. The article on Tsai Ing-wen, which was deleted two years after its publication, is an example.

There are interactions between the authors, the internet service provider (here Tencent), and the state apparatus throughout this process. Different authors, internet service providers, officials from various regions and levels of government, and their interactions can lead to varied outcomes through a dynamic process.

The strength of censorship may also change based on changes in the macro-environment. The number of articles published each month fluctuates (see fig. 6.1), but the percentage of unpublished and deleted articles typically rises prior to or during sensitive events (see fig. 6.2). It is clear that whenever there is a prominent political event, the percentage of articles censored goes up around the time of the event. For example, the 19th National Congress of the Chinese Communist Party was held on October 18–24, 2017. There was a spike in the percentage of articles censored in October and November of 2017. There were no articles censored between March and September and December during that year. Every year during early March, the "Two Sessions" (the meetings of the National People's Congress and Chinese People's Political Consultative Conference) are held in Beijing, and around the same time, particularly leading up to the meetings, the percentage of censorship rises. Other specific occasions such as Kim Jong Un's visit to China (May 2018), the one-hundred-year anniversary of May 4 (May 2019), and the thirty-year anniversary of the 1989 Tiananmen incident (June 2019) all had increased censorship during those periods. Sometimes censoring articles may not be the only means of intervention during major events. The editing page of the WeChat public account crashed for a short period during the 19th Party Congress, which did not happen at other times.

Our editorial work verified that these correlations are not merely coincidences. Besides the example of the AB test of Kim Jong Un's name, mentioned at the beginning of this chapter, additional evidence supports the "incident-related" dynamic nature of censorship. On May 7, 2019, an article directly commented on then American president Donald Trump's Twitter announcement of new tariffs against China. The article was blocked for publication on WeChat. The *Global China* website, however, is not subjected to censorship, since the server is outside of mainland China. I informed a major news outlet that often reprints our articles that this particular commentary had just been posted on our website and that the outlet could feel free to reprint. The editor said, "At this moment, this topic should not be discussed" (目前还不能谈这事). I followed up with amazement and asked, "So there is a dynamic list of forbidden topics that you have access to?" He answered in the affirmative. I inquired about how to get access to that list, but his vague reply suggested that only when the Cyberspace Affairs Office pays exceptionally close attention to a publication (usually an extremely influential one) do they take preemptive measures by offering this dynamic "banned list." "Trump's tweets to raise another round of tariffs" was one of those topics on

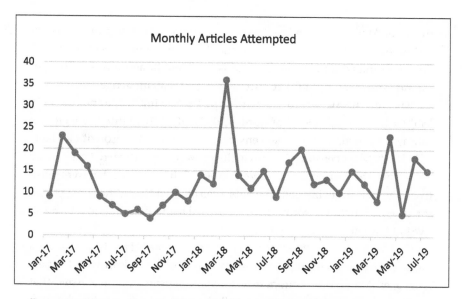

Figure 6.1. Articles attempted for publication each month (from January 2017 to August 2019)

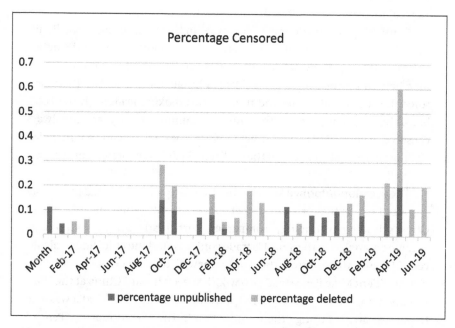

Figure 6.2. Percentage censored by month (from January 2017 to August 2019)

the list on May 7. Two days later, on May 9, the editor sent me a message indicating that the list had changed and that the topic could now be discussed. Therefore, our editorial team tried our WeChat public account, and the article was immediately published successfully and remains active today.

Based on the AB tests conducted during the "saving" stage and the "publish" stage, I compiled a list of words and classified them into three groups: "always censored," "sometimes censored," and "not yet censored" (see table 6.3). The "always censored" group includes words that triggered censorship every time; the "sometimes censored" group includes words that were sensitive only a few times but could be published at other times; the "not yet censored" group includes words that the editorial team thought might be sensitive but have never triggered the censorship.

On the "always censored" list, it is clear that names of foreign anti-China media outlets are censored, particularly those that broadcast with Chinese languages (Mandarin, Cantonese, etc.). Some censored political issues that are placed in quotation marks ("so-called") might reduce the likelihood of censorship, but making a complete statement or hinting at a stance ("the South China Sea is not a part of China," and Tsai Ing-wen as the president of Taiwan) increase the likelihood.

Censorship is also a double-edged sword in that while it can block discussion of individuals' scandals, it may also reduce opportunities for the public to praise the top leaders. Therefore, it is interesting that some Politburo members and former top leaders (like Hu Jintao and Hu Yaobang) are censored, but the number one and number two ranking leaders on the Politburo, the top ruling body of the Chinese Communist Party, are not always censored. *Global China* successfully published several articles that included Xi Jinping (general secretary of the CCP) and Li Keqiang (premier of the State Council).

The occasion-informed keyword bank adjustment mentioned previously produced words that are only sometimes censored. When Huawei, one of China's leading technology companies, particularly on 5G technology, became entangled in the Sino-US trade conflicts, and the chief financial officer of Huawei was arrested, the word "Huawei" became censored. After US vice president Mike Pence made a hawkish speech toward China at the Hudson Institute, "Pence" was censored, although a friend's self-media was able to publish articles using "the number two in the US" to replace "Pence." These keywords were not censored prior to those incidents, and some keywords became uncensored after the incidents.

TABLE 6.3. Classification of keywords censorship

Always censored	Sometimes censored	Not yet censored
朝鲜劳动党 (The North Korean Labor Party)	金正恩，文在寅 (Kim Jong Un, Moon Jae-In)	文革 (The Cultural Revolution)
蔡英文总统 (President Tsai Ing-Wen)	彭斯，蔡英文 (Pence, Tsai Ing-Wen)	大跃进 (The Great Leap Forward)
西藏独立 (Tibet Independence)	公民，萨德 (Citizen, THAAD)	李登辉 (Lee Teng-hui)
南海不是中国的 (The South China Sea is not a part of China)	关键词加引号，如"台独"、"台湾主权独立"、"法理台独"、"太阳花学运" ("Taiwan independence," "Taiwan's sovereign independence," "De Jure Taiwan Independence," "Sunflower Movement")	共产党，中国共产党 (Communist Party, Chinese Communist Party)
胡锦涛 (Hu Jintao)	李克强、李总理 (Li Keqiang, Premier Li)	温家宝 (Wen Jiabao)
胡耀邦 (Hu Yaobang)	中国国家主席、习主席，最高领导人 (President of China, Chairman Xi, Supreme leader)	
栗战书、汪洋、王沪宁、赵乐际、韩正 (Names of all Politburo Standing Committee members except Xi Jinping and Li Keqiang)	习近平, 特习，习特，特金 (Xi Jinping, Xi and Trump, Trump and Xi, Trump and Kim)	
大纪元 (the *Epoch Times*)	华为 (Huawei)	
新唐人电视台 (the New Tang Dynasty TV)	十九大 (19th Party Congress)	
亚洲自由电台 (Radio Free Asia)	毛泽东，周恩来，邓小平，时任总书记 (Mao Zedong, Zhou Enlai, Deng Xiaoping, then general secretary)	
撸 (Rub one's palm along)	G20	

Interestingly, some of the words that people intuitively consider sensitive and could be censored are not yet censored in any of the articles published so far. This includes individuals such as Taiwan's controversial former leader Lee Teng-hui and former Chinese premier Wen Jiabao as well as major controversial incidents in China, such as the Cultural Revolution and the Great Leap Forward. Significant events such as the 17th and 18th Party Congresses are not censored, and the Chinese Communist Party itself is not censored.

INSIDE THE BELTWAY ON WECHAT, WEIBO, AND TOUTIAO

The experience of *Inside the Beltway*, which is simultaneously published every day on WeChat, Weibo, and Toutiao, is slightly different from that of *Global China*. First, there are no internal communications, as I am the only person involved in producing the contents. The publication process is streamlined for both Weibo and Toutiao, as the articles are tweet-length short summaries, so there is also no within-platform editing or saving. Thus, the only points of intervention during the life of the articles are publishing and post-publication, although the articles published on WeChat are similar in length to those of *Global China*, since summaries are grouped into one article and published once a day.

The scenarios within Weibo are binary; an article is either allowed to be published or not allowed to be published. If an article encounters censorship, the message states, "Sorry, there is a violation of relevant laws and regulations." The messages in Toutiao, on the other hand, are individualized. A typical censorship message might state:

> "Dear content creator, according to the 'Internet News Information Service Management Regulations,' **the platform only supports qualified media to publish news on current affairs**. Thus, the article XXX you published at XX/XX/XXXX <u>will no longer be recommended to others</u>."

While the above message is often the template, the specific reason to censor an article (bold in the above text) and the outcome of the censorship (underlined in the above text) can vary. I have listed the reasons and outcomes that *Inside the Beltway* has encountered in table 6.4. Any combination of a reason and an outcome is possible, and this may not be an exhaustive list:

TABLE 6.4. Reasons and outcomes of censorship from Toutiao

Reasons	Outcomes
The platform supports only qualified media to publish news on current affairs	Will be recommended to your followers only
Because we are unable to verify the authenticity of the content	
Because the post contains inappropriate content	Will stop being recommended
Because the usage of expressions are not the norm	
Involving exaggerated descriptions, inaccurate information, or inconsistent titles, etc., which can easily cause misunderstandings or cause imagination that does not match the facts	Was not approved to publish
Because it involves risk information in the financial sector or contains content that induces transactions	
Suspected of containing uncomfortable text descriptions or pictures, such as bloody, violent, dense, visually impactful pictures, descriptions looking for the exotic and strange, etc.	

Although the reasons do not always accurately point out the most relevant issue of why an article is censored, the outcomes reflect gradually intensifying censorship levels. Toutiao uses algorithms to recommend articles to its users. Without censorship, the algorithms would recommend each article to those readers who are most likely to be interested in the content. When the article is recommended only to an author's followers, other people who click on the author's profile can still see the article but have to take that initiative; otherwise, only those who have already followed the author receive a recommendation to see that specific article. At the next level, even followers don't get the recommendation, and only those who regularly check the author's profile are able to see the censored article. The strictest level is complete censorship, meaning no one at all can see the article. If there are downsides of censorship, this more nuanced mechanism might be intended to address some of the downsides. For example, if followers can still see the published material, the author might not resent the censorship regime as much.

The "survival rate" for *Inside the Beltway* articles is significantly higher than it is for those of *Global China*. Using the WeChat platform for comparison, out of the 558 articles published from June 2020 to December 2021, 13 (6.81%) had to be desensitized; otherwise, they would not be allowed to get

TABLE 6.5. Articles going through censorship on Inside the Beltway

(From June 2020 to December 2021)

Starting total	Sign of sensitivity	Stopped from publication (0.18%)	Published	Deleted after publication (0.90%)	Survived	Survived Total
558	13 sensitive and with keyword adjustments (6.81%)	1	12	2	10	552 (98.92%)
	545 no sign	0	545	3	542	
Total		1	557	5		

saved or published. Then 557 articles were published; only 1 article (or 0.18%) did not pass the initial censorship and was never allowed to be published. Among the 557 articles that were published, 5 were deleted (0.90%). Therefore, there are 552 articles that remain published as of December 2021, with a 98.92 percent survival rate (or 1.08% deleted rate), compared to the 89.59 percent survival rate of articles from *Global China*—meaning the deleted rate is ten times as high on *Global China* (see table 6.5).

The censored rate can be different when different types of materials are published on the same platform. The same material published on different platforms can also face different treatments. The censored rate for *Inside the Beltway* is 2.87 percent, 1.29 percent, and 2.24 percent on WeChat, Weibo, and Toutiao, respectively. The eventual survival rate ranges from 98.71 percent to 98.92 percent (see table 6.6).

On the surface, the censored and survival rates seem close when the same material is published on different self-media platforms, thus pointing toward a unified and consistent censorship apparatus. In reality, however, this cannot be further from the truth. When looking at the specific articles censored, the overlap is minimal. Among the total of ninety articles censored across the three platforms for *Inside the Beltway*, only one article was censored by two platforms, and no article was censored by all three. The censoring of an article by both WeChat and Toutiao could be due to different reasons, as the one censorerd article included a description of US legislators visiting Taiwan and a picture of Tsai Ing-wen and the Taiwanese flag, and pictures are often subject to censorship as well.

The censored articles can generally be divided into two broad categories.

TABLE 6.6. A cross-platform comparison of censored and survival rate

Contents	Platform	Censored rate (including any degree of restriction)	Survival Rate
Global China	WeChat	17.68%	89.59%
Inside the Beltway	WeChat	2.87%	98.92%
	Weibo	1.29%	98.71%
	Toutiao	2.24%	98.90%

The first is a discussion of US politics that might have implications for Chinese politics or might be misunderstood by Chinese readers to have domestic political implications. For example, an article discussed then president Trump entertaining the idea of staying in office for more than two terms, which could be interpreted to have implications for Xi's tenure in China. A discussion on the US Democratic Party infighting could be picked up by the automatic keyword bank, as conflict within a party does not only happen to US parties. Even when an article describes US domestic politics, sometimes the idea is relatable when discussing protests, freedom of speech, and free elections, among other topics.

The censorship process is not one-sided. A few months after the *Inside the Beltway* account was created, staff members from both Weibo and Toutiao contacted me privately. Weibo's staff member praised me for publishing valuable information every day and asked me to message him whenever I think an article is worth being promoted so that he can use the platform's resources to make the article more widely read. Toutiao had a more complex interaction with me. The platform first invited me to be a "content rater" due to "the high-quality content having been published." I ignored the message, assuming that the platform mobilizes social resources to support its in-house censorship apparatus. Then the platform informed me that due to the high-quality articles I publish every day, the platform was lifting the "eight times a day" publication limit so that I could publish as many articles as I wish, encouraging me to produce more content. Later, a staff member contacted me directly. Besides thanking me for the high-quality content I have published consistently, she invited me to join a messaging group titled "International Scholars and Journalists VIP Group" (国

际学者记者VIP群). The 240 or so people in this group are primarily international scholars and journalists who produce content on Toutiao. The function of the group is that if anyone's article is censored by the system (based on the algorithm or the automatic keyword bank), the author can make an appeal within this group, and the in-group staff from Toutiao immediately processes the request to potentially reverse the censorship decision. Although I have never made an appeal, it seems that the success rate is exceptionally high. I had previously tried the official appeal mechanism on WeChat a few times when first publishing material on *Global China* and never once heard back from the platform. It is fascinating to know that there could be a group of authors with such special privileges that a request to cancel censorship could be made and granted at ease.

INTERACTIVE AUTHORITARIANISM IN VIRTUAL SPACE

The self-media experiences in virtual space are consistent with the interactive authoritarianism model with toleration, differentiation, and legalization. New players are tolerated and monitored, repeated interactions lead to a differentiation of treatment, and then the experiences and lessons learned from the interactions are solidified through legalization.

Toleration

On February 9, 2021, an article titled "The Great Firewall Cracked, Briefly. A People Shined Through" was published in the *New York Times*, capturing the social media app Clubhouse's "uncensored" status for a while.[47] Although the author of the article claimed that Clubhouse "emerged faster than the censors could block it," in reality the gate of the great firewall was intentionally left open so that the Chinese censorship could monitor and study this new actor that had emerged recently after an institutional disruption and that created a platform combining audio and social network and allowed users to discuss political and social issues.

Toleration is the initial status quo whenever new players or phenomena emerge in the virtual space. The popularization of social media, particularly self-media, is a new phenomenon in the past decade; Sina Weibo had its first internal testing on August 14, 2009,[48] and both the WeChat public account and Toutiao platforms were introduced in 2012.[49] The state's approach is toleration when a new phenomenon arises, especially before the activities become sophisticated or solidly anti-regime. This is true for both those platforms and the self-media publishers. The regulators understand that the free flow of information is no longer containable, and much of the information that people publish on self-media is with good intentions; therefore, it is essential to allow people to speak and collect their ideas and suggestions.[50] The state is also confident that the media environment is much less hostile than it is in the West, for the media is not a direct check against the ruling party.[51]

Allowing self-media to make adjustments and then try to publish again is in itself a great example of toleration during censorship. It does not point toward inadequate censorship, as some keyword changes (such as moving from "Xi Jinping" to "Xi") would obviously be easy to catch if the real purpose is to prevent the article from being published. Instead, the process is executed intentionally to train self-media for habits of self-censorship. It is also a way to remind the societal participants who the boss really is—just like the example of removing church crosses without shutting down churches.

Toleration happens more likely when newcomers enter the public sphere. One piece of evidence pointing to this initial phase is the tolerance on newly created and smaller media accounts. For example, a newly created account that reported the firing of a professor for his research claimed that the center for anti-Japan war in the 1940s was not Yan'an but Chongqing. Such a topic directly challenges the political security of the CCP—and the firing of the professor is a testament—but the account still managed to publish the article because it was still a small (with only a few followers) and new account. Some political activists have utilized this property and created new accounts constantly whenever the old account becomes banned. A self-media publisher I interviewed informed me that he had created dozens of new accounts, as every time the old one is banned, the newly registered one was created and tolerated, even though the registration requires the account owner's real ID.[52]

The toleration of small and newer accounts could also be proved by *Global China*'s experience, as logistic regression indicates that censorship tightens on the account as the number of publications grows (see table 6.7). I code the "censored" variable as "blocked or deleted." If an article was not published successfully or was later deleted after publication, it was coded as "1"; otherwise, it was coded as "0" for the "censored" variable. Because of the desensitizing mechanism, which replaces censored keywords with uncen-

TABLE 6.7. Factors and censorship

	Censored (~)	Deleted	Full Model
main			
number	0.00310**	0.00454**	0.00532***
	(0.027)	(0.012)	(0.005)
desenspub			1.656***
			(0.001)
viewed			–0.0000344
			(0.540)
Constant	–2.848***	–3.679***	–4.095***
	(0.000)	(0.000)	(0.000)
Observations	413	397	397

p-values in parentheses
* $p < 0.10$, ** $p < 0.05$, *** $p < 0.01$

sored ones (homophones, puns, etc.), I also included a binary variable I called "desenspub," which indicates an article that had been desensitized and still published. The "number" variable indicates the order of the publications and therefore is an ordinal variable from 1 to 413; the larger number indicates a newer publication. The "viewed" and "shared" variables look at how popular the article was, but since the two variables are highly correlated, I have included one in the model in order to demonstrate how replacing one with the other does not change the outcome. Newer articles are more likely to be censored across models.

This outcome could be due to a variety of potential factors, including a change in censorship strategy, the tightening of the control of the society, or a change in coverage by our writers, among others. The editorial experiences from *Global China* suggest that the more mature a publication becomes, the more likely it is to face censorship.

An article titled "How China Could Learn from the Democratic Opposition in Its Interaction with Trump" commented on US Speaker of the House Nancy Pelosi's interactions with Trump during the government shutdown from December 22, 2018, to January 25, 2019. The article was blocked for publication because *Global China* already had over six thousand followers at the time, and a single article's viewership was as high as forty thousand by then. *Global China* was no longer a small and new account, but other smaller accounts successfully reprinted the same article on our official website. This means the censorship on *Global China*—by this time a more developed and influential account—is different from that of smaller and newer accounts. Such incidents happened multiple times.

Differentiation

One typical type of toleration in the virtual space is turning a blind eye to the use of the Virtual Private Network, often referred to as "climbing over the firewall" (*fanqiang* 翻墙). Many Chinese netizens I spoke to believe that as long as they are not doing anything criminal while using the VPN but are simply viewing information and increasing their productivity, there will not be any consequences. However, the state differentiates individual users and sometimes intentionally chooses not to intervene until the intervention will be tactically more effective—for instance, when doing so could set an example for others or achieve other political goals. Interview with officials also confirmed that the penalties are selectively applied.[53] If we look at Zhejiang province alone, a province with over 64.5 million people,[54] the provincial online service platform (在线政务服务平台) indicates only 292 cases of individuals penalized for connecting to the international internet (国际联网) from February 2017 to December 2021, a five-year period.[55] Yet, the use of VPN is almost ubiquitous among the well-educated, especially in the high-tech sector. Based on the evidence from this chapter, the practice and logic of differentiation are clear.

Looking at self-media, not many of them could outlive the initial stage of toleration (many stop publishing content due to their own reasons), but once they grow into more developed and mature sources of information and opinions, the state treatment toward them changes. The state differentiates the regime-challenging ones and regime-supporting ones on multiple dimensions at various stages of publication.[56]

The experiences of *Global China* and *Inside the Beltway* point toward two different paths; the deleted rate of the former is about ten times as high as that of the latter within the same platform. There are several important distinctions between the two accounts. *Global China*'s contents are political commentaries that are largely analyses and opinions and are normative by nature. This means that the arguments made or the results of the analyses could directly contradict policy decisions of the state. The delete rate in absolute terms is not that high because sometimes that material serves a consultation purpose. Because authors are scholars trying to be objective, they are also not perceived to have an anti-Beijing agenda.

The experience from *Inside the Beltway* is quite different. The content is mainly informational, providing timely insights about the developments and sometimes foreign policy making of the United States relevant to China. The content's positive nature (as opposed to normative) can lead to a very

different type of censorship. It is usually platform-specific and often triggered by specific keywords. For example, many of the censored articles on
Toutiao covered the development of how TikTok was facing crackdowns in
the United States under Trump (Toutiao and TikTok originated from the
same parent company, ByteDance). Thus, the company itself wished to censor the discussion for business interests rather than the state doing the job.
Indeed, different service providers have their own keyword banks, and the
officials at different levels in different regions reach different conclusions
when determining whether an article should be censored or not. This is why
some other studies that use a self-generated list of keywords to test censorship might not be reliable.

"Being potentially helpful" is an important standard during the differentiation stage. After starting *Inside the Beltway*, major news outlets, including
the *Global Times* and *China Global Television Network (CGTN)*, contacted me
for more information or a quote, indicating that the information provided
in self-media is valuable. However, the material would have to have at least
some potential usefulness in order to be tolerated in the long term. For example, *Inside the Beltway* wrote about the secretary of state of Georgia, a US election battleground, releasing phone conversations with Trump, who complained about privacy violations for making the records public. The original
article, which cited the law 18 USC 2511(2)(d), was not allowed to be published, but as soon as this series of numbers and letters, which were probably
foreign to the Chinese censorship, were removed, the article was published
successfully. The numbers and letters from the US Code probably had no
potential to be helpful and therefore triggered the censorship.

In addition, many other indicators would lead to differentiated outcomes for articles and platforms. The author's identity could be utilized for
differentiation. For example, an article published by a Taiwanese scholar, Dr.
Su Chi, was initially blocked for publication, and the editing team could not
find the keyword that was blocking the publication. Then our editorial team
added an extra sentence to the introduction, indicating that the author was
the inventor of the concept "92 Consensus" (the bedrock of Beijing's Taiwan
policy), and the article was then successfully published. It seems that the
staff did not know who Dr. Su was, and the extra introduction reassured the
censors that the author had good intentions and was not an enemy.

A self-media and an article could also be censored if the comments section was not managed well, letting discussions get out of control.[57] It could
be due to the inclusion of a specific analysis within an article, resulting in

the deletion of just one or two paragraphs but not the entire article—for example, one article was not deleted in its entirety but had just two paragraphs (discussing Michael Pillsbury's and Graham Allison's arguments) deleted. If the editors do not go back to articles already published, one would not be able to notice that the article was even censored. A self-media and an article could also be tolerated because the state is also intentionally preventing the Tacitus Trap from happening, a phenomenon in which people consider whatever the government says to be lies or a bad deed.[58] Therefore, getting the suitable "helpers" to produce and propel "helpful" information is as important, if not more important, than preventing specific contents. The Cyberspace Affairs Office actively encourages government offices and agencies to register their own social media accounts on major platforms so that society's "helpful voices" can be augmented. Of course, the timing of major political events could lead to the scale of differentiation to tip toward either more censorship or more toleration.

Even though the two publications studied in this chapter were treated quite differently based on the deletion rates, the differentiation at various stages of the articles' lives is similar within the two publications, although *Global China* has more stages in its publication process, which might contribute to the lower survival rate of its articles. At the pre-editing stage, communications are differentiated based on location. Instead of blocking all messages and alerting the sender, censorship may prevent messages from being received or shared in a group chat or personal pages (such as 朋友圈 or a circle of friends on WeChat) while misleading the sender that the message was sent or posted. It has been reported by the authors that occasionally when the group chat or personal pages censorship is on, those who registered their WeChat account while outside of mainland China, whether they used a mainland or abroad cell phone number, would be able to see messages sent by others, while those who registered their account inside China would be blocked. This is why even if a foreign-registered user is in mainland China, the person can still access information that many other members of the same chat group cannot. Not only can a person's location of registering an account lead to differentiation in censorship, but the assessment of public opinion can lead to different levels of freedom of expression. For example, protests in Hong Kong in the summer of 2019 were a major discussion topic within chat groups. For several weeks, messages were virtually uncensored because much of the mainland public opinion was moving in Beijing's favor. However, members of a few groups reported that they would not be able to send or receive any messages in certain groups, but others who used the same group continued to have a conversation. The group members then realized that all the remaining active members had registered their accounts while outside of mainland China.

The process of transferring articles among editors faces the same challenge. The sender might assume the article has been sent, while many, if not all, of the members of the WeChat group cannot receive the file. This scenario can occur because of the differentiated censorship toward the sender due to the transferring history of the sender—the person might have previously sent many sensitive articles to others—the content of the article, or the location of the sender. This is not a temporary technical glitch but an integral part of censorship. For instance, one cannot type the three characters "大纪元" (the *Epoch Times*, an anti-Beijing publication) in WeChat.

Even after an article has been published, censorship can control the viewership. Sometimes an article one publishes or shares can be seen only by oneself or a few others—a controlled viewership. The Toutiao censorship messages pointed toward those different levels of outcomes. Self-media users on other platforms such as "简书" (the Chinese version of Medium) went as far as directly including "Your article has been turned to be visible only to you; if you have any questions, please contact . . ." in the error message.

One of the primary purposes for differentiation is to better adapt to new situations and challenges, especially after institutional disruptions. Continuing to tolerate some actors in the virtual space provides ongoing opportunities to test pilot governance methods, while applying pressure or completely censoring others reduces the potential challenge to the regime.

The interactions between the state, the delegated private internet companies, and individual self-media can make censorship more effective. The actions and contents from those who are tolerated can be used to train the censorship apparatus; if everything is shut down completely, there is no learning opportunity, so it does not help when a real threat in the virtual space comes about. This is also why users who register their WeChat accounts outside of mainland China may be tolerated for the most part; interactions with them provide valuable data for the internet companies and the state.[59] However, even those who have been censored can provide useful information to the censorship apparatus. They may try tactics such as using homophones or turning text into pictures to evade censorship,[60] but the censorship is likely to eventually notice some of those tactics and include such practices in their evolved automatic keyword bank and picture bank.

More importantly, the state has mobilized societal resources to join the censorship apparatus during this interactive process. Internet companies sometimes willingly pledge self-discipline in order to continue to survive,[61] and the occasional crackdowns by the state toward online platforms[62] are not only testing the state's tool kits of controlling the society but also providing credible threats to those who are still being tolerated without having to spend a significant amount of political capital. Therefore, such crackdowns are not meant to destroy an entire industry or completely shut down the virtual space but to set a few examples and target specific actors. For example, after Weibo allowed the Chinese tennis star Peng Shuai's tweet against a former CCP Politburo member to go viral, Weibo was hit with a penalty of about $471,000 for "spreading illegal information." Even though Weibo said that it would clean up its content, the fine would hardly affect Weibo's business.[63] The Peterson Institute for International Economics assessment suggests that China's tech crackdown in 2021 has affected only a small share of its digital economy and total GDP.[64]

The logic of these differentiations on various dimensions is not to block the flow of information but to identify and utilize the forces that could potentially contribute to the regime's legitimacy. On the one hand, the government is actively creating a team of commenters, but on the other hand, it also realizes that the government staff is not sufficient to manage the explosion of information.[65] Therefore, it is important to rely on the forces in society to strengthen the state's narrative or help with the state's agenda; scholars did find that online political expression can enhance regime support through nationalism.[66] Therefore, rather than seeing the existing censorship regime as an information blocker, it is more accurate to see it as an "ally" identifier.

Legalization

The process of moving from toleration to differentiation is only a part of the evolving censorship mechanism. These stages mainly happen in a legal gray area where the new activities (or newly registered accounts) may be violating some existing laws or acting within a domain where no laws or rules govern. But such new activities or players could be utilized as potential allies of the state, or motivations to improve the legal system. Let us take a look at how the interactions between the new activities online, censorship and differentiation, and the legalization of the domain have worked.

Before social media, many of the internet laws were about protecting the physical computer systems[67] and preventing the spread of national secrets and harmful information.[68] Once online activities started to pick up in the late 1990s, the government started to deploy a special group of police—internet police—to regulate the internet. The idea was initially experimented with at the provincial level and mainly targeted at online rumors and scams.[69] Laws regulating internet companies were made in 2000, which started to require internet companies to provide credentials.[70]

With the rise of social media, especially self-media on WeChat and Weibo, old laws and regulations could no longer govern the new activities and were updated/revised based on new developments. For example, the 2011 revision of the 2000 "Temporary Decree on the Management of Computer Information Network International Connectivity in the People's Republic of China" included specific topics that are banned from production, replication, publication, and distribution—in other words, guidance for censorship.[71] Based on the new challenges the censorship faced, the Supreme People's Court and the Supreme People's Procuratorate published updated interpretations of the censorship rules in 2013.[72] Further rules were announced to require real-name registration and banning publications of current affairs and commentaries unless accompanied by relevant credentials in 2014, when WeChat public accounts and Weibo self-media flooded the Chinese internet with current affairs discussions.[73] This provides legal grounds whenever the censorship regime wants to delete content or suppress content providers for most self-media users, who do not have such credentials. The Cyberspace Affairs Office intentionally does not eliminate all of the content providers, which could be potential allies.

While some content providers are genuine allies, others simply use tools and methods to circumvent censorship. The use of homophones, puns, long picture texts (so that texts are turned into pictures), upside-down long picture texts, upside-down long picture texts with random markers (to interfere with detections by artificial intelligence), and various other tactics have been used. The censorship mechanism initially neglected or tolerated certain developments, then differentiated accounts and articles, and eventually made new laws to tackle the specific tactics used. For example, the "Internet Information Search Service Management Regulations" published by the Cyberspace Affairs Office mentioned explicitly that "Internet information search service providers shall not provide information content prohibited by laws and regulations in the form of links, abstracts, snapshots, association words, related searches, and related recommendations."[74] Knowing that certain publications are shared only within WeChat groups, the People's Republic of China Cyber Security Law included new provisions governing communication groups.[75]

As the laws and rules have covered social media in general, and as WeChat public account publications became popular, specific laws were drafted to tackle censorship and credential issues on WeChat. On June 1, 2017, six months after *Global China* started its publications, the Cyberspace Affairs Office announced the "Internet News Information Service Management Regulations," which stipulate that "if the service provider allows users to open public accounts, the internet news information service provider shall review the account information, service qualification, service scope, and other information, and classify and record it to the local cyberspace affairs office of the province, autonomous region or municipality directly under the Central Government."[76] These regulations also specifically ask people involved in censorship to pay attention to information that is news propaganda in nature or has social mobilization abilities. On the same day, the state clarified that service providers should have designated staff members to review content and provide technical support by publishing the "Internet News Information Service License Management Regulations."[77] Moreover, the "Interim Provisions on the Development Management of Public Information Services for Instant Messaging Tools," published on August 7, 2017, further clearly placed the burden of censorship on the service providers. Companies could face a direct penalty if not doing the censorship properly or missing content that later caused problems.[78]

Once the responsibility of censorship was clear and platform-specific laws were made, the state went further in depth vertically to perfect the censorship regime. For example, the "Internet Post Comment Service Management Regulations" would govern the censorship of comments after articles,[79] and the "Internet Forum Community Service Management Regulations" would govern censorship in online forums and communities.[80] In the meantime, new regulations were also published to affirm the differentiation and categorization of different WeChat groups[81] and WeChat public account publications.[82] A few weeks later, even regulations governing the management of censorship staff were drafted.[83] New laws and regulations that tackle specific actors, actions, and issues are being drafted, circulated, and passed continuously based on the state-society interactions.[84] For example, as short videos on platforms such as TikTok are becoming popular, standards and rules are also being drafted.[85]

It is clear that once new rules and laws are made on specific activities and actors previously operating in legal gray areas, the strength and frequency of censorship and penalties can change. Previously differentiated approaches by different keyword banks, staff members of service providers, and officials from different regions and levels of the government may gradually unify.[86] This is a highly dynamic process, with new apps and services being invented and new tools and methods of circumventing censorship being deployed on the one hand, and a learning government that employs toleration, differentiation, and legalization on the other hand. Such a multilayered dynamic process is complex and evolving.

CONCLUSION

Censorship is becoming more and more important in the study of politics and governance as it becomes more intertwined with political activities worldwide. However, most countries' censorship simply switches the internet off and on or deletes information and accounts. What has been observed in the censorship regime in China is more nuanced, sophisticated, and interactive. There is authoritarian learning by the Chinese state, and the state is responsive to different actors at different stages of development, at different locations, with content-specific individualized tactics.

This chapter has examined the interactive nature of how China governs its virtual civil society, which includes the world's largest internet population (by June 2021, there were 1.011 billion internet users in China[87]). The results perhaps also reflect the logic of politics and governance in China in general. The logic of interactive authoritarianism indicates the differentiation of societal forces by the state. The purpose of such an approach is to maintain regime stability and legitimacy. Rather than blocking all free flow of information and players, the state recognizes its technical and bureaucratic limits and realizes that a certain degree of toleration might bring some benefits. The method used in this approach is interactive differentiation mainly based on the perception of the state. Rather than focusing on tackling regime-challenging information (such as information that could incite collective actions), the state is also actively utilizing users and content that could help improve the state's legitimacy. Sometimes, the state might even actively engage in guiding and shaping the behaviors of individuals in society through interactions. In sum, the state would identify and differentiate the regime-supporting voices at various stages of the life of the articles and content providers. Different parties are involved in the censorship regime and actively interact with the players involved. After capturing enough data, the state would make new rules and laws to adapt to new developments. Such a process allows the state to harness support and reduce risk, which ultimately improves its legitimacy. The result, therefore, is a seemingly more active media environment rather than the complete prevention of the flow of information and the halt of social, political, and economic activities in general. Thus, the cost of repression is limited and localized on only a small group of activists and elites, while the vast majority in the public is still satisfied. This more sophisticated interactive censorship under Xi reflects the more sophisticated governance of the authoritarian regime. Even though the cases described in this chapter are from the virtual space and much of the background conditions are different from the earthquake case, it is clear that the logic of authoritarian governance of the society after an institutional disruption is similar, and the outcomes are comparable. The more supportive forces or contents are differentiated—and even encouraged—after the legalization processes, thus contributing to authoritarian resilience.

The evolving three-stage interactive censorship also means that tactics used to manage the flow of information are adjusted and updated constantly. For example, before the 2022 Beijing Winter Olympic Games, platforms such as Weibo and Toutiao sent out messages warning users against posting any content from the games that belonged to broadcast rights holders or risk being blocked. The preemptive notices mainly targeted copyrights violations, but such warnings obviously makes self-media users warier about discussing the Olympic Games, resulting in increased self-censorship. Thus, censorship was carried out preemptively without content having ever appeared.

The interactive authoritarian state does not block all information or completely suffocate society based on the empirical data presented above. It is expected by all participants that some information and actions are allowed—at least tolerated, if not encouraged—while others are prohibited. This minimizes the cost of repression while soliciting the most help from society. A friend of mine subscribes to *The Economist* magazine within mainland China. He recently posted a picture of the magazine he received, with the entire "China" section cut out. Logistically, it would be much easier to ban the subscription entirely rather than having to cut those specific pages from each magazine manually, but the situation reflects the governance logic that this chapter, and this book, have described.

Censorship is not a taboo in state-society relations in China. *People's Daily*, a state-affiliated media in China, has tripled its stock price in the first four months of 2019, mainly due to the censorship service it provides to other content providers who do not have the budget to maintain their own censorship teams.[88] *People's Daily* even provides a training camp about "content reviewing," which charges 4,500 RMB (about 643 USD) for two days. A "content reviewing" industry is also emerging in the city of Jinan, the capital of Shandong province, as multiple companies similar to *People's Daily* have set up their censorship business in Jinan.[89] Furthermore, it is not only Chinese companies or media groups that are participating in this interactive authoritarian censorship. US researchers have also found that the California-based tech giant Apple also uses censored word lists from mainland China sources to populate its own list of forbidden terms and then apply them to regions including Taiwan and Hong Kong.[90] The interactive authoritarian censorship thus has implications outside of authoritarian states.

While censorship is an ordinary, everyday experience for anyone living in China or paying attention to China, the study of censorship has been fragmented. In this chapter, I have made an attempt to provide a holistic view of the multilayered dynamic process. I presented firsthand data from *Global China* and *Inside the Beltway* across multiple self-media platforms and depicted the life of an article and each moment possible of encountering censorship as well as describing the detailed interactions between the self-media publisher and the censorship apparatus. I then provided evidence and methods of circumventing censorship, such as tweaking the keywords, changing the publication time, and adding a new introduction of the author, among many others. Many of the AB tests could provide certainty, which most related studies lack. Furthermore, I provided the details of the censorship process, including revealing the logic of evolution from toleration, to differentiation, and eventually, legalization. Legalization is not the end of the process, as new activities and players continue to emerge, and the censorship system continues to evolve through such dynamic processes.

Although my focus is on political censorship, it should be mentioned that Chinese censorship also targets pornography, violation of laws and regulations, vulgar information, malicious pop-up windows, and malicious speculations.[91] Besides targeting individual articles, it is also possible for any content producer to be banned from publishing for a short period or even for life. Given the scope of this research and the data available to us, I have focused only on censorship over active publishers.[92] The dynamic nature of

Chinese censorship also means that what is valid during the time of data collection may be different at a future time, but the logic of censorship is likely to remain relevant.

The main contribution of this chapter to the literature is that it uses the editorial experiences of an actual online publication to reveal the multilayered dynamic nature of interactive censorship in China. Rather than using a predetermined sensitive keywords list and extremely narrow hypotheses to test the censorship at a specific point, I followed the lives of articles and found that the strength and choices of censorship vary throughout the life of a publication and are subject to the status of the author, the publisher, the timing, the different censorship staff that are involved, and the macro-political environment. Thus, instead of contradicting the existing literature, I have provided a more unified overview of the censorship regime that is less dependent on the observation choices of time and content. The variations presented by the existing literature are often not contradictions but indicate different stages and levels within the interactive authoritarianism framework.

A second significant contribution is the direct utilization of interviews with officials and staff members in charge of censorship to directly capture their logic and actions. The censorship regime is often seen as mysterious and inaccessible to researchers because of the nature of their work. These rare opportunities for interviews were used in this research to reveal the intricacy and detailed process of interactive censorship, which could be valuable for related future studies.

Methodologically, this chapter has provided a new way of analyzing censorship. Instead of capturing data from material published by others and not being able to include prepublication censorship—including self-censorship and denial of publication—being editors of an online journal and publishing actual articles written by experts in the field could help us reveal the internal logic and the dynamic nature of the interactive censorship regime. The AB tests I adopted through tweaking keywords to turn blocked articles into those that are publishable also gave us deterministic, rather than probabilistic, conclusions about which keywords triggered censorship at specific moments and which did not. As Chinese censorship continues to evolve and adapt, some of the specific keywords and tactics may change. However, the logic and process of interactive censorship will continue to help us better understand the future iterations of the censorship regime in China and the logic of governing the society.

CHAPTER 7

Case III

Internet-Facilitated Guerrilla Resistance of the Ride-Sharing Networks

On June 2, 2015, I rode in an Uber car in Hangzhou, China. The driver was very eager to show me a few videos on his cell phone, asking, "Did you hear about how we ride-sharing drivers fight transportation officials (*yunguan* 运管)? Check these out!" In one of the videos, a man in uniform was surrounded by dozens of (presumably) Uber drivers asking him to confess to how he had used entrapment to criminalize an Uber driver in order to charge the driver with a fine. This video was shot in Hangzhou, a major urban center, during broad daylight. The official of an authoritarian country specializing in cracking down protests does not seem authoritative at all; the protesters were, however, emboldened and demanded that the official give up and leave. When the police arrived, they did not arrest any of the protesters but accompanied the official in leaving the scene without receiving the fine he had demanded. My driver had dozens of those videos with almost the same plot and results, and with different crowds and transportation officials. Why were these ride-sharing drivers able to repeatedly organize grassroots protests and successfully achieve their purposes in an authoritarian state that is quite good at quashing protests? How did the state respond?

Ride-sharing drivers can be seen as part of the Chinese civil society, given the broad definition provided in the introduction. They not only share information and build relationships using the WeChat groups in the virtual space and organize leisure activities, but they also often organize collective actions and other gatherings when one community member faces injustice from the state. They create informal union-like associations that can turn shared grievances into mini social movements—what I call "guerrilla resistance"—reacting to officials' predation.

Those repeated successful grassroots protests against the Chinese authoritarian government are unique and noteworthy, especially after Xi Jinping took office in 2012. Among the sweeping transformations of the Chinese political institutions, the crackdown on grassroots civil society, including villagers,[1] labor activists,[2] lawyers,[3] feminists,[4] journalists,[5] environmental activists,[6] entrepreneurs,[7] and religious groups,[8] is well documented. During Xi's second term, the space for civil society and social activism in China has further diminished,[9] leaving only a few institutionalized channels viable, such as writing emails to officials.[10] However, the ride-sharing drivers have been able to organize frequent and effective protests beyond what Ching Kwan Lee and other scholars had previously observed from labor struggles in China, in which protesters were confined within their dormitories and organized only "cellular activism" that excluded workers from other factories.[11] The ride-sharing drivers empathize with drivers from other WeChat groups, even if they have never interacted with them, and take risks to help one another beyond their "cells." Why are the ride-sharing drivers' protests able to move beyond cellular activism and survive the contentious political environment while achieving their goals over and over again, even under a state that is tightening its grip on society?

The state's interactions with the ride-sharing industry follow a logic that is similar to that of the interactive authoritarianism framework discussed in this book, with a toleration, differentiation, and legalization process. The key actors interact within both virtual spaces and physical spaces. When the institutional disruptions of technological breakthroughs and significant new supply and demand for services occurred, the government was unsure about the potential consequences of having such new, sometimes organized, forces in the society. However, it did recognize the potential benefits that those new societal forces could bring to economic growth. For a modernizing authoritarian state like China, one of the primary sources of legitimacy comes from the growth of the economy and the people's rising standards of living. The direct benefits of keeping the ride-sharing networks as a new growth point were as evident as (if not more obvious than) the local governance and regime-stabilizing narratives that the social organizations and self-media could provide, respectively (discussed in the preceding chapters). Thus, individual entrapment guerilla protests were initially allowed as the government monitored and learned about ride-sharing drivers' behaviors in those urban areas. Then, after major mass incidents, the government differentiated drivers, cars, and platforms based on potential costs and benefits—not just economically but also politically. Some had to face harsher inspections, while others were encouraged to create benefits more effectively. After repeated interactions, the legalization of certain standards and procedures were tested during the differentiation stage. So the state solidified the contribution of some participants of this new economy while minimizing risks and costs from potentially regime-challenging or less productive actors.

Such associational behaviors and collective actions occur both online and in physical spaces. By employing process tracing and four years of participant observation of Uber and Didi (the Chinese ride-sharing company that bought Uber China in 2015) drivers' city-wide messaging groups, including in-depth interviews with organizers and government officials, I argue that collective action for rights protection is achievable in today's China after institutional disruptions emerge. In this case, institutional disruptions are caused by new technologies and methods of conducting business. When there are repeated opportunities for within-network group support so that social capital (trust and norms of reciprocity) can be created, and the potential economic benefits of the newly emerged sector are desirable, the state tolerates the activities. However, deliberate differentiation by the state occurs when major social disruptions take place so that the more cost-effective individuals are favored over the less cost-effective individuals (i.e., the troublemakers, who also happen to be less productive.) Then new laws and rules are made once critical features of the more desirable and less desirable groups become apparent. Of course, for toleration to happen in the first place, rights claims must not challenge the whole state bureaucracy but must be aimed at individual officials or a specific industry, making the state less likely to repress them immediately.

PROTESTS AND THE POLITICS OF RIDE-SHARING IN CHINA

The government describes organized protests in China as "mass incidents" (*quntixing shijian* 群体性事件). There is no strict definition of what counts as a "mass incident," and the Ministry of Public Security (MPS) stopped publishing data on mass incidents in 2005. To make the case even more complicated, sometimes the Chinese government treats such incidents as "disturb-ing the public order" (*raoluan gonggong zhixu* 扰乱公共秩序). Yu Jianrong interprets "mass incidents," based on the description of "The Rules of Han-dling Mass Incidents by the Public Security Organs,"[12] as incidents not clearly approved by law, with at least five people gathered together with common goals, and disturbing the social order.[13] Some scholars consider only incidents with more than five hundred participants as mass incidents.[14] With different methodologies and definitions, scholars have very different estimates about how many mass incidents occur in China every year. How-ever, most sources point to the rapid increase in the frequency of mass inci-dents from 1993 to 2011.[15]

Since Xi Jinping took office in 2012, there have been qualitative changes to the treatment of mass incidents by the Chinese state. Even though Hu Jintao's administration (2002–2012) was quite assertive in regulating civil society and used the state corporatist model to limit the activities of civil society organizations and their activities,[16] local officials still had discretion and variation in their implementation of state repression. Xi Jinping, how-ever, saw mass incidents as a challenge to national security, and the suppres-sion of mass incidents became a priority in safeguarding the survival of the country and the regime. Diana Fu and Greg Distelhorst describe this transi-tion from Hu to Xi as moving from "fragmented repression" to "consoli-dated repression."[17] With the fragmented repression under Hu, scholars have documented various ways contentious protest organizers achieve their goals, whether through using the right tactics,[18] providing the appropriate fram-ing,[19] getting the right timing,[20] or finding an angle for complementarity.[21] Such factors may no longer be effective under Xi's consolidated repression.

This more consolidated state treatment toward protests makes organiz-ing collective actions more difficult in China today. If there are two modes of grassroots participation in collective action—contentious and institution-alized—China today has less room for contentious participation (for exam-ple, disruptive protests, petitioning, and strikes) and has only limited room for institutionalized participation (for example, hotlines, mailboxes, and local elections).[22]

Besides the difficulties of organizing contentious mass incidents in authoritarian China, the trend toward a sharing economy itself may not be ideal for social and labor movements in general, regardless of regime types. Drawing from studies on the sharing economy worker's psyche and the business mind-set of the stakeholders, Peterson Nnajiofor points out that the lack of long-term engagement and physical communication may render collective social movements and labor struggles unfeasible.[23] Although creative protests using the mobility of vehicles had been used in other countries, such as the blue bucket protests in Russia[24] and the Automaidan protests in Ukraine,[25] they were mainly acting as part of a larger protest, and their efforts are often directly deterred by the state.

While the existing literature suggests that organizing contentious protests in China is becoming more challenging and that the ride-sharing sector may weaken the social base for labor and other social movements,[26] this chapter shows that the Chinese ride-sharing industry has produced numerous contentious protests. In multiple cities, Uber and Didi drivers organize quick and clean protests. These may not always be "important mass incidents" (those involving between one thousand and five thousand people) or "extraordinary mass incidents" (those involving more than five thousand participants),[27] but they usually achieve their purpose and successfully force the transportation officials to back off. What factors made it possible for the ride-sharing industry in China to produce abundant collective actions despite the increased constraints imposed by the state and the suboptimal conditions for organized labor protests?

To put the data into perspective, according to the *China Labor Bulletin*, organized labor protests in the manufacturing industry and construction industry are, in general, more frequent than those in the transportation industry (see fig. 7.1), especially with the drastic increase of labor protests in those industries since 2014. However, if we look at the actual cases within the transportation industry, most of them were organized by taxi drivers unless the ride-sharing drivers' protests made it onto the news. This was especially true when Uber and Didi still operated within the legal gray areas before 2016. Most of the smaller-scale guerilla protests have not been recorded. Therefore, the number of labor protests in the transportation industry is likely underestimated. Nevertheless, drivers' protests are among the top three most frequent types of protests by labor in China. Why does labor in the ride-sharing industry organize protests so frequently? And how do state-society interactions evolve in this particular relationship? Below, I first summarize the history and main stakeholders of the ride-sharing industry and then utilize the data I collected from participant observation and interviews to address these questions.

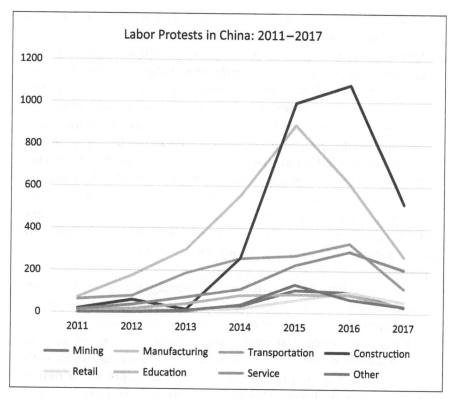

Figure 7.1. Labor protests in China from 2011 to 2017 by industry. Chart compiled based on raw data provided by the *China Labor Bulletin*. See *China Labor Bulletin*'s interactive data here: http://maps.clb.org.hk/strikes/zh-cn#/

THE LEGAL GRAY AREA CREATED BY THE INSTITUTIONAL DISRUPTIONS

During the first decade of the twenty-first century, the private transportation industry in China was mainly made up of the taxi sector plus some regulated (and sometimes unregulated) ride services. However, with the growth of smartphone applications and the ride-sharing sector, the existing institutional arrangements were suddenly disrupted.

In 2012 Didi (aka Didi Chuxing, or Didi Dache) started to test the waters for its business in the city of Beijing. The company was then designated as a platform for taxi drivers. Realizing that there might be a mismatch between demand and supply of taxi rides, Didi provided significant financial incentives for taxi drivers who would install the app on their cell phones and use Didi's system for managing reservations and rides. The number of registered drivers on Didi grew to 350,000, with over 20 million users by the end of 2013.[28] By 2015 Didi had already covered 360 major cities in China with 1.35 million drivers. About 80 percent of the taxi drivers in China use Didi.[29]

Around the same time Didi was launched, a company called Kuaidi started its own driving service in Hangzhou and was soon backed by Alibaba, one of China's most influential tech giants. The competition for market share has led both companies to burn through investors' cash by offering drivers and riders bonuses when using their platforms. Most drivers I interviewed said that their monthly incomes had at least tripled between 2012 and 2014, although some cautioned that this trend would not last long. So they wanted to get as much money out of the business as quickly as possible.

The drivers' assessments were not far from reality. In July 2014 both Didi and Kuaidi launched the private car-share service called Didi Zhuanche (or "specialized cars"). Private cars that met the standards (usually luxury cars with a specified minimal wheelbase) were tapped by the platform, and targets for bonuses started to shift from taxi drivers to private car drivers. With Uber also entering the Chinese market in July 2014, private car owners started to enjoy the benefits that taxi drivers had enjoyed for the past year and a half. This led to the initial resentment between taxi drivers and private car owners. As taxi drivers' incomes went back to the pre-2012 level, they were no longer content. The taxi drivers suddenly realized that they had to defend their interests and that the law seemed to be on their side.

In October 2014 the city of Shenyang announced that Didi Zhuanche was illegal and that drivers of private cars running as service cars would be fined if caught. In the next few months, a few other cities followed suit. However, when I asked multiple Didi Zhuanche drivers how they would react to such announcements by the city transportation bureaus, all of them said they would continue with Didi Zhuanche because the benefits outweighed the costs; some even said the platform had privately agreed to pay their fines if they were caught.

To further complicate the situation, the announcements made by several city governments had no legal base, as there were no laws at the time that pertained to ride-sharing platforms. A few months later, in May 2015, Didi kept its luxury private car fleet and launched the Didi Kuaiche (or "quick car") service, which allowed cars that had slightly lower standards than Didi Zhuanche with much cheaper fares, to join the platform. To many riders, Didi Kuaiche is a much more cost-effective option than taxi services, because they are cheaper and cleaner and because the quality of the cars is better than that of the taxis. Didi merged with Kuaidi in February 2015 and acquired Uber China in August 2016, becoming the de facto monopoly of the Chinese private car ride-sharing industry. As the 2018 report published by the China Information Center states, by 2017 Didi had 21 million registered drivers and 450 million users, all of which operate in a legally gray area.[30]

METHODS AND DATA

A few weeks after Didi Kuaiche was introduced, I encountered the driver mentioned at the beginning of this chapter. I was fascinated by the videos he showed me. So I asked him if he could add me to the Didi drivers' WeChat group. (Many of the drivers used both Uber China and Didi before Didi acquired Uber China in 2016. To simplify things, I refer to those drivers as "Didi drivers" in this chapter.) After learning that I was a researcher interested in the organizational behaviors of Didi drivers' organized resistance, he immediately added me to the group and offered to send me fascinating videos and inform me about major protests.

Following that encounter, I got myself invited to three other city-wide Didi drivers' WeChat groups in Hangzhou. The number of members in these groups ranged from 41 to 254 as of March 2018 (the membership has stayed relatively the same since I joined in June 2015). There are hundreds, if not thousands, of such WeChat groups in the city of Hangzhou (estimated by several drivers), but most of their conversations are quite similar: sharing information about the level of customer demand by area, sharing information about fellow drivers being entrapped by transportation officials, discussing current events, and organizing offline gatherings— whether for entertainment or protests. Realizing the content in the four groups that I had already joined was quite similar and that adding myself to more groups might raise suspicions among some drivers in multiple groups—certain drivers are members of many groups, and they often spread important messages across different groups—joining four groups was sufficient for this research. I mainly focused on the largest group, as it was a hub for many smaller groups.

Therefore, I conducted ethnographic participant observations in those WeChat groups and conducted open-ended interviews with more than one hundred Didi drivers in Hangzhou, Shanghai, Nanjing, and Chengdu between 2015 and 2018. I have used the June 12, 2015, anti-entrapment protest as a case study to capture the evolution of a major protest from its beginning to end.

As discussed in the preceding chapter, WeChat is a "better WhatsApp crossed with the social features of Facebook, and Instagram, mixed with Skype and a walkie-talkie."[31] WeChat's group messaging function allows participants to post pictures, videos, and send text or voice messages. The private networks in WeChat provide a comfortable space for discussions and can cultivate alternative public spheres[32] facilitated by the robust internet in China.[33] The conversations in those WeChat groups are usually in audio formats. Drivers constantly have their hands on the wheels, and typing is possible only when their cars are parked. Most drivers are also aware that typed texts are easily censored and prefer the audio option. Thus, even with the presence of censorship, due to the sheer volume of audio conversations and the local dialects used in those audio conversations, the censorship cannot monitor them effectively.

This creates significant obstacles for censorship, as one government official once revealed during an interview that the government does not have an effective way of capturing and censoring audio data. It is virtually impossible to assign enough people to listen to all the conversations in those WeChat groups. In the first twelve months that I joined the 254-person group, there were 33,798 voice messages (in addition to videos, pictures, and text messages). These voice messages were also not concentrated within a short period but were spread out during a day, as drivers work different shifts, thus creating more difficulties for censorship. A typical voice message lasted about 20 seconds. This means that to censor a WeChat group like this, a censorship staff would need to spend 30 minutes a day listening to all of the conversations, and that 30 minutes would be spread throughout the day in 180 ten-second segments. Such work is not within the scope of the local government. Therefore, we can assume that audio conversations were likely to be uncensored during regular times.

As a researcher, I faced the same challenge the censorship staff faces. It would be virtually impossible for me to listen to all of the messages in the WeChat group. Therefore, I first listened to the entire month worth of conversations from June 2015 and then randomly selected 5 percent of the days from June 2, 2015, to March 20, 2018, and listened to every message in those

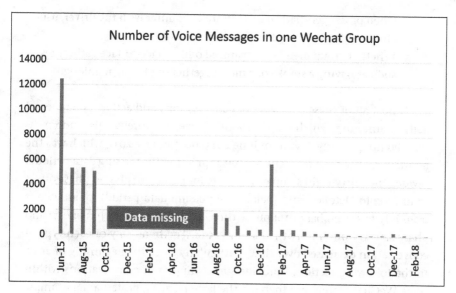

Figure 7.2. Frequency of voice messages

days. My cell phone had an accident on July 7, 2016, and conversations from October 19, 2015, to July 6, 2016, were not backed up, and therefore that part of the data was lost. The voice messages were also concentrated within the first few months. After July 2016, the number of conversations significantly decreased, with January 2017 being an exception.

Among the 5 percent days randomly selected (thirty-eight days of voice messages), I coded the existence of the following conversations:

1. Whether there was an anti-entrapment protest organized or partici- pated in by members of the group. This means that a member was entrapped by a transportation official, asked for help in the group, and other members in the group showed up to protest and drove out the official. Sometimes the original victim of entrapment was from another WeChat group.
2. Whether there were complaints against the Didi platform—usually conversations complaining about Didi taking too large a cut or not offering enough of a bonus for drivers.
3. Whether there were complaints against competitors, especially taxi drivers.
4. Whether there were complaints against customers. This happened

when passengers had an unpleasant encounter with the driver, usually resulting in a negative review of the driver.
5. Whether group members organized offline, face-to-face gatherings,
   such as having a smoke or a meal together or playing mahjong.

Almost all of these five types of conversations and activities happened
daily in June 2015, which was the month I covered entirely. This randomization did not pick any days from June 2015, nor January 2017, which was the
month with the most frequent conversations after the missing data period. I
divided the thirty-eight sampled days into four different phases: phase one is
from June to October 2015 (before the missing data period); phase two is
from July to December 2016; phase three is from January to June 2017; and
phase four is from July 2017 to March 2018. The frequency of each type of
conversation decreased over time, particularly since the beginning of 2017.
In the following section, I provide some snippets of conversations within
these WeChat groups and then use the June 12, 2015, protest as an example
to demonstrate why contentious participation in the ride-sharing industry
is possible and can even be successful.

It is worth reminding readers that this case is also the third of a set of
"most-different cases," which look at different types of institutional disruptions (earthquakes, media innovations, market demands, and technological
innovations), happen in different spaces (physical, virtual, and combined)
and regions (rural, urban, national, and international), with different key
actors. However, the very different cases all share the same process of interactive authoritarianism, moving from toleration to differentiation to legalization without institutionalization. Moreover, similar outcomes from these
very different cases point toward more public service provision and regime
resilience and more creative ways for the societal actors to survive. I discuss
the third of the three cases below.

INTERNET-FACILITATED RESISTANCE IN THE
RIDE-SHARING INDUSTRY

The toleration of the drivers' activities naturally became the status quo
approach initially, for this newly emerged industry could bring new economic benefits. This section discusses how that status quo treatment turned
into deliberate differentiation and then eventually legalization of the ride-

TABLE 7.1. Type of conversations in the WeChat group

	Date range	Days sampled	Anti-entrapment	Anti-platform	Anti-taxi	Anti-customer	Offline gathering
Phase one	Jun 2015-Oct 2015	8	4	5	3	4	1
Phase two	July 2016-Dec 2016	8	5	4	0	1	1
Phase three	Jan 2017-June 2017	10	1	2	0	0	0
Phase four	July 2017-Mar 2018	12	2	0	0	0	0

sharing industry. I also use the June 12 protest in 2015 to illustrate how a major stimulus to the status quo escalated the process from toleration to differentiation and then to legalization.

Toleration

When Didi started to grow, the extensive state apparatus tolerated the new developments and wanted to wait and see the economic, political, and social impacts the new sector could bring. Therefore, on the government side, only the Transportation Management Office (运输管理处)—a secondary office under the Transportation Bureau—was involved. The Transportation Management Office is mainly responsible for facilitating transportation (and collecting fees from fines as a source of income) rather than maintaining regime stability and controlling the society, which are responsibilities of Public Security, a much more powerful "lump" discussed in chapter 1.

During the toleration stage, activities between the ride-sharing drivers and the Transportation Management officials were mostly entrapments, and anti-entrapment activities and the opposition they faced were mainly taxi drivers—competitors—and city Transportation Management officials. In the view of taxi drivers, it was unfair that their competitors did not have to pay the taxi licensing fees (thus, bore lower costs) yet received much higher bonuses and customer volume (higher incomes). As for city Transportation Management officials, they wanted to follow the orders of their superiors to catch the "illegal" ride-sharing drivers and collect fines as additional sources of revenue for the office. However, since they did not have the necessary laws and regulations to back them, they started using entrapment.

Transportation Management officials usually work alone and are predominantly male. An officer first uses the Didi app to request a car. When the car arrives at the final destination, the officer shows his Transportation Bureau badge and fines the driver. Based on my interviews, the fine ranged from 3,000 RMB (about 500 USD) to 20,000 RMB (a bit over 3,000 USD). Taxi drivers might do the same, giving up a few hours of earnings to pretend to be Didi passengers. The taxi drivers record detailed information about the Didi driver and then report him or her to the Transportation Bureau. These entrapment tactics by government officials and taxi drivers have resulted in huge financial losses for many Didi drivers. My research is mainly based on Didi drivers' organized protests as responses to this entrapment.

When individual Didi drivers realized that any one of them could be the next victim of entrapment and that there were no explicit laws against their ride-sharing activities, they decided to use WeChat groups to organize protests. As soon as a driver was about to be fined by a Transportation Management official, the driver sent a message, including a GPS location, to the drivers' WeChat group and asked for help. Since these drivers were mainly on the road and very mobile, they could quickly arrive at the scene, park their cars, and surround the Transportation Management official to cause a traffic jam. The Didi drivers then questioned the authority of the official and demanded explanations about the official's behaviors. Many Transportation Management officials usually patrolled alone and did not want to take responsibility for causing a traffic jam, as they might not only be blamed by their superiors from the Transportation Bureau but may also be challenged by the more powerful Public Security Bureau for creating a scene and disturbing social stability. So the officer would leave, if possible. If the crowd of drivers was big enough, the Didi drivers usually formed a thick circle around the official and protested against him. In the case mentioned earlier, the official had to be rescued by police, who arrived later during the incident.

The Didi drivers usually not only showed restraint while making sure not to assault the official verbally or physically, but they also tried to calm each other down so that they were not violating any laws. What they did mostly was to ask the official questions and demand answers. Drivers have repeatedly succeeded in avoiding paying fines through this mechanism, and the state apparatus continues to tolerate incidences of anti-entrapment, especially since these incidents tend to target only individual officials—a conscious decision by the drivers—so the regime does not feel threatened. The government was also quite satisfied with the improved resource allocation within the transportation industry and the additional benefits the sector has brought to the economy.

The June 12th Protest and Differentiation

After joining the drivers' WeChat groups, my informer left me messages almost every day about anti-entrapment incidents in the city during the first few days we got to know each other. He sent me videos and let me know where an incident was happening, anticipating that I probably would not have time to listen to their voice messages in the WeChat group every day. Occasionally, the videos he sent me had nothing to do with Didi drivers but were about how repressed individuals, when faced with brutality or harassment from the government, were able to strike back. One video shows a person hitting an official with a shovel after the official verbally abused him. Such videos were used in the WeChat group to encourage others to fight back when repressed.

On June 12, 2015, a major incident alerted the state apparatus more than the usual anti-entrapment incidents. In the evening, my informer left me a message saying that thousands of people had gathered near Yuhangtang Road, which he believed might interest me. I immediately opened the WeChat group and followed the development of this incident. It started with a message left by a Didi driver at 10:21 p.m. saying that another WeChat group he was part of was going to save a fellow driver being entrapped by a taxi driver and a Transportation Management official, and he was wondering whether that entrapped driver was also a member of this group. About six drivers immediately responded that even though they did not know if the entrapped driver was from this group, they rushed to Yuhangtang Road to show support, and a GPS location was quickly shared within the group.

About five minutes later, one driver questioned whether they should go, since it had become apparent that the driver entrapped was not from this group. Quite a few drivers started to comment and discuss this issue of who was the "us" in this fight: "As long as it is a Didi driver, and as long as you are not too far away, you should go. Next time when members of our group are in trouble, and we send a message to other groups, they will also come to rescue us." Multiple drivers reasoned that not all of their members would be nearby when an incident like this happened. Therefore, helping members from other groups when nearby was the right thing to do. It was clear that the norm of reciprocity operated not only within this particular WeChat

group but also across different groups as long as they had the same grievances and interests.

Those who arrived at the scene quickly started broadcasting the developments through videos, pictures, and narrations. Within about twenty minutes, more than thirty members of the group had joined the conversation.
Furthermore, through their descriptions, it was clear that even more people
from this group had arrived at the scene. The more experienced organizers in
the group started to repeat tactics: "Park your car with some distance and
then go surround the scene. Do not speak to them—let alone get into direct
confrontations with the official. Just surround and watch (*weiguan* 围观)."

At 10:43 p.m. those at the scene reported that there were so many people
at the scene and that it was "fiery." Some drivers in the group started to suggest that they should flip the transportation official's vehicle in order to esca-
late, while others suggested that they should protect their rights rationally
(*lixing weiquan* 理性维权). Around this time, one driver reported that armed
SWAT teams were arriving at the scene. About four blocks of roads were completely jammed by that moment.

There was usually a customer service representative from the Didi Company
within these groups. That representative usually did not participate in conversations, but whenever someone had a question about the company's operations,
they could use the "@" function to directly alert the representative so that the
representative could provide answers. At 11:06 p.m. the representative said, "Do
not cause trouble and watch for your own safety!" These words were basically
ignored as videos from the scene continued to flood the WeChat group. Only
one person replied to the representative: "We are not causing trouble."

At 11:11 p.m. the discussion was focused on the conditions the drivers
should demand. It was quickly agreed that the transportation official should
release both the driver and his car without punishment or retribution. At
this time, the Didi representative started discouraging people from going to
the scene—"Do not go to the scene anymore; the nature of this event has
changed!"—suggesting that it was no longer a simple protest by a few drivers
but might have escalated to a mass incident. It was quite clear that by this
time there were more than five hundred drivers at the scene. The Didi drivers, however, continued to arrive, and the WeChat group was full of encouragement, shouting, "Unity is a strength!" (*Tuanjie jiushi liliang* 团结就是力量!)
and "The power of the team is endless!" (*Tuandui de Liliang shi Wuqiong de* 团
队的力量是无穷的).

At 11:21 p.m., exactly one hour after the incident was first brought up in this group, one driver estimated that over three thousand people were already at the scene. And another ten minutes later, another driver reported that both the taxi driver and the transportation official had been taken into custody by the police as a tactic to calm the crowd and protect the two of them who had no support at the scene.

At 11:37 p.m. the police used a loudspeaker to ask the entrapped Didi driver to come and get the keys to his car so that he could leave. Members of the group, however, were not satisfied. A person mentioned that "the law cannot be enforced when everyone is an offender" (*fabuzezhong* 法不责众), and most people wanted to continue the protest and demand punishment for the government official conducting the entrapment.

At 11:47 p.m. the Didi representative sent a message to the group:

> Dear Hangzhou Didi drivers, please be sure to stay calm and do not get into conflicts with law enforcement. Please actively cooperate and promptly withdraw from the gathering. We will have to use GPS to locate car owners who continue to stay at the scene and cancel our service to them, to cope with public security. . . . If you are still on-site, please evacuate immediately!

While the original driver was released before midnight, the crowd had grown to about ten to twenty thousand. The GPS threat did not deter drivers, as people within WeChat groups started asking others at the scene to turn off their GPS or turn off their cell phone entirely. It was also reported that government tow trucks had started to tow away cars parked in the vicinity. Media also started to cover the story at midnight.

At 12:03 a.m. the experienced organizer asked other drivers in the WeChat group to pull out, as he anticipated the entire region would be blocked, and it would become difficult to retreat later. Members of the group also started to assess how they had done that day, and the consensus was that the protesters had won the battle: "The transportation official did not dare to say a word throughout!" "We showed solidarity, and the protest was very effective!" A few other members questioned whether they had made the incident too big and made too many demands; they also had concerns about whether the entire industry would be banned because of this incident. The Didi representative sent another message to the group at 1:03 a.m.:

Dear Didi drivers, our company is currently having a dialogue with the relevant government departments. If you encounter routine law enforcement, please cooperate with them calmly and then contact us afterward with this phone number XXX-XXXX-XXXX. . . . If you spread the information over the internet and cause other drivers to gather, our company will no longer be able to help you. If you participate in those gatherings, we will deduct your pay and bonus from that week and terminate our service.

The warning was again ignored, and the discussion within the WeChat group lasted for at least one more hour before the conversation ended for that day. The conclusion was that if similar events happened in the future, they would repeat what they did that day.

The June 12 incident was not an anomaly in 2015, as events of similar scope in Guangzhou and Wuhan were also discussed in drivers' WeChat groups. In Hangzhou another major incident (although involving a slightly smaller crowd) took place near the Hangzhou East Railway station only three days later. Water bottles were thrown at the government officials, and many WeChat group members showed up at the scene. Much smaller incidents happened daily, and usually dozens of drivers were able to scare away the transportation official. About a month later, drivers in the WeChat group started discussions about forming their own labor unions to protect their interests.

The mass incidents in different cities did caution the local authorities, and the period of toleration also made it clear to the governments that the different parties involved might bring different levels of costs and benefits. Therefore, the state started differentiating between drivers, cars, and platforms based on potential costs and benefits.

First of all, taxi drivers and ride-sharing drivers are treated differently. For taxi drivers, providing rides is usually their primary income source, and competition from the new ride-sharing sector, could mean unemployment for them. Since maintaining lower unemployment is an important goal of the Chinese state, the interests of taxi drivers should be satisfied. Many cities even asked taxi companies and their reservation platforms to lower the fees for taxi drivers so that taxis could remain economically relevant or even competitive. Many ride-sharing drivers, on the other hand, provide rides for extra income, so the main policy goal when regulating them is to help meet transportation demand and provide high-quality service rather than protecting employment. Therefore, the state can afford to be harsher against ride-sharing drivers. Taxis also have the specific privilege of being able to provide service to whomever hails them at roadside, whereas ride-sharing services are used only on a reservation basis.

Institutional hurdles were also created targeting the ride-sharing drivers, especially to screen the drivers. Those who do not wish to cooperate are eliminated. For example, the local governments screen drivers before granting them credentials. Ride-sharing drivers have to go through background checks using the Ministry of Public Security's database. Anyone with a criminal record is deterred from receiving or renewing their credentials. The government has also asked companies to organize monthly study sessions to review the "security problems" of the previous month and the precautions for the future, even though that means the loss of a whole day's worth of income for each driver. These study sessions are opportunities for the indoctrination of new regulations and policies, including speeches made by top leaders.

The differentiation also includes hurdles during licensing for the cars. During the toleration stage, virtually any car could participate in ride-sharing. During the differentiation stage, each car needs a commercial operating license. Even though this license does not cost additional money, the cars must be scrapped after 60,000 kilometers (about 37,282 miles). That means private car owners are reluctant to use the same car for personal use and business use, since the per-mile cost for personal use will have increased tremendously. The rationale for the government was to have only the newest and safest cars on the road. During interviews, many drivers also reported that their insurance costs had tripled compared to when they first joined the ride-sharing sector. For example, one driver mentioned that his insurance was 6,000 RMB before the government took any action and had increased to 18,500 RMB. In this case, whenever there are any accidents or legal disputes, society and the private sector pick up the tab. Of course, such new institutional hurdles push out some ride-sharing drivers that drive older (and therefore less safe) cars and are less insured. Those who remain have more to lose if they participate in organized collective actions.

Interestingly, the WeChat groups were not banned or dissolved after major incidents. It is important that there is a way for the government and the companies to maintain channels for direct communication and utilize such channels to assert control. Relevant officials also mentioned during interviews that they have the confidence and capacity to prevent mass incidents from happening, but the costs would be much higher if they pursued that more ambitious goal. With such incidents, it would be easier for them to differentiate between the more obedient drivers and the more rebellious ones through GPS locations and in-group messages. Such differentiation could help them minimize the cost and maximize the economic and social benefits of the new ride-sharing industry. Thus, officials often intentionally allow the closely monitored and controlled mass incidents to play out and use them to differentiate actors.

Legalization

China's rules and laws regulating the transportation industry have long ignored the taxi industry, not to mention the newly emerged ride-sharing sector. The "Road Transportation Regulations of the People's Republic of China," passed in 2004, also excluded the taxi industry.[34] Therefore, before the emergence of the ride-sharing sector, the government mainly used policy tools to tackle specific problems within the taxi industry. For example, the "Notice on Further Cracking Down on the Illegal Operation of Taxis, Such as 'Black Cars'" was announced in 2013 by the Ministry of Transportation to tackle "black cars"—meaning unlicensed cars that offer rides in exchange for money.[35] When the ride-sharing apps initially emerged, they mainly facilitated the reservation of taxis rather than private drivers. Therefore, patch regulations such as the "Notice on Promoting the Orderly Development of Taxi Calling Services Such as Mobile Phone Software Calls"[36] and "Taxi Management Service Regulations"[37] were introduced in 2014 to provide some guidelines for the taxi industry and the new app-based services. Based on these regulations, private car owners who provide rides to others may be considered illegal, but the local governments mainly tolerated such incidents when the ride-sharing sector first emerged, as discussed in the previous sections.

When the institutional disruptions occurred in the taxi industry, especially with the robust growth of the ride-sharing sector, the government started to pay close attention to the developments and sometimes used various new strategies and rules to test their effects. New laws were drafted and introduced once certain strategies and rules were deemed effective in the state's cost-benefit assessment. In June 2015 the Ministry of Transportation started to organize public hearings and symposiums about potential regulations for the ride-sharing industry. By the end of 2015, two government documents—the "Guiding Opinion on Deepening Reform and Further Promoting the Healthy Development of the Taxi Industry"[38] and the "Interim Measures for the Management of Online Booking of Taxi Business Services"[39]—were announced and suggestions and comments from the public were solicited. The legislation moved forward quickly, and China became the first country in the world to legalize the online booking of cars on July 28, 2016; the law became effective on November 1, 2016. In these regulations that had the ride-sharing sector in mind, the idea of "differentiating traditional and new services while creating a diverse and differentiated travel system" was introduced. These developments provided the legal ground for treating the taxi industry and the ride-sharing services differently. The name of the law that previously governed the taxi industry was also changed in November 2016 so that traditional taxis are now referred to as "cruise taxis" (巡游出租车), since ride-sharing cars are also considered as a part of the taxi industry.

Just as new self-media laws were made that would target specific players, the ride-sharing industry created such laws based on the experiences of differentiation. Regarding the drivers, laws on the service capability,[40] drivers' credentials, exam procedures,[41] and background checks[42] were made. There were also laws created that directly target the platforms/companies that operate the ride-sharing reservations.[43] Once legalization is pushed forward regarding drivers and platforms, laws to constrain the supervisors were also made in order to guide and provide limits for the local bureaucracy.[44]

The new regulations created multiple hurdles for private car owners to operate their vehicles in the sharing economy, including passing major tests, sometimes having to have a local Hukou (city residential registration), and stricter requirements for their cars. The new regulations also provided a path for these drivers to legalize their behaviors so that they can have a license and no longer need to operate in the gray area, fearing entrapment by transportation officials.

These new regulations also destroyed the basic fabric of the Didi drivers' WeChat groups. Some drivers went on and got the new licenses; others could not meet the qualifications. Those who have a license no longer need to protest against entrapments, since they are now legal. With the remaining smaller percentage of Didi drivers not qualified for the license (cannot pass the exam, do not have a qualified car, or do not have a local residential registration), the adaptive local governments have also figured out how to deal with them. When transportation officials got into these cars and found out that the driver had no ride-sharing license, he would tell the driver, "You don't need to summon other drivers in your WeChat group, because Didi is going to pay your fine. All you need to do is to cooperate with us." The WeChat groups are still used for information sharing, but messages no longer receive enthusiastic responses from other group members. The legalization of the industry and the experiences accumulated by government officials and companies in dealing with the protesters have internalized the institutional disruptions and got the ride-sharing sector under control while serving as a new growth point contributing to the GDP.

CONCLUSION

The rise and fall of the short-lived internet-facilitated guerrilla resistance from the ride-sharing industry is another example of how the Chinese authoritarian state manages institutional disruptions in society. The state could have intervened when the new ride-sharing sector emerged but decided to temporarily retreat from that space. Local officials were also not sure about how to deal with the new rules and constraints of the game initially and chose to let the course develop on its own while closely monitoring it. With this window of opportunity, Didi drivers had the space to organize protests against entrapment, believing that they were not violating any laws and that, therefore, they should not be penalized.

The virtual space of WeChat groups also provided the technology and resources for Didi drivers to interact with one another and create trust, networks, and norms of reciprocity within and between WeChat groups. Such accumulation of social capital played an important role in quickly bringing drivers to specific protest locations to help one another in the name of justice and fairness. Didi drivers were also able to learn lessons and improve their tactics after repeated protests to maximize group benefits and minimize individual risks and costs.

However, differentiation began once the local government acquired enough information and knowledge during the toleration stage. Unlike the CSO case after the earthquakes, and unlike the self-media censorship case, the ride-sharing industry provides a new point of economic growth, while the scope of their target and demands are limited. The drivers made it clear that they were not against the government or existing laws but were targeting only the misbehaving transportation official. Since all that they wanted was to be released without a fine, the state can satisfy that quite easily while continuing to take advantage of its contribution to the economy. Of course, those who are local residents who have better and safer cars and are willing to take the required exams and sit in for the monthly training sessions are prioritized and differentiated. Like the self-media case, the state is often not directly involved in controlling the societal actors but creates the institutional constraints to get the actors in society, especially private companies, to implement the differentiation on their behalf.

Legalizing this "zone of indifference" poses a fundamental threat to the internet-enabled guerrilla protests as participants are divided into different legal statuses after laws regulating the gray area are implemented. The participants no longer have as much motive and willpower to organize. On the one hand, they have smaller numbers; on the other hand, they are now clearly violating the laws. With the rapid transformation of the state, society, the public sphere, and the market, new institutional disruptions will continue to arise. It is expected that the Chinese state will implement a similar adaptive approach of toleration, differentiation, and legalization in order to meet future changes and challenges.

PART IV

Conclusion

CHAPTER 8

Conclusion

Governing as an Interactive Authoritarian State

Andrew Nathan popularized the concept of "authoritarian resilience," arguing that the institutionalization of Chinese politics—particularly the norm-bounded nature of its succession politics, its merit-based promotion, functional specialization, and formalized channels of political participation—could provide resilience to the Chinese regime. However, as many of those institutions are no longer stable, if not completely eroded, the Chinese regime is still surviving, if not thriving. Apparently, a resilient Chinese regime can continue without Nathan's key institutionalizations. This book has provided an alternative in arguing that rather than relying on institutionalizations, the Chinese state utilizes a process that repeatedly and dynamically creates new rules and laws that meet the newest challenges and prolong the regime, especially with institutional disruptions.

The COVID-19 pandemic was an institutional disruption felt by people of almost all countries in the world. The public health crisis, accompanied by economic, social, and political challenges, tested the governance of countries regardless of cultural norms, regime types, and the level of modernization. When the world saw the city of Wuhan locked down at the beginning of the pandemic and the strict and costly "zero COVID" policies the Chinese government put in place, many predicted that the pandemic-induced halt of a nearly half-century run of growth[1] could lead to the stalling of the standard of living for China's middle class, who may thus turn against the CCP.[2] Others directly pronounced the death of Xi's "China Dream" due to COVID-19.[3]

However, even though such a major crisis disrupted the economic and social orders (and likely political orders as well), the regime took full advantage of this institutional disruption—comparing the unscientific and chaotic approaches by some Western countries to the relatively normal lives that most Chinese people were living even during the pandemic, contrasting the drastic different death tolls (especially deaths as a percentage of the population) between China and many Western countries, and bragging about China being the only major economy in 2020 to have positive GDP growth.

The interactions between the Chinese state and some of the social actors and voices that emerged during COVID-19 also fit the three-stage interactive authoritarianism model described in this book. Many voices, including the whistleblower Dr. Li Wenliang's voice, that initially warned about a possible coronavirus outbreak were tolerated initially, until there was a major crackdown on certain actors (such as Fang Fang, who documented what was happening on the ground) and the promotion of others (including outspoken doctors such as Zhong Nanshan). Faced with social pressure with many state-society interactions, Dr. Li Wenliang's name was cleared and he received a posthumous award as an "advanced individual in epidemic prevention and control work."[4] Even during lockdowns, the state observed and differentiated how societal actors behaved so that some actors would be trusted to take on more responsibilities in future endeavors. The lessons learned during the interactions also led to pilot legalizations of infectious disease prevention and control procedures in places like Shanghai[5] and Guangdong[6] that could eventually be adopted nationally. Such a process was repeated in 2022 after lockdowns in cities such as Xi'an and Shanghai.

In terms of the survival and durability of the regime, many scholars had predicted the collapse of the Chinese state or the extinction of Communism in its entirety toward the end of the twentieth century, following the collapse of the Soviet Union and the changes after the color revolutions, seen as democratization's "third wave." Some of them have long anticipated the democratization of the People's Republic of China, following the paths of South Korea and Taiwan.[7] However, what we are witnessing is the continuation of one of the most durable authoritarian regimes in modern history. While some observers remain puzzled as China has surpassed the "70-year itch" mark—the point of collapse for the longest-running one-party regimes like the USSR under the Soviet Communist Party or Mexico under the Institutional Revolutionary Party—one must stop and ask, Why is the Chinese authoritarian system resilient, if not thriving?

Scholars have provided various reasons to explain this resilience, particularly the unique institutions of the Chinese system,[8] but few can explain why the political system still endures when specific institutions are disrupted. As informal leadership succession institutions are disrupted under the Xi Jinping regime, as new civil society organizations continue to grow despite the intention of the state to micro-manage, as social networks riding on the rapid technological innovations of the internet make the spread of information and ideas much easier, and as new industries arise and new dynamics of labor-employer-state relationships emerge, why is the Chinese state capable of overcoming these challenges in the forms of institutional disruptions? In particular, how does the Chinese state manage a particular type of change and manage its emerging nascent civil society?

We have seen in this book that China is no longer a totalitarian system nor a static corporatist system in which the party penetrates every corner of the private sphere and controls the vast majority of its people's behaviors. On the other hand, no one would naively believe that a mature and robust civil society is naturally emerging now that we have seen some growth of the nascent civil society activities. Instead, what we are seeing is an interactive authoritarian regime that can adjust to institutional disruptions and adapt to the new environments and institutional settings after such disruptions.

This book argues that a key factor in the ability of the Chinese state to prolong its regime and have the resiliency that many other authoritarian countries lack is the approach of *interactive authoritarian* governance. Moments of institutional disruptions that rearrange the constraints and incentives of players amid state-society interactions are normally vulnerable times for authoritarian regimes. However, the Chinese state has managed to take advantage of such moments to observe, learn, intervene, and evolve. This interactive approach typically involves three stages: toleration, differentiation, and legalization.

The toleration stage allows the government to observe and understand the new phenomena that occur immediately after institutional disruptions. If we use the example of internet censorship (discussed in chapter 6), China allows certain anti-government sensitive discourses to be expressed initially so that the state apparatus knows the nature and the scope of the issue and can prepare for the second stage of differentiation. This is unlike countries like India, which happens to be the world's largest democracy, where the government completely shuts down the internet after such disruptions. The rationale is that if regime-challenging ideas, speeches, and actions are not expected to be completely contained anyway, why not figure out an adequate way to most efficiently reduce the risks while these challenges are still rudimentary and manageable? This is also why nascent civil society activities and ride-sharing protests are able to emerge and sustain, at least for a certain period, as long as the state is still at the "toleration" stage.

Once the second stage, differentiation, is reached, the state is ready to use its limited resources most effectively. The differentiation of regime-supporting and regime-challenging speeches, activities, and actors is necessary to neutralize the potential challenges to the state and, equally important, to outsource responsibilities to the non-challenging social forces. For civil society organizations, this means shouldering tasks the government assigns through service purchases as well as taking the blame in the case that the jobs are not done well. Occasionally, *this is also a way to let one part of the society check on another part of the society*.

When the practices of differentiation become routine in a particular sector after major institutional disruptions, the legalization process emerges. Quite often, the laws being drafted are aimed explicitly at governing a particular new type of activity so that the differentiation mechanisms can be formalized. Laws, rather than institutions, are tools for governance used to constrain all players within the state. This is why I refer to this process as "legalization without institutionalization."

The above three-stage process is highly interactive between the state and the actors within the society. The state constantly adjusts its behaviors and reactions based on new developments that emerge. This means the progression of the toleration-differentiation-legalization trajectory does not always move toward one direction or in that order. Nevertheless, the ultimate consequence is that the state could utilize a rather small amount of necessary resources, take a minimal hit to its legitimacy, and make use of the most help and support from the society when faced with new phenomena that arise after institutional disruptions. Therefore, the typically vulnerable moments for many other authoritarian regimes become moments of reeducation, adaptation, and evolution.

This is not to say that the Chinese interactive authoritarian state may be able to weather all crises regardless of the scope and condition. Instead, the Chinese state utilizes moments of crisis, follows a specific coherent three-stage process, adapts to new conditions and emerging actors, and cultivates new resources, helpers, and methods to improve its legitimacy. As the Chinese Communist Party revitalizes itself during its second centennial, it is relying less and less on its revolutionary legitimacy; even the continued economic growth and the subsequent rises of the standard of living for a typical modernizing authoritarian state are not a must. The more sustainable source of legitimacy comes from the state's effective and meticulous handling of new challenges. During the repeated state-society interactions, the toleration stage signals that the state can be benevolent and not despotic. The differentiation stage not only separates the potential regime-challenging actors from those who are regime-supporting, but the creativity and resources of the latter are used to help better governance. Thus, a big part of the society feels a sense of ownership and accomplishment after successfully tackling major challenges alongside the state. After citizens vote in many democracies, the agency to act is often transferred to the representative, and citizens may sometimes feel powerless between elections. Under Chinese interactive authoritarianism, even though voting is often a formality and kept at the local level, societal forces are continuously empowered to help tackle governance challenges, although sometimes the so-called challenges come from other parts of the society. Once best practices are tested in pilot cases and particular governance methods are promoted widely, they are legalized. The state relies on the legalization process to maintain stability but without the actual institutionalization process that would constrain the state and the elites in terms of government flexibility and maneuverability. Thus, legalization provides a sense of temporary policy stability cohesion until the next round of the toleration-differentiation-legalization process repeats itself after new institutional disruptions.

The interactive authoritarianism model does not directly challenge theories of corporatism, graduated control, contingent symbiosis, and consultative authoritarianism. Instead, it provides a more dynamic and comprehensive framework to point out which theory is relatively more dominant at different stages and how state-society relations evolve through repeated interactions via a recognizable pattern of three stages. This new model is not as constrained by specific conditions and is not region-specific, level-specific, case-specific, or time-specific, but it captures an organic and holistic unification of many existing theories. It provides us with the flexible understanding that organizations and individuals can be at different stages within this unifying model, so one should not be naïve when observing toleration, thinking the state is liberalizing society, but should also not be desperate when brutal crackdowns occur, believing the state is reverting to totalitarianism. They are all part of the process.

FINDINGS

This book has been structured using the "most different case" design, for the cases are similar in just one independent variable (the three-stage approach of toleration, differentiation, and legalization) and the dependent variable (authoritarian resilience in terms of improved service, more effective propaganda, and more areas for economic growth and job creation) while all other plausible factors show different values. The three cases had different types of institutional disruptions, occupied different spaces within the public sphere, occurred in different regions, and focused on different key actors.

The post-earthquake CSOs' case investigated the governance of CSOs after major earthquakes, which are the institutional disruptions in this case. This case mainly focused on rural physical spaces with CSOs as key actors. The second case, of internet self-media, examined the censorship on the internet after major media and technological innovations. This case mostly focused on the virtual space and was not bounded by physical boundaries. The third case, of ride-sharing communities, explored the governance of disruptions in the market after technological and commercial breakthroughs. This case interwove the virtual and physical spaces and targets groups of drivers. It is worth noting that the selection of cases was conditioned on specific constraints, and factors of the relative power of state versus society and the alignment of goals (discussed in chapter 5) had to be within a certain range. During this process, stress and break points also existed that could collapse into localized scenarios of society entirely dominated by the local government. As the model points out, the long-term outcome of state-society relations for specific sectors is likely co-optation, constrained by legal tools with minimal free and autonomous CSOs, until another institutional disruption or new players and conditions emerge.

Even though the settings of these three cases were quite different, the interactive authoritarian approach was consistent. For the first stage of "toleration," newer and unregistered illegal associations were allowed to exist, just as critical and diverse discourses and perspectives were tolerated in newer self-media publications, and scattered individual anti-entrapment guerilla protests by the ride-sharing drivers had local authority's acquiescence. Once the local state observed and learned, they started to differentiate. For the state-CSO interactions, a complex and dynamic typology of relationships was presented in chapter 5. Besides those that were cracked down upon, plenty of CSOs also received help from the government during their initial registration and obtained government contracts. For the self-media, only a proportion of accounts and articles have been taken down. There is also a complex mechanism (discussed in chapter 6) that informs the timing and decision of censorship. For the ride-sharing drivers, the harsher inspections affect only a fraction of drivers, while a significant number of drivers are still providing rides to passengers and contributing to the growth of the Chinese economy. We also saw the legalization of all three cases as evidence that laws are used to further strengthen the governance of the actors and phenomena that emerge after institutional disruptions.

Underneath this overarching most different case design are individual studies that provide additional nuances to the theory using original data and a set of mixed research designs. Through process tracing, I demonstrated the historical roots and the logic of authoritarian tolerance (chapter 2). Using an original field experiment, I provided systematic evidence of deliberate differentiation and the rationale for such differentiation by the state (chapter 3). The comparison of the management of domestic and foreign CSOs and the process and reasoning of their respective legalization without institutionalization were explained (chapter 4). After exploring the three key stages of the interactive authoritarian approach, I used a natural experiment (utilizing earthquakes as the as-if-random treatment), and through surveys and interviews in 126 villages in Sichuan, I showed how CSOs are governed under this framework (chapter 5). Then I used the self-media publication that I manage to reveal, through repeated AB tests as the publications grew, how self-media are governed under this framework (chapter 6). Finally, through participant observation, I documented how ride-sharing drivers' collective actions are managed, again, through interactive governance (chapter 7). It is apparent that this approach is not unique to just one industry or one type of institutional disruption but is intrinsic to the logic of the Chinese state's governance strategy.

INTERACTIVE AUTHORITARIANISM

Since Xi Jinping took office in 2012 as China's top leader, the general sense among the scholarly and journalistic communities is that the Chinese state is tightening its grip on society. What is puzzling and usually ignored is that the perception of the societal space by the vast majority of the Chinese people may not be consistent with this claim. The preliminary survey results from the China Internet Survey (2018), for example, indicate that the vast majority of the people in China perceive online space as becoming more open and diverse.[9] Such a puzzling outcome is precisely the result of the interactive authoritarianism approach discussed in this book. Instead of conducting the traditional indiscriminate repression against the entire society, which is easier to carry out and might be cost-effective in the short run, the state has chosen a process to carefully study the situation, identify the actual rebels and risky individuals, and then use discriminate repression against them and make laws to solidify a new status quo order. More importantly, the differentiation tactic also has allowed societal forces to participate in public goods provision (the CSOs from Case I), help control society (the internet companies from Case II), and balance or mediate unstable forces (the taxi drivers and ride-sharing platforms from Case III), which all lead to regime stability. Such a process does not create as many enemies but requires strong state capacity. This also means that the state needs to have an acute sense of the situation when tolerating and monitoring new developments so that the potential regime-challenging actions do not grow out of control, while regime-supporting forces can be utilized in the meantime.

Therefore, the interactive authoritarianism approach is China's solution to manage risks without enlarging the backlash from the entire society. When large protests broke out in the streets of Hong Kong in the summer of 2019, many observers feared that the Beijing government might send troops immediately to oppose the regime-challenging forces. However, the Chinese state used this moment to observe and study the situation, tolerating the behaviors, especially since such behaviors did not directly threaten the Beijing government; the situation was still manageable in the eyes of the leaders. When the National Basketball Association's Houston Rockets general manager Daryl Morey tweeted, "Fight for freedom, stand with Hong Kong,"[10] the state did not ban the NBA completely but stopped broadcasting the Houston Rockets' games only in China. Differentiating the Houston Rockets from the other twenty-nine teams minimized the commercial damage many of the NBA's Chinese partners would suffer but sent a strong enough signal to others tempted to be critical of the Chinese state's handling of the Hong Kong situation. Here, we can also see that the logic of how the Chinese state governs its society is transferrable to how it governs businesses, as individual private companies are viewed as societal and political actors first and economic actors second. The crackdowns on the education sector and online platforms reflect the logic similar to that of interactive authoritarianism—

toleration, differentiation, and then legalization. The state's intention is not to eliminate an entire industry or even specific actors, although elimination could still be the outcome for many organizations.

It is tempting to ask whether the Xi Jinping administration is bringing China back to the Mao era, which tightly controlled the society, de-privatized the economy, and used permanent social mobilizations and revolutions to propel legitimacy.[11] I have presented evidence in this book that it is not a reversal back to Mao but, rather, an evolution of governing strategies. During the Mao era, China was a closed society where information was completely controlled, and the state managed the political discourses entirely. From Mao to Deng, one could see China moving away from the totalitarian regime in order to liberalize, particularly in the 1980s. Freedom of expression was not only allowed but also encouraged during some periods, and the society was beginning to open up, although the 1989 Tiananmen incident briefly disrupted such trends. Then, throughout the 1990s and 2000s, the opening up and toleration of free speech continued. After Xi Jinping took office in 2012, the trend of opening up halted, but it did not revert to the totalitarian approach under Mao. Instead, interactive authoritarianism was tested and continued to be implemented.

Much of China's nonthreatening society continues to enjoy toleration by the state and the fruits of sustained economic growth. However, the tightening grip of the carefully differentiated "dangerous elements" continues, and the already limited political and civil rights of regime-challenging actors will continue to diminish. This is the tale of two societies under one state: a growing number of non-regime-challenging civil society activities that are tolerated, if not promoted, by the state, and the emerging civil society that attempts to check and monitor the state that is being strangled in its cradle. The institutional disruptions that will continue to arise may not always weaken the state, but they might further strengthen the governance capacity of the ruling bureaucracy and make the regime even more resilient.

Appendix

Eight Useful Tips of Conducting Fieldwork on China

As I was reading the first round of reviews of this book, one of the series editors, Mary Gallagher, encouraged me to write a separate chapter about conducting fieldwork on China because I used several methods, such as experiments, ethnographic interviews and fieldwork, online ethnography, and survey research, to triangulate findings and develop the theories. As flattered as I was, I did not think I was suitable for this task. There are so many giants in the field who are much more experienced and erudite on the subject than a newcomer like me. However, I quickly realized that many of the methods I used in this book—and much of how I implemented the project—were due to unreserved guidance from, and interactions with, true experts such as Joseph Fewsmith, Robert Weller, Roderick MacFarquhar, and Ezra Vogel, and rising stars such as Jennifer Pan, Greg Distelhorst, and Yue Hou when I was still a PhD candidate in Boston. It would be meaningful to share what I learned from them. In addition, as I am finishing this book, I have spent exactly half of my life growing up in China and the other half being educated and working in the United States. If the two cents I share could be helpful to anyone who researches China, then it will have been worthwhile.

The Sino-US relationship had deteriorated since the 2010s with no sign of improving immediately. Scholars working on China are facing tremendous challenges conducting research there. However, it is essential to point out that limited access to mainland China is not new. Many of the legends in the field had to deal with a China that was almost completely closed to the outside world and had to face significant risks and challenges, especially before the 1980s. Just as Ezra Vogel managed to conduct interviews in Hong Kong to put the pieces together in capturing Guangdong under reform, there are innovative ways and opportunities that we should continue to use and explore. Given China's presence in the world today, Chinese officials, scholars, employees of

Chinese state-owned enterprises (SOEs) can be accessed virtually everywhere in the world. That is why I named this chapter "Eight Useful Tips of Conducting Fieldwork *on* China" (rather than *in* China), since fieldwork outside of China is an important channel. Finding the right moment to conduct research could also be helpful. Studying state-society relations after institutional disruptions in different domains in this book was not only a theoretical choice but also a methodological one. When the state is bogged down by dealing with crises or new phenomena, it may not apply the same level of control and repression to society and researchers (toleration). Therefore, the interactive authoritarianism model also points out the possibility of conducting fieldwork in China during the right moments/stages.

We should also not take anything for granted. Before I became a disciple of Joseph Fewsmith, I never thought there would be any justification to read the CCP propaganda publications such as *People's Daily* and *Qiushi*. Later, Professor Fewsmith taught me how to read a paper properly, and I realized that some of the elite political exchanges and conflicts were happening right in front of our eyes. The treasure has always been hidden in plain sight. Even more recently, that was how we first learned about the Chinese government's intentions to crack down on major companies like Alibaba and its plans to implement important policies such as "dual circulation."

Methods and data should be appropriate and targeted to the specific research question when we conduct research, so when we face challenges of collecting data about China, it is never a good strategy to avoid difficulties right away and use only familiar and comfortable tools. How Vogel and Fewsmith think about methods and data continues to be valuable and effective. Here, I summarize eight tips for conducting fieldwork on China as I reflect on the lessons I have learned through my research on this project. The first four are about interacting with others and accumulating social capital when conducting fieldwork; the next three tips are about data and methods of collecting it; and the last one is about creating the agency to impact our research environment positively.

TIP NO. 1: TREAT INTERVIEWEES AS HUMANS
RATHER THAN PARTS OF A MACHINE

As students and researchers of politics and governments, we sometimes cannot help but treat the state and government as the primary unit of analysis.

As a result, when we speak to Chinese government officials, some people naturally think about them as parts of a giant authoritarian machine. Many Western media outlets are not shy about depicting the negative images of the Chinese government, and this government is, of course, made up by those officials. While understanding that politics is often involved, as scholars we need to first treat our interview subjects as humans with feelings and interests of their own. Although the Weberian bureaucracy is at its best when it is impersonal, the principal-agent problem under authoritarian context is prevalent and valuable to researchers.

I co-founded a student organization at Harvard around 2012, and we organized workshops of civic engagement to train Chinese youth leaders. When we ran such workshops in China, it was common that some Chinese government officials would sit in the back, observe, and take notes.[1] Many of us might automatically assume that their only interest would be to assess the political risks of such events and then decide whether to shut the events down. However, one day an official came up to our event organizer at the end of a workshop and asked if it was possible to allow his son to participate in the upcoming workshop at Harvard. At that moment, his role as a father was more important than his role as a government official. Understanding such complexity of individuals helped us to motivate cooperation from our interviewees and research subjects.

Everyone has the desire to share. We just need to make sure we become someone our subjects are comfortable speaking with. The ride-sharing drivers wanted to share their grievances against the transportation officials and were proud of their successful guerrilla protests; many government officials felt misunderstood by the people and their superiors and wanted to share the challenges they were facing given the limited resources; NGO leaders were often nostalgic about the struggles they made during difficult times and the joy they experienced after making even just small accomplishments. We should not expect to hear the whole story from everyone, and we should not expect everything they say to be relevant to our research. Treating interviewees with respect and being mindful of any opportunity to push for more details would get us a long way. Of course, if we want to hear extensively about the inside stories and assessments, it is best to speak with recently retired government officials or scholar-officials, as the former will have fewer concerns while the latter are more likely to trust what we are doing. Overall, demonstrating that we are serious scholars doing important research and genuinely believe what they share is meaningful can go a long way. Of course, researchers and subjects may disagree on many issues and opinions, but it is important for researchers to understand what their subjects are saying, not to debate or, even worse, belittle their ideas.

TIP NO. 2: SPEAK THE INTERVIEWEE'S LANGUAGE AND HAVE EMPATHY

Before any interactions with subjects during fieldwork, I always ask myself, How will the subjects view me? Will they think I am someone who's suspicious and going to hurt their careers? If they cannot trust me, the data quality will not be very high, and I would rather have fewer but higher-quality data points than the other way around. For example, when I rode alone in an Uber/Didi car, I usually passed up the opportunity to interview the driver unless the casual conversation had built enough trust—a middle-age male riding alone asking many questions about drivers' organized collective actions might look a lot like a transportation official on an entrapment mission. If I went ahead and asked a lot of questions anyway, the driver could alert his WeChat group members about a guy claiming to be conducting research and asking a lot of sensitive questions, and that might hurt my chances of conducting interviews in the future. However, if I was riding in the car with my family or friends, that would appear much less suspicious. The group conversations might even be livelier. More important, what was more valuable is when such conversations led to an invitation from the driver for me to join their WeChat group so that I could observe their communications and how they organize collective actions live.

Along the same lines, I learned from many CSO leaders to try to speak the government's language. I needed to be familiar with the key talking points of the recent CCP documents and policies, especially those coming out of important conferences such as a plenum. That way the government officials I spoke with would feel that I wasn't a troublemaker, since we already spoke the same language. Such a tactic also informed the field experiment I did when sending out emails to officials in Sichuan province. In the email, I first stated how greatly encouraged I was after studying the "Chinese Communist Party's Third Plenum decision about deepening reform" and reading "to ask social organizations to set up various enterprises in villages," "motivate the vitality of social organizations," and "let social organizations provide public service" and other quotes. The response rate was slightly higher than it was in other, similar experiments, and I think framing it by "speaking the official language" might have helped.

Having empathy in mind is critical when conducting fieldwork, and speaking the language of our subject is one of many ways to demonstrate empathy. Related to tip number one, caring about the individual as a human being, paying attention to the person's life and work, knowing where she or he comes from, and researching the individual's background beforehand could not only lead to more conversations and thus higher-quality data but also build relations.

TIP NO. 3: BUILD SOCIAL CAPITAL WHENEVER POSSIBLE

"Social capital" refers to the norms, trust, and networks embedded in communities that improve the efficiency of civic lives by facilitating coordinated actions.[2] If we look at it from a specific individual's perspective, the term refers to a person's relational resources. Such resources can be crucial when conducting fieldwork in China—related to the idea of *Guanxi* (关系)—and should be accumulated whenever possible. Thus, much of the rewarding fieldwork successes can happen before the fieldwork starts.

The process I used to recruit my fieldwork team members was crucial to the effective outcome. I first circulated a recruitment announcement in my WeChat friend circle so that my friends and their friends could forward the announcement to each of their own friend circles. The announcement listed clearly my expectations and the potential benefits to candidates. I received about fifty high-quality applications for about three to five positions. Thus, I was able to conduct about a dozen interviews to assess who fit the research project the most. To my surprise, I found team members who not only met all of my expectations but also some who had family members that were well connected in the government. One team member had an uncle in the provincial government who helped me to secure more than a dozen interviews with county-level government officials; another team member was even more resourceful, as she had a relative who, I suspect, made it possible that no Public Security or National Security official ever bothered us during the entire trip.

I was able to expand my existing social capital during the field trip as well. For example, a friend's father was taking a temporary post at one of the counties in my sample; it is a common practice in China that government

officials temporarily hone their skills and gain experience in different localities. So he got me a few interviews and introduced me to more people who
would be helpful to my project. In a snowball effect, strong ties led to weak
ties, and eventually I had a solid network of people to work with.

I was also never hesitant to provide help when any of the individuals in
my network needed it. Some of them have kids who would like me to take a
look at their college applications; others wanted me to promote their agricultural produce in my friend circle. What is important to note is that when
a researcher helps someone during fieldwork and is offered something in
return, money is likely the least valuable mode of exchange. It is almost
always a good idea to deny payments but ask for unique resources, especially
personal connections, they can provide. We are there to do research and
probably already have a budget. It is not a good time to make money, but it is
an excellent time to further accumulate social capital. When I was in
Chengdu, the capital of Sichuan province, I even organized game nights so
that people who were already in my friend circle could invite their friends
and become a part of my potential social network. You never know who
might play a crucial role in helping your research project succeed.

Whether conducting fieldwork or not, building social capital should be a
constant practice. Whenever a friend asked me for a favor and wanted to
return a favor, I thought about whether I could get any help to further my
research. Many friends of mine had introduced me to their relatives who
work at the Chinese government at different levels in different regions, and
such access would otherwise be impossible to get.

In a moment when China and many Western countries have tensions,
we should always pay attention to accumulating social capital outside of
China during various opportunities and do not dismiss any individual, even
if our opinions and ideology differ significantly. I can never forget how Professor Roderick MacFarquhar interacted with his visiting scholars. I was the
co-organizer of the Harvard-MIT-BU Chinese Politics Research Workshop for
several years, and Professor MacFarquhar once had a mid-level Chinese official presenting his study at our workshop. Based on previous interactions
with this official, some of us thought it would not be valuable, as we often
heard opinions and propaganda rather than serious research. Nevertheless,
Professor MacFarquhar not only had the official present and stayed for his
entire presentation, asking sharp questions, but he also encouraged the official to continue to polish his research. I realized that it was both an intellectual exercise that could benefit everyone in the room and, perhaps more

important, an opportunity to build relationships and encourage critical thinking in people who are opinionated and not used to doing empirical research. Even if the research was not perfect yet, the interaction was at least a potential data point (in terms of what the official said) and a new relationship.

TIP NO. 4: FIND LOCAL SUPPORT AND EMBED ONESELF IN THE LOCAL NETWORK

This tip is probably easier to achieve for someone who grew up in China, speaks authentic Mandarin, and already has a network of people in China. However, there are still recommendations that could be beneficial to most researchers regardless of individual experience and background.

Having local institutional support would be extremely valuable. I first went to Sichuan to interview CSO leaders because Professors Qiang (Braven) Zhang and Qibin Lu invited me to join their Beijing Normal University team on their fieldwork. I met Zhang in Boston when he was a visiting scholar at Harvard, and knowing I was interested in Chinese civil society development after major disasters, he kindly recruited me as one of his team members. We conducted individual interviews together and organized symposiums in which dozens of active CSO leaders were invited to the Southwestern University of Finance and Economics (whose vice president became an important partner in my projects later on) to share their experiences with state-society interactions. I was also able to give a presentation during the symposium and provided my assessments. This made me a somewhat familiar face in the Sichuan CSO community.

By the time I was leading my own team the next year, not only did I have support from the Southwestern University of Finance and Economics and a letter of recommendation from Beijing Normal University explaining what I was doing (in case any local officials would ask), but also Sichuan University sent an experienced staff member to join my team and assist my work. If we got stopped by police or guards at checkpoints, she could show her university ID and explain in Sichuan dialect about the academic work we were doing. We ended up being stopped only once at a checkpoint, and having her on my team was crucial. The letter of recommendation was never necessary during my interviews with government officials, but some villagers did want to see it. Some had suspected that we were officials in disguise sent down by Xi Jinping; others wanted to make sure we were not people from multilevel marketing companies who were after their money.

CSO leaders were not only my interview subjects but also provided valuable knowledge and insights logistically. For example, one CSO leader recommended a driver for my fieldwork. This driver had an extended version of the Wuling van that could fit my entire team of seven, plus our luggage. More importantly, this driver was a volunteer hauling supplies to quake-stricken regions after each of the major earthquakes and was often hired by the CSO community. Therefore, everywhere we went, he knew where I could find a local CSO, and he could also share his experiences interacting with CSOs. This way, the extended time on the road also became valuable time for me to learn more about the localities and civil society there.

TIP NO. 5: LEARN FROM THE PIONEERS

The challenges we are facing today in conducting fieldwork on China is not entirely novel, and even if it is, someone might have already found an angle to tackle them before we can. We do not need to come up with innovative and creative solutions every time on our own. Quite often, the most effective way is to see if someone has already used a method that we could imitate. This approach is not limited to the most recent studies. Examples like how Ezra Vogel researched Guangdong in Hong Kong are still relevant today.

I learned extensively from my peers. As I was starting this project, Greg Distelhorst and Yue Hou sampled their friends about ethnic-sounding names in preparation for their field experiment in China. I was fascinated by their approach and immediately realized that such a method was also applicable to my project. Of course, this method of sending emails to subjects under an experimental setting can be traced from Marianne Bertrand and Sendhil Mullainathan's experiment on the labor market's discrimination against people with African American–sounding names. It also means we can learn a lot from other scholars who do not work on China or are in other disciplines.

We do need to pay attention to the ethical consequences involved when using innovative methods or borrowing, but not completely replicating, others' methods. When I discussed my research with Professor Elizabeth Perry, she half-jokingly told me that Chinese officials would all be busy replying to our emails. She was very kind, as she wanted to protect the curiosity and enthusiasm of a young scholar, but her point was loud and clear: we should seriously assess the ethical consequences of our research and should not place a significant burden on our subjects; with China, this also involves the potential political risks for our study subjects. After assessing my research under the guidance of my university's Institutional Review Board, I ended up doing the experiment only with officials in Sichuan province in order to limit the scope.

TIP NO. 6: NO RESPONSE AND BEING CENSORED ARE ALSO DATA

We often face not-so-cooperative government officials and even censorship when studying Chinese politics (or authoritarian politics in general). Such responses should not easily be dismissed. Since the state's control of the society is also an integral aspect of state-society interactions, we should pay attention to the degree, condition, and exceptions of state control. I studied censorship of self-media in chapter 6. Having censorship as one type of response allowed me to do AB tests to identify critical relevant issues at specific moments, and the different degrees of censorship responses provided a more nuanced observation of authoritarian control. A laissez-faire government is probably more difficult to study, as one could never grasp important government actions. Under an authoritarian regime, on the other hand, when we are being controlled, it is also a valuable opportunity to study how and why specific control measures are applied.

Similarly, the lack of access in itself could be valuable sometimes. When a specific government official does not want to speak to you, and you get a chance to interview someone else who might have some knowledge about the official, the "no access" or "no comment" condition itself could be a subject of the conversation. Furthermore, when everyone has the understanding that getting access to China is challenging, it gives us excuses to interact with China and Chinese individuals whenever and wherever possible. If a Chinese person knows that they are the only person who can help you because it is likely no one else would be able to do so, they might be more willing to help you out. Even if they can't, they might be willing to introduce you to someone who can. We just need to have the mentality to pay attention that whether a person says yes or no, there is value in the response.

TIP NO. 7: RELYING ON ORIGINAL BUT TEDIOUS WORK

In the difficult time when Sino-US relations deteriorate, many scholars naturally switch to collecting data online. However, we still don't always have to rely on secondhand data, even when the data are from the internet—we are all producers of content. To make one's work unique, we sometimes have to put in a lot of hours facilitating the data-generation process or generating the data independently. Running self-media *Global China* and *Inside the Beltway* takes at least two hours a day. However, what I have obtained are the real experiences of being a content creator and interacting with the censorship apparatus.

During my research on China, there were also positive externalities, as creating platforms for political commentaries and information about political developments for other scholars and making it free for our readers could be considered a public good. I was not doing it entirely altruistically, as I acquired valuable data from such experiences. When we think about the incentives for public goods provision, we tend to think about the hegemonic stability theory, where the hegemony would be benefiting much more than other potential free-riders and thus still have the incentive to do so. In reality, scholars conducting research might also find the incentives to provide public goods because that process of producing public goods could be documented and studied.

TIP NO. 8: SPEAK OUT AND POTENTIALLY SHAPE THE ENVIRONMENT IN WHICH WE CONDUCT FIELDWORK

Scholars are not only takers of rules but might also have the potential to shape them. Most of us probably benefited from the public intellectuals who came before us who shaped and reshaped China's domestic and foreign policies and other relevant countries, especially the United States. On the one hand, junior scholars like me have to understand our limitations; on the other hand, we should not lose our agency to act.

When more prestigious scholars and public intellectuals speak out, we should not let them feel alone. For example, when Professor Jia Qingguo of Beijing University, who is a standing committee member of the Chinese People's Political Consultative Conference, published his proposal on improving the management of foreign exchanges between experts/scholars titled

"Let the Voice of the Chinese People Be Heard More Conveniently and Effectively" on our *Global China* platform,[3] I wrote a commentary supporting his proposal.[4] Having fewer hurdles for Chinese scholars to participate in academic conferences and symposiums where non-Chinese scholars are present is crucial to academic exchanges, joint research, and quite often doing field-work in China. 天下兴亡，匹夫有责. As we conduct research on politics, we should also try to contribute, even just slightly, to a more suitable political environment for researchers for generations to come.

Notes

Introduction

1. "Cross Removal Returns in Zhejiang Province," *Persecution.org*, July 11, 2020 https://www.persecution.org/2020/07/11/cross-removal-returns-zhejiang-prov ince.

2. "China removes crosses from 500 churches, religious staff afraid to cause trouble," *Gospel Herald* (in Chinese), July 10, 2020, https://chinese.gospelherald .com/articles/28998/20200710/%E4%B8%AD%E5%9C%8B%E6%8B%86%E4 %BA%94%E7%99%BE%E6%95%99%E5%A0%82%E5%8D%81%E5%AD%97 %E6%9E%B6-%E5%82%B3%E9%81%93%E6%96%A5%E7%A5%9E%E8%81 %B7%E4%BA%BA%E5%93%A1%E6%80%95%E6%83%B9%E4%BA%8B%E5 %99%A4%E8%81%B2.htm.

3. Emily Feng, "China is removing domes from mosques as part of a push to make them more 'Chinese'," *NPR*, October 24, 2021, https://www.npr.org/2021 /10/24/1047054983/china-muslims-sinicization

4. "Religious Affairs Regulations (2017)," *The Central Government of the People's Republic of China*, September 7, 2017, http://www.gov.cn/zhengce/content/2017 -09/07/content_5223282.htm.

5. "Measures for the Management of Religious Groups," *National Religious Affairs Administration*, February 1, 2020, http://www.sara.gov.cn/ywdt/322201.jhtml.

6. "Religious Affairs Regulations (2004)," *The Central Government of the People's Republic of China*, November 30, 2004, http://www.gov.cn/gongbao/conte nt/2005/content_63293.htm.

7. Barbara Geddes, *Paradigms and Sand Castles: Theory Building and Research Design in Comparative Politics* (Ann Arbor: University of Michigan Press, 2003).

8. Jason Brownlee, *Authoritarianism in an Age of Democratization* (New York: Cambridge University Press, 2007).

9. Johannes Gerschewski, "The three pillars of stability: Legitimation, repression, and co-optation in autocratic regimes," *Democratization* 20, no. 1 (January 2013): 13–38, https://doi.org/10.1080/13510347.2013.738860.

10. Max Weber, "Politics as a Vocation," in *From Max Weber: Essays in Sociology*, ed. H. H. Gerth and C. Wright Mills (eds.), (London: Routledge, 1991).

11. Iza Ding, *Performative Governance*, Working Paper, University of Pittsburgh, (2017).

12. Wenfang Tang, *Populist Authoritarianism: Chinese Political Culture and Regime Sustainability* (Oxford University Press, 2016).

13. David Kelly and X. I. N. Gu, "New Conservatism: Ideological Program of a 'New Elite,'" in *China's Quiet Revolution: New Interactions between State and Society*, ed. David S. Goodman and Beverly Hooper, (Melbourne: Longman Cheshire, 1994): 219–33.

14. Suisheng Zhao, *A nation-state by construction: Dynamics of modern Chinese nationalism*, (Stanford University Press, 2004).

15. Hongxing Yang and Dingxin Zhao, "Performance legitimacy, state autonomy and China's economic miracle," *Journal of Contemporary China* 24, no. 91 (2015): 64–82.

16. Rongbin Han, "Cyber Nationalism and Regime Support under Xi Jinping: The Effects of the 2018 Constitutional Revision," *Journal of Contemporary China* (2021): 1–17.

17. A. J. Nathan, "China's Changing of the Guard: Authoritarian Resilience," *Journal of Democracy* 14, no.1 (2003): 6–17; also see R. Truex, "The returns to office in a 'rubber stamp' parliament," *American Political Science Review* 108, no. 2 (2014): 235; E. Perry, *Challenging the Mandate of Heaven: Social Protests and State Power in China*, (Armonk, NY: M.E. Sharpe, 2002); K. O'Brien and L. Li, *Rightful Resistance in the Chinese Countryside*, (New York: Cambridge University Press, 2006); G. King, J. Pan, and M. E. Roberts, "Reverse engineering Chinese censorship: randomized experimentation and participant observation," *Science* 345, no. 6199 (2014), 1–10; J. Chen, J. Pan, and Y. Xu, "Sources of authoritarian responsiveness: a field experiment in China," *American Journal of Political Science* 60, no. 2 (2016): 383–400.

18. V. C. Shih, *Economic Shocks and Authoritarian Stability: Duration, Financial Control, and Institutions*, (Ann Arbor: University of Michigan Press, 2020).

19. J. Gandhi, *Political institutions under dictatorship*, (New York: New York University, 2004).

20. T.B. Pepinsky, *Economic Crises and the Breakdown and Authoritarian Regimes: Indonesia and Malaysia in Comparative Perspective*, (New York: Cambridge University Press, 2009).

21. M. K. Dimitrov, ed., *Why communism did not collapse: Understanding authoritarian regime resilience in Asia and Europe*, (Cambridge University Press, 2013).

22. V. Shue, "Legitimacy Crisis in China?" in *Chinese Politics: State, Society, and the Market*, ed. Peter Hays Gries and Stanley Rosen (New York: Routledge, 2010), 41–68.

23. J. Teets, *Civil Society under Authoritarianism: The China Model*, (New York: Cambridge University Press, 2014).

24. A. Mertha, "'Fragmented Authoritarianism 2.0': Political Pluralization in the Chinese Policy Process," *China Quarterly* 200 (December 2009): 995–1012.

25. X. Kang, and H. Han, "Graduated Controls: The State-Society Relationship in Contemporary China," *Modern China* 34, no.1 (Jan. 2008): 36–55.

26. Taiyi Sun, "Importing Civic Education into Authoritarian China," in *Teaching Civic Engagement Globally*, ed. Elizabeth C. Matto, Allison Rios Millett McCartney, Elizabeth A. Bennion, Alasdair Blair, Taiyi Sun, and Dawn Michele Whitehead (Washington D.C.: American Political Science Association, 2021), 53–72.

27. J. Fewsmith, *The Logic and Limits of Political Reform in China* (New York: Cambridge University Press, 2013).

28. G. Montinola, Y. Qian, and B.R. Weingast, "Federalism, Chinese Style: The Political Basis for Economic Success," *World Politics* 48, no. 1 (1996): 50–81.

29. J. Gandhi and A. Przeworski, "Cooperation, cooptation, and rebellion under dictatorship," *Economics & Politics* 18, no. 1 (2006): 1–26.

30. P. C. Schmitter, "Still the Century of Corporatism?" *The Review of Politics* 36, no. 1 (1974): 85–131.

31. B. J. Dickson, *Wealth into power: The Communist Party's embrace of China's private sector*, (Cambridge: Cambridge University Press, 2008); J. Unger and Anita Chan, "China, Corporatism, and the East Asian Model," *The Australian Journal of Chinese Affairs*, no.33 (January 1995): 29–53.

32. D. C. Mattingly, *The Art of Political Control in China*, (Cambridge: Cambridge University Press, 2019).

33. Hank Johnston and Sheldon X. Zhang, "Repertoires of Protest and Repression in Contemporary China," *Mobilization: An International Quarterly* 25, no. SI (2020): 601–622.

34. Feng Chen, and Xin Xu, "'Active judiciary': Judicial dismantling of workers' collective action in China," *The China Journal* 67 (2012): 87–108; Yang Su and Xin He, "Street as courtroom: state accommodation of labor protest in South China," *Law & Society Review* 44, no. 1 (2010): 157–184.

35. Julia Chuang, "China's rural land politics: bureaucratic absorption and the muting of rightful resistance," *The China Quarterly* 219 (2014): 649–669.

36. Juan Wang, "Managing social stability: The perspective of a local government in China," *Journal of East Asian Studies* 15, no. 1 (2015): 1–25.

37. Chongyi Feng, "Preserving stability and rights protection: conflict or coherence?" *Journal of Current Chinese Affairs* 42, no. 2 (2013): 21–50.

38. Kevin J. O'Brien and Yanhua Deng, "Preventing protest one person at a time: Psychological coercion and relational repression in China," *China Review* 17, no. 2 (2017): 179–201.

39. Lynette H. Ong, "Thugs and outsourcing of state repression in China," *The China Journal* 80, no. 1 (2018): 94–110.

40. Tony Saich, "What Explains the Resilience of Chinese Communist Party Rule?," *Brown J. World Aff.* 27 (2020): 105.

41. R. Weatherley and Q. Zhang, *History and Nationalist Legitimacy in Contemporary China: A Double-Edged Sword*, (Springer, 2017).

42. L. Diamond, "Thinking about Hybrid Regimes," *Journal of Democracy* 13, no.2 (April 2002): 21–35.

43. J. Fewsmith and A. Nathan, "Authoritarian Resilience Revisited: Joseph Fewsmith with Response from Andrew J. Nathan," *Journal of Contemporary China*, 28, no. 116 (2018): 167–179.

44. O. A. Lewis, "Net inclusion: New media's impact on deliberative politics in China," *Journal of Contemporary Asia* 43, no. 4 (2013): 678–708. Also see K. S. Tsai, *Capitalism without democracy: The private sector in contemporary China*, (Cornell University Press, 2007), 36; V. Shue, *The reach of the state*, (Stanford CA, Stanford University Press, 1988).

45. X. Kang, and H. Han, "Graduated Controls: The State-Society Relationship in Contemporary China," *Modern China* 34, no. 1, (January 2008): 36–55.

46. J. Teets, *Civil Society under Authoritarianism: The China Model*, (New York: Cambridge University Press, 2014).

47. C. Heurlin, *Responsive authoritarianism in China*, (Cambridge University Press, 2016).

48. D. C. North, *Institutions, Institutional Change and Economic Performance*, (Cambridge: Cambridge University Press 1990), 3.

49. Douglass North, *Institutions, Institutional Change and Economic Performance* (Cambridge: Cambridge University Press, 1990).

50. A. Boin and P. T. Hart, "The Crisis Approach," in *Handbook of Disaster Research* (New York: Springer, 2007), 42–54.

51. C. Gilbert, "Studying Disaster: Changes in the main conceptual tools," in: What Is a Disaster? Ed. E. L. Quarantelli (London: Routledge, 1998), 3–12.

52. A. McConnell, "Overview: Crisis Management, Influences, Responses and Evaluation," *Parliamentary Affairs* 56: no. 3 (2003): 393–409; there are other approaches, for example, dividing different crises into sudden and cumulative, see D. Hwang and J.D. Lichtenthal, "Anatomy of Organisational Crises," *Journal of Contingency and Crisis Management* 8, no. 3 (2000): 129–140.

53. S.J. Gould and N. Eldredge, "Punctuated Equilibria: The Tempo and Mode of Evolution Reconsidered," *Paleobiology* 3, no. 1 (1977): 115–151.

54. F. R. Baumgartner and B.D. Jones, *Agendas and Instability in American Politics*, (Chicago: University of Chicago Press, 1993).

55. M. Blyth, *Great transformations: Economic ideas and institutional change in the twentieth century*, (Cambridge University Press, 2002).

56. J. Hogan and D. Doyle, "A Comparative Framework: How Broadly Applicable is a 'Rigorous' Critical Junctures Framework?" *Acta Politica* 44, no. 2 (2009): 211–240.

57. J.S. Migdal, *State in Society: Studying How States and Societies Transform and Constitute One Another* (Cambridge: Cambridge University Press, 2004), 24.

58. E. Ostrom, *Understanding Institutional Diversity* (Princeton: Princeton University Press, 2005); H. Ingram, A. Schneider, and P. deLeon, "Social Construction and Policy Design," in: *Theories of the Policy Process*, second edition, ed. Paul Sabatier (Boulder, Colorado: Westview Press, 2007), 93–128.

59. J. Kingdon, *Agendas, Alternatives, and Public policies* (Amsterdam: Longman, 1995); T. A. Birkland, *After Disaster: Agenda setting, public policy and focusing events* (Cambridge: Cambridge University Press, 1997); and N. Zaharidis, "The Multiple Streams Framework: Structure, Limitations, Prospects," in: *Theories of the Policy Process*, second edition, ed. Paul Sabatier (Boulder, Colorado: Westview Press, 2007), 65–92.

60. H. Jenkins-Smith and P. Sabatier, "The Dynamics of Policy-Oriented Learning," in: *Policy Change and Learning: An Advocacy Coalition Approach*, ed. Paul Sabatier and Hank Jenkins-Smith (Boulder, Colorado: Westview Press, 1993), 41-56.

61. See an extensive discussion on this literature in M. Blyth, *Great Transformations: Economic Ideas and Institutional Change in the Twentieth Century* (New York: Cambridge University Press, 2002).

62. C. Gilbert, "Studying Disaster: Changes in the main conceptual tools."

63. C. Gilbert, "Politique et complexite: les crises sans ennemi," in *Colloque International: Le Cadre Theorique de la Gestion des Crises dans les Societes Complexes: Etat de la Question* (Grenoble, Fance: CRISE).

64. C. Gilbert, "Politique et complexite: les crises sans ennemi."

65. C.F. Hermann, "Some Consequences of Crisis Which Limit the Viability of Organizations," *Administrative Science Quarterly* 8, no. 1 (1963): 61-82; J.T.S. Keeler, "Opening the Window for Reform: Mandates, Crises and Extraordinary Policy-making," *Comparative Political Studies* 25, no. 4 (1993): 433-486; U. Rosenthal and A. Kouzmin, "Crises and Crisis Management: Toward Comprehensive Government Decision Making," *Journal of Public Administration Research and Theory* 7, no. 2 (1997), 277-304.

66. S. Saurugger and F. Terpan, "Do crises lead to policy change? The multiple streams framework and the European Union's economic governance instruments," *Policy Sciences* 49, no. 1 (March 2016): 35-53.

67. B. Xu, *The Politics of Compassion: The Sichuan Earthquake and Civic Engagement in China* (Stanford: Stanford University Press, 2017).

68. G.M. Luebbert, *Liberalism, Fascism or Social Democracy* (New York, NY: Oxford University Press, 1991).

69. J. Smith and D. Wiest, "Social Movements in the World-System: The Politics of Crisis and Transformation."

70. R. A. Boin and M. H.P. Otten, "Beyond the Crisis Window for Reform: Some Ramifications for Implementation," *Journal of Contingencies and Crisis Management* 4, no. 3 (September 1996): 149-161.

71. D. Slater, *Ordering power: Contentious politics and authoritarian leviathans in Southeast Asia*, (New York: Cambridge University Press, 2010)

72. H. Chan, "Crisis Politics in Authoritarian Regimes: How Crises Catalyse Changes under the State-Society Interactive Framework," *Journal of Contingencies and Crisis Management* 21, no. 4, (December 2013): 200-210.

73. G. Capano, "Understanding Policy Change as an Epistemological and Theoretical Problem," *Journal of Comparative Policy Analysi* 11, no. 1 (2009): 7-31.

74. For a more comprehensive description of this literature, see: D. Nohrstedt and C. M. Weible, "The Logic and Policy Change after Crisis: Proximity and Subsystem Interaction," *Risk, Hazards, & Crisis in Public Policy* 1, no. 2 (July 2010).

75. North, *Institutions, Institutional Change and Economic Performance*, 91.

76. There are also about four counties that we passed by and conducted surveys but did not include the data in this particular sample because those county-level administrative regions are urban districts of major cities.

77. J. Gerring, Case Study Research: Principles and Practices, (Cambridge: Cambridge University Press, 2007), 139.

78. Y. Y. Ang, *How China escaped the poverty trap*, (Cornell University Press, 2016).

Chapter 1

1. The Book of Rites (礼记), about 400 B.C.

2. Song Dynasty also has state-sponsored charities such as 居养院、安济坊、慈幼局、漏泽园. From Ming Dynasty (1368–1644) to Qing Dynasty (1644–1912), there are state-sponsored charities such as 普济堂、育婴堂、救生局、恻隐堂、积善堂.

3. J. Gernet, *A History of Chinese Civilization* 2nd Ed. (New York: Cambridge University Press, 1999), 393.

4. X. Zhi, 中国各朝人口数量 *("Zhongguo Gechao Renkou Shuliang: Chinese Population in Each Dynasty")*, https://wenku.baidu.com/view/cc5c7e91941ea76e59fa040b .html.

5. L. Tsai, *Accountability Without Democracy: Solidary Groups and Public Goods Provision in Rural China* (New York: Cambridge University Press, 2007).

6. L. He, "中国农村变革的先驱和开拓者邓子恢,"《党史文苑》, 2008, no. 23, http://news.ifeng.com/history/zhongguoxiandaishi/detail_2012_11/13/19099 395_0.shtml.

7. Clemens Ostergaard, "Citizens, groups, and nascent civil society in China: towards an understanding of the 1989 student demonstrations," *China Information* 4, (1989): 28–41; L. Sullivan, "The emergence of civil society in China, spring 1989." In: Tony Saich (eds.) *The Chinese People's Movement: Perspectives on Spring 1989.* (Armonk, NY: M.E. Sharpe, 1990), 126–144; A. J. Nathan, *China's Transition*, (New York: Columbia University Press, 1997), 11.

8. K. Simon, *Civil society in China: the legal framework from ancient times to the 'new reform era,'* (New York: Oxford University Press, 2013), xl. Also see: H. Azhar, Haris, "The human rights struggle in Indonesia: international advances, domestic deadlocks," *International Journal on Human Rights* 11, no. 20 (2014): 227–234; John J. Casey, "Comparing nonprofit sectors around the world: what do we know and how do we know it," *Journal of Nonprofit Education and Leadership* 6, no. 3 (2016): 187–223.

9. M. E. Gallagher, "China: the limits of civil society in a late Leninist state," in: *Civil Society and Political Change in Asia*, ed. Muthiah Alagappa (Stanford: Stanford University Press, 2004); J. Fewsmith, *Blurring the Lines: The Logic and Limits of Political Reform in China*, (New York: Cambridge University Press, 2013); A. Nathan, "China's challenge," *Journal of Democracy* 26, no. 1 (2015): 156–170.

10. Q. Ma, "Defining Chinese nongovernmental organizations," *International Journal of Voluntary and Nonprofit Organizations* 13, no. 2 (2002): 113–130; *X. Kang and H. Han*, "Graduated controls: the state-society relationship in contemporary China," *Modern China* 34, no. 1 (2008): 36–55; Z. Deng and Y. Jing, "Civil society in China: a theoretical reflection," in *State and Civil Society: The Chinese Perspec-*

tive, ed. Deng Zhenglai (Shanghai: World Scientific, 2011); J. Teets, *Civil Society under Authoritarianism*, (Cambridge, US: Cambridge University Press, 2014), 176.

11. A. D. Tocqueville, *Democracy in America*, (Penguin Books, 2003).

12. F. Wakeman, Jr., "The Civil Society and Public Sphere Debate: Western Reflections on Chinese Political Culture," *Modern China* 19, no. 2 (1993): 108–138.

13. T. B. Gold, "The Resurgence of Civil Society in China," *Journal of Democracy* 1, no. 1 (1990): 18–31.

14. P. C. Schmitter, "Still the Century of Corporatism?" *The Review of Politics* 36, no. 1 (1974): 85–131.

15. J. Unger and A. Chan, "China, Corporatism, and the East Asian Model," *The Australian Journal of Chinese Affairs*, no.33 (1995): 29–53.

16. Fewsmith, *Blurring the Lines: The Logic and Limits of Political Reform in China*.

17. C. Hsu, "Beyond Civil Society: An Organizational Perspective on State-NGO Relations in the People's Republic of China," *Journal of Civil Society*, no. 3 (2010): 259–277.

18. J. Fewsmith, *Blurring the Lines: The Logic and Limits of Political Reform in China* (New York: Cambridge University Press, 2013).

19. E. Perry, "Trends in the Study of Chinese Politics: State-society relations," *China Quarterly* 139, (1994): 704–713; V. Shue, *The Reach of the State: Sketches of the Chinese Body Politic* (Stanford: Stanford University Press, 1988).

20. C. Lee, "Daily active users for WeChat exceeds 1 billion," *ZDNet*, January 9, 2018, https://www.zdnet.com/article/daily-active-user-of-messaging-app-wechat-exceeds-1-billion/.

21. J. Horwitz, "In China, you can now hail a taxi and pay the driver on Wechat," *Tech in Asia*, 2014, https://www.techinasia.com/china-hail-taxi-pay-driver-WeChat.

22. J. Gao and Q. Duan, "New rules from the ministry of transport on taxi reform: regulate Internet-enabled hires," *21st Century Business Herald*, October 12, 2015.

23. J. Zhang, "Didi by the numbers: ride-hailing firm covered more miles in 2018 than 5 Earth-to-Neptune round-trips," *South China Morning Post*, January 23, 2019, https://www.scmp.com/tech/start-ups/article/2181542/didi-numbers-ride-hailing-firm-covered-more-miles-2018-5-earth.

24. Note: the Chinese constitution lists four (*de jure*) levels of local government: provincial, municipal, county level, and townships. See "the Constitution of the People's Republic of China" http://www.npc.gov.cn/npc/xinwen/2018-03/22/content_2052489.htm. However, in practice (*de facto*), and including the central government, there are five and a half levels.

25. Note: village governments perform and function as a government, but their existence and authority are not guaranteed by the Chinese constitution. Quite often, the village level is treated as a "quasi-official" level. This is also why it is much easier to have village democratic elections in China than having township or county level elections to select the leaders of that level.

26. 基金会条例(Regulation on Foundation Administration) (2004) http://www
.lawinfochina.com/display.aspx?lib=law&id=3463&CGid=, last accessed on
June 24, 2017.

27. L. Li, "The direct registration of four types of social organizations: halting
unnecessary procedures," The Ministry of Civil Affairs of the People's Republic of
China, December, 2013, http://www.mca.gov.cn/article/mxht/mtgz/201312/20
131200556602.shtml.

28. A household registration system that identifies the residence status and origin of a person. The Hukou system is associated with certain privileges such as
access to public schools, lower insurance premiums, housing subsidies and many
more.

29. Interview 19GO01.

30. Y. Hao, "People's Daily's Stock Tripled mainly due to this new service," (人
民网股价暴涨三倍,背后最大的"功臣"是这个新业务), *Sohu.com* (April 8, 2019),
http://www.sohu.com/a/306599320_250147.

Chapter 2

1. Interview 16GN42.

2. Interview 14SN08.

3. Interview 14HG47.

4. Marquis, Christopher and Yanhua Bir, "The paradox of responsive authoritarianism: How civic activism spurs environmental penalties in China." *Organization Science* 29, no. 5 (2018): 948–968.

5. Jidong Chen, Jennifer Pan, and Yiqing Xu. "Sources of authoritarian
responsiveness: A field experiment in China." *American Journal of Political Science*
60, no. 2 (2016): 383–400. Also see, Gary King, Jennifer Pan, and Margaret E. Roberts. "Reverse-engineering censorship in China: Randomized experimentation
and participant observation." *Science* 345, no. 6199 (2014).

6. Runya Qiaoan and Jessica C. Teets. "Responsive Authoritarianism in
China—a Review of Responsiveness in Xi and Hu Administrations." *Journal of
Chinese Political Science* 25, no. 1 (2020): 139–153.

7. Marie-Eve Reny. *Authoritarian containment: Public security bureaus and Protestant House churches in urban China* (Oxford University Press, 2018), 64.

8. B. He and S. Thogersen, "Giving the people a voice? Experiments with consultative authoritarian institutions in China," *Journal of Contemporary China* 19,
no. 66 (2010): 675–692.

9. J. Teets, *Civil Society under Authoritarianism: The China Model*, (New York:
Cambridge University Press, 2014).

10. H. Han, "Legal governance of NGOs in China under Xi Jinping: Reinforcing
Divide and rule," *Asian Journal of Political Science* 26, no. 3 (2018): 390–409.

11. A.J. Spires, "Contingent Symbiosis and Civil Society in an Authoritarian
State: Understanding the Survival of China's Grassroots NGOs," *American Journal
of Sociology* 117, no. 1 (July 2011): 1–45.

12. Y. Shen and J. Yu, "Local Government and NGOs in China: Performance-Based Collaboration," *China: An International Journal* 15, no.2 (May 2017): 177–191.

13. J.W. Tai, "Embedded Civil Society: NGO Leadership and Organizational Effectiveness in Authoritarian China," Author's dissertation (2012).

14. C. Hsu, "Beyond Civil Society: An Organizational Perspective on State-NGO Relations in the People's Republic of China," *Journal of Civil Society* 6, no. 3 (2010): 259–277.

15. Q. Wang, "Co-Optation or Restriction: The Differentiated Government Control over Foundations in China," October 2, 2016, https://papers.ssrn.com/sol3/papers.cfm?abstract_id=2846635#.

16. Daniela Stockmann. *Media commercialization and authoritarian rule in China* (Cambridge University Press, 2013), 151.

17. Jessica Chen Weiss,. "Authoritarian signaling, mass audiences, and nationalist protest in China." *International Organization* 67, no. 1 (2013): 1–35.

18. James Reilly. *Strong Society, Smart State* (Columbia University Press, 2011).

19. T. Johnson, "Extending environmental governance: China's environmental state and civil society," Ph.D. thesis (University of Glasgow, 2009).

20. H. Gao and A. Tyson, "Administrative Reform and the Transfer of Authority to Social Organizations in China," *The China Quarterly* 232 (December 2017): 1050–1069.

21. Z. Li and A. Ong, *Privatizing China: Socialism from Afar*, (Ithaca, NY: Cornell University Press, 2008).

22. G. Wood, "New partners or old brothers? GONGOs in transnational environmental advocacy in China," *China Environmental Series* 5 (1996): 45–58.

23. Hsu, "Beyond Civil Society: An Organizational Perspective on State-NGO Relations in the People's Republic of China."

24. Zhao, Yuezhi. *Communication in China: Political economy, power, and conflict.* Rowman & Littlefield Publishers, 2008.

25. Interview 12SB35.

26. Interview 16GGO18.

27. Interview 14SGO03.

28. Interview 14SN06.

29. Interview 14SN08.

30. Based on interviews with dozens of local government officials.

31. Interview 14SGO17.

32. Interview 14SN07.

33. Interview 14SN08.

34. Interviews 12SN40, 15SGO08.

35. Interview 14HG47.

36. Interview 14SGO14.

37. Interview 14SN08.

38. Interview 14HG47.

39. Interviews 14SGO03, 16GGO18.

40. Interview 14SN07.
41. Interview 14SN08.
42. Interviews 16GN42, 18GN01.
43. Interview 14SGO03.
44. Interview 18GN01.
45. Interview 18GN02.
46. Interview 18GN02.
47. Interview 14SGO03.
48. Interview 14SN08.
49. Interview 14SN06.
50. Interview 14SGO17.
51. Interview 12SN40.

Chapter 3

1. B. J. Dickson, *Red Capitalists in China: The Party, Private Entrepreneurs, and the Prospects for Political Change*, (Cambridge: Cambridge University Press, 2003).

2. Kang and Han, "Graduated controls: the state-society relationship in contemporary China."

3. G. King, J. Pan, and M. E. Roberts, "How Censorship in China Allows Government Criticism but Silences Collective Expression," *American Political Science Review* 107, no. 2 (2013): 1–18; Also see: G. King, J. Pan, and M. E. Roberts, "Reverse Engineering Chinese Censorship: Randomized Experimentation and Participant Observation." *Science* 345, no. 6199 (2014): 1–10.

4. M. S. Gleiss, "How Chinese labour NGOs legitimize their identity and voice," China Information 28, no. 3 (October 1, 2014): 362–381.

5. F. Wu and K. Chan, "Graduated control and beyond: The evolving government-NGO relations," *China Perspective*, no. 3 (2012): 9–17.

6. L. Zhang, "A Commentary on 'Beyond Civil Society,'" *Journal of Civil Society* 7, no.1 (April 2011): 119–122.

7. Wu and Chan, "Graduated control and beyond: The evolving government-NGO relations."

8. C.L. Hsu and Y. Jiang, "An Institutional Approach to Chinese NGOs: State Alliance versus State Avoidance Resource Strategies," *The China Quarterly* 221 (March 2015): 100–122.

9. X. Zhan and S. Tang, "Understanding the Implications of Government Ties for Nonprofit Operations and Functions," *Public Administration Review* 76, no. 4 (February 01, 2016): 589–600.

10. C. Song, S. Wang, and P. Kristen, "All Roads Lead to Rome: Autonomy, Political Connections and Organisational Strategies of NGOs in China," *China: An International Journal* 13, no.3 (December 2015): 72–93.

11. R. Hasmath and J. Y.J. Hsu, "Isomorphic Pressures, Epistemic communities and State-NGO Collaboration in China," *The China Quarterly* 220 (December 2014): 936–954.

12. X. Zhou, "Unorganized interests and collective action in Communist China," *American Sociological Review* 58, no. 1, (1993): 54–73.

13. E. Perry, *Challenging the Mandate of Heaven: Social Protests and State Power in China*, (Armonk, NY: M.E. Sharpe, 2002); K. O'Brien and L. Li, *Rightful Resistance in the Chinese Countryside*, (New York: Cambridge University Press, 2006); P. Lorentzen, "Regularizing rioting: permitting public protest in an authoritarian regime," *Quarterly Journal of Political Science* 8, (2013); G. King, J. Pan, and M. E. Roberts, "Reverse engineering Chinese censorship: randomized experimentation and participant observation," *Science* 345, no. 6199 (2014): 1–10; J. Chen, J. Pan, and Y. Xu, "Sources of authoritarian responsiveness: a field experiment in China," *American Journal of Political Science* 60, no. 2 (2016): 383–400.

14. B. Magaloni and J. Wallace, "Citizen loyalty, mass protest and authoritarian survival," paper presented at the conference on "Dictatorship: Their Governance and Social Consequences," Stanford University, California (April 25–26, 2008); D.M. Butler and D.E. Brockman, "Do politicians racially discriminate against constituents: a field experiment on state legislators," *American Journal of Political Science* 55, no. 3 (2011): 463–477; D. E. Broockman, "Advance blacks' interests: a field experiment manipulating political incentives," *American Journal of Political Science* 57, no. 3 (2013): 521–536.

15. J. Zhang, "Will the government 'serve' the people: the development of Chinese e-government," *New Media & Society* 4, no. 2 (2002): 163–184; M. Edin, "State capacity and local agent control in China: CCP cadre management from a township perspective," *The China Quarterly* 173, (2013): 35–52; X. Lu and P.F. Landry, "Show me the money: interjurisdiction political competition and fiscal extraction in China," *American Political Science Review* 108, no. 3 (2014): 706–722.

16. A.J. Nathan, "Authoritarian Resilience," *Journal of Democracy* 14, no. 1 (2003): 6–17; B. He and S. Thogersen, "Giving the people a voice? Experiments with consultative authoritarian institutions in China," *Journal of Contemporary China* 19, no. 66 (2010): 675–692; P. Lorentzen, "Regularizing rioting: permitting public protest in an authoritarian regime," *Quarterly Journal of Political Science* 8, (2013); M.K. Dimitrov, "What the party wanted to know: citizen complaints as a 'barometer of public opinion' in communist Bulgaria," *East European Politics and Societies and Cultures* 28, no. 2 (2014): 271–295; J.L. Wallace, "Information politics in dictatorship," in Robert Scott and Stephen Kosslyn (eds.), *Emerging Trends in the Social and Behavioral Sciences: An Interdisciplinary, Searchable, and Linkable Resource*, (Hoboken, NJ: Wiley and Sons, 2015), 1–11.

17. R. Truex, "Consultative authoritarianism and its limits," *Comparative Political Studies* 50, no. 3 (2014): 329–361; I. Ding, "Invisible Sky, Visible State: Environmental Governance and Political Support in China," Doctoral dissertation, Harvard University, Graduate School of Arts & Sciences, 2016.

18. T. Sun, "Earthquakes and the typologies of state-society relations in China," *China Information* 31, no. 3: 304–326.

19. E. Perry, "A new rights consciousness?" *Journal of Democracy* 20, no. 3 (2009): 17–20; K.J. O'Brien, "Rightful resistance revisited," *Journal of Peasant Stud-*

ies 40, no. 6 (2013): 1051–62; D. Fu, "Disguised collective action in China," *Comparative Political Studies* 50, no. 4 (2016): 499–527.

20. A. Mertha, "'Fragmented authoritarianism2.0': political pluralization in the Chinese policy process," *The China Quarterly* 200, (2009): 995–1012.

21. Similar strategies have been used by other scholars doing research in China, see Hartford 2005 and Distelhorst and Hou 2013.

22. Interview 14SGO01.

23. Interviews 14SGO14, 14SGO01, and 14SGO03.

24. Interview 16GGO18.

25. Interviews 14SGO03, 14SGO04, and 15SGO13.

26. Interview 16GGO18.

27. Interviews 14SGO01, 14SGO02, 14SGO03, 14SGO05, and 14SGO17.

28. J. Yinger, "Measuring racial discrimination with fair housing audits: caught in the act," *The American Economic Review* 76, no. 5 (1986): 881–93; D. Neumark, R.J. Bank and K.D. Van Nort, "Sex discrimination in restaurant hiring: an audit study," *The Quarterly Journal of Economics* 111, no. 3 (1996): 915–941; M. Bertrand and S. Mullainathan, "Are Emily and Greg more employable than Lakisha and Jamal: a field experiment on labor market discrimination," *American Economic Review* 94, no. 4 (2004): 991–1013; M. Arai and P.S. Thoursie, "Renouncing personal names: an empirical examination of surname change and earnings," *Journal of Labor Economics* 27, no. 1 (2009): 127–147.

29. "Zhonghua renmin gongheguo guowuyuan ling di 492 hao: Zhonghua renmin gongheguo zhengfu xinxi gongkai tiaoli," Open Government Information Ordinance, April 2007, Accessed 31 July 2019, http://www.gov.cn/zwgk/20 07-04/24/content_592937.htm.

30. P.R. Rosenbaum, *Design of Observational Studies, Springer Series in Statistics,* (New York: Springer Verlag, 2010).

31. G. Yang, "The internet and civil society in China: a preliminary assessment," *Journal of Contemporary China* 12, no. 36 (2003): 453–475.

32. J. Zhang, "Will the government 'serve' the people: the development of Chinese e-government."

33. X. Chen, "China at the tipping point? The rising cost of stability," *Journal of Democracy* 24, no. 1 (2013): 57–64.

34. L.M. Luehrmann, "Facing citizen complaints in China, 1951–1996," *Asian Survey* 43, no. 5 (2003): 845–866.

35. M. Edin, "State capacity and local agent control in China: CCP cadre management from a township perspective;" Lu and P.F. Landry, "Show me the money: interjurisdiction political competition and fiscal extraction in China."

36. T. Meng, J. Pan and P. Yang, "Conditional receptivity to citizen participation: evidence from a survey experiment in china," *Comparative Political Studies* 50, no. 4 (2014): 399–433.

37. Interview 12SN40.

38. Interview 14SGO03.

39. Similar work by Chen, Pan and Xu (2016) introduces a potential threat (of

collective action or tattling to superiors). Such threats burden officials because they may need to take action before replying, such as trying to solve the problem before providing a satisfactory response. This approach also introduces noise to the "non-response" category as there may originally be an intention to respond but since the action taken would not meet the demand anyway, the official could have decided not to bother to respond.

40. J. Chen, J. Pan, and Y. Xu, "Sources of authoritarian responsiveness: a field experiment in China."

41. Chen, Pan and Xu (2016).

42. The lower response rate from Chen, Pan and Xu's (2016) study can also be attributed to the difference in this procedure as they randomized the identification numbers and phone numbers. Both identification numbers and phone numbers contain direct information about the person's locality, and if the local officials are immediately aware that the sender is not from their own jurisdiction, then it is easy to disregard the request.

43. The variables used here were provided by Chinese government officials who conduct geological surveys, and the data were specified before any of the data used in this research were collected.

44. To have fewer parametric assumptions, I tested again by using the "xbalance" command in "RItools" package designed by Bowers, Fredrickson and Hansen (2014). The model p-value is 0.97 and each covariate's p-value is much larger than the 0.05 level, therefore indicating the assignment of the treatments were balanced.

45. G. Distelhorst and Y. Hou, "Ingroup bias in official behavior: a national field experiment in China," *Quarterly Journal of Political Science* 9, no. 2 (2013): 203–230.

46. To test whether the t-test is adequate here (with the assumptions of a normal t-distribution), 1,000,000 permutations were conducted to construct replicated confidence intervals. The coverage rate is about 0.945, indicating that the t-test is performing properly and I can rely on the central limit theorem here.

47. Bowers, Fredrickson and Hansen 2014. RItools package in R. Here setting p-value at 0.025 for this test. Note that the confidence interval for the model of effect also does not cover 0, meaning there is a significant negative treatment effect.

48. Interview 15SGO13.

49. P. Lorentzen, "Regularizing rioting: permitting public protest in an authoritarian regime;" M.K. Dimitrov, "What the party wanted to know: citizen complaints as a 'barometer of public opinion' in communist Bulgaria," *East European Politics and Societies and Cultures.*

50. J. Chen, J. Pan, and Y. Xu, "Sources of authoritarian responsiveness: a field experiment in China."

51. G. King, J. Pan, and M. E. Roberts, "Reverse engineering Chinese censorship: randomized experimentation and participant observation."

52. Interview 14SGO03.

53. Interview 14SGO03.
54. Interview 16GGO18.
55. Interview 16GN42.
56. Interview 14SGO03; Interview 15SGO12.
57. Interview 12SJ34.
58. Interview 14SGO14.
59. Interviews 13SJ33, 14SGO14, and 16GGO18, among many.
60. There are several provinces in China that have loosened the policy, and in 2011, the minister of Civil Affairs Li Liguo announced that, nationally, four types of organizations no longer need to have a "sponsor organization": industry associations, science and technology organizations, charities, and entities providing community social services. Yet, most CSOs still need a "sponsor organization" to operate in China today.
61. Interview 16GGO18.
62. Interview 16GN42.
63. Interview 13SN39.
64. C.H. Steinhardt and F. Wu, "In the name of the public: environmental protest and the changing landscape of popular contention in China," *The China Journal* 75 (2015): 61–82.
65. Interviews 12SI38, 13SN25, 13SB35, and 13SN41.
66. T. Hildebrandt, *Social Organization and the Authoritarian State in China*, (New York: Cambridge University Press, 2013).
67. "Zhonghua renmin gongheguo jingwai feizhengfu zuzhi jingnei huodong guanlifa" (Law of the Management of Foreign NGOs in the PRC), Accessed 31 July, 2019, http://www.npc.gov.cn/npc/xinwen/2017-11/28/content_2032719.htm. For the original draft of the text, see National People's Congress of the People's Republic of China (2015).
68. J. Teets, "The test of a civilization: social management and the future of philanthropy in China," Paper presented at the conference on "Chinese Philanthropy: Past, Present and Future," Fudan University, Shanghai, (9–10 June 2015).
69. AONGOMPS, "Statistics on foreign NGO registration and official events documentation for the first nine months of 2017 in China," *Gongyi cishan zhoukan* (Public Welfare and Charity Week), 37, Accessed 31 July, 2019, http://mp.weixin.qq.com/s/WtIakQgj0sNNQ4wkfFRLfw.
70. Interview 14 SGO17; Interview 14SGO03; Interview 13SN40.
71. Xu, Bin. *The politics of compassion: The Sichuan earthquake and civic engagement in China*. Stanford University Press, 2017.
72. Interview 12HO01.
73. Interviews 12SJ34, 12SN39, 13SN39, and 14SGO03.
74. Interview 09SF11.
75. Interview 15SGO03.
76. Interview 15SN40; Interview 15SGO16.

Chapter 4

1. G. Montinola, Y. Qian, and B.R. Weingast, "Federalism, Chinese Style: The Political Basis for Economic Success," *World Politics* 48, no. 1 (1996): 50–81.

2. S. Heilmann, "Policy-Making through Experimentation: The Formation of a Distinctive Policy Process," In *Mao's Invisible Hand: The Political Foundations of Adaptive Governance in China*, eds. Sebastian Heilmann and Elizabeth J. Perry (Harvard University Press, 2011).

3. Tsai, Wen-Hsuan, and Nicola Dean. "Experimentation under hierarchy in local conditions: cases of political reform in Guangdong and Sichuan, China." *The China Quarterly* 218 (2014): 339–358.

4. G. Roland, Gerard, *Transition and Economics: Politics, Markets, and Firms.* (Cambridge and London: The MIT Press, 2000).

5. H. Cai and D. Treisman, "Did Government Decentralization Cause China's Economic Miracle?" *World Politics* 58, no.4 (2006): 505–535.

6. D. Yang, *Beyond Beijing: Liberalization and the regions in China*, (Routledge 2002).

7. Performative legitimacy is slightly different from performance legitimacy. While performance legitimacy still aims at producing meaningful outcomes (such as higher GDP), performative legitimacy is simply aiming at putting on a believable show (such as pollution investigation without necessarily having to treat the pollution). See I. Ding, "Performative Governance", working paper presented at Harvard-MIT-BU Chinese Politics Research Workshop (2016).

8. J. Zeng, "Did Policy Experimentation in China Always Seek Efficiency? A case study of Wenzhou Financial reform in 2012." *Journal of Contemporary China* 24, no. 92 (2014): 338–356.

9. P. Liu, "Experimentation based on the center's selective control" (基于中央选择性控制的试验—中国改革"实践"机制的一种新解释), *kaifang shidai*, no. 4 (2010).

10. S. Wang, "Learning through Practice and Experimentation: The Financing of Rural Health Care," In *Mao's Invisible Hand: The Political Foundations of Adaptive Governance in China*, eds. Sebastian Heilmann and Elizabeth J. Perry (Harvard University Press, 2011).

11. T. Hao, "Benign Violation of the Constitution" (论良性违宪), *Faxue yanjiu* 18, no. 4 (1996); Z. Tong, "One should not affirm the concept of 'Benign Violation of the Constitution'" ("良性违宪"不宜肯定—对郝铁川同志有关主张的不同看法), *Faxue yanjiu* 18, no. 6 (1996).

12. S. Heilmann, "Policy Experimentation in China's Economic Rise," *Study of Comparative and International Development* 43, (2008): 1–26.

13. Tsai and Dean.

14. Tsou, Tang. 1986. *The Cultural Revolution and Post-Mao Reforms: A Historical Perspective*, The University of Chicago Press, Chicago: xxiv.

15. 外国商会管理暂行规定 (Provisional Regulations for the Administration of Foreign Chambers of Commerce in China, 1989), last accessed on 24 June, 2017. http://www.mca.gov.cn/article/gk/fg/shzzgl/201507/20150700847911.shtm.

16. 社会团体登记管理条例 (Regulation on Registration and Administration of Social Organizations), 1989.

17. J. Han, "Foreign NGO's development and governance since the reform and opening era" (改革开放以来在华NGO的发展及其治理), in *Blue Book of Philanthropy: Annual Report on China's Philanthropy Development* (2013), Yang Tuan ed. *Social Sciences Academic Press* (China) (2013), 188.

18. N. Wheeler, "Nurturing Civil Society: A Joint Venture," in *The Role of American NGOs in China's Modernization: Invited Influence*, (New York: Routledge, 2012), 168.

19. 98洪水的损失及外来的捐款 (Damages and Donations from the 98 flood), 2009, http://news.xilu.com/2009/0909/news_112_14702.html, last accessed on 25 June, 2017.

20. 汶川地震8年，600亿捐款都花哪里去了(Eight years after the Wenchuan earthquake, where did the 60 billion donations go?), wenxuecity news, 2016, http://www.wenxuecity.com/news/2016/05/12/5198847.html, last accessed on 25 June, 2017.

21. 民办非企业单位登记管理暂行条例 (The Interim Regulations on Registration Administration of Private Non-enterprise Units), 1998 http://www.pkulaw.cn/fulltext_form.aspx?Db=chl&Gid=21052, last accessed on 24 June, 2017.

22. 中华人民共和国公益事业捐赠法 (Law of the People's Republic of China on Donations for Public Welfare) http://www.lawinfochina.com/display.aspx?lib=law&id=6238&CGid=, last accessed on 24 June, 2017.

23. 基金会条例(Regulation on Foundation Administration), 2004 http://www.lawinfochina.com/display.aspx?lib=law&id=3463&CGid=, last accessed on 24 June, 2017.

24. G. Zheng, *Zhonghua Renmin Gongheguo Cishanfa: Jiedu yu yingyong (中华人民共和国慈善法：解读与应用)*, (People's Publishing 人民出版社, 2016).

25. Interview 12SJ34.

26. Interview 15SN40.

27. Interview 12SJ34.

28. Codename of the person is used here to avoid direct identification of the interviewee.

29. Interview 09SJ33.

30. From here on, material regarding Zhang Guoyuan's case came from the following interviews: Interview 09SJ33, 09SN25, 12SJ34, 12SN39, 12SN40, 13SJ33, 13SN40, 13SN25, 13SN39, and 15SN40.

31. Material of the 512 Center case mainly come from Interview 12SJ34 unless otherwise noted.

32. See Shangming Gongyi's website, http://www.512ngo.org.cn, last accessed on 24 June, 2017.

33. Bian Huimin, Zhenyao Wang, Puqu Wang, and Yan Feng. *Social Management and Innovation in Disaster Response* (灾害应对重的社会管理创新：绵竹市灾后援助社会资源协调平台项目的探索)，People's Publishing (人民出版社), 2011: 76–77.

34. Interview 14SGO02.

35. See Xieli Gongyi's website, http://www.ixieli.org/, last accessed on 24 June 2017.

36. "Report on the work of the Mass Organizations Social Service Centers in Sichuan Province," (四川省基层群团组织社会服务中心工作汇报) Sichuan Women's Federations, 2015 http://www.scfl.org.cn/Article/ShowArticle.asp?ArticleID =8302.

37. Zou Yi. "Trade Unions should firmly grasp the advanced nature and keep pace with the times" (工会要牢牢把握先进性 与时俱进), *Trade Union's Half Month Paper* 20, 2015, Hangzhou http://www.hzgh.org/byt/view.aspx?id=29005.

38. Wang Jiexiu. Blue Book of Civil Affairs (2014): Annual Report on Development of China's Civil Affairs (中国民政发展报告 (2014)), China Social Publishing House (中国社会出版社), 2014: 129-131.

39. Wang Jiexiu, 2014: 129-131.

40. Wang Ming. "On Improving the Mechanisms of Social Supervisors" (关于完善社会监督员机智的建议案), in *Reports on the Civil Society Action in Wenchuan Earthquake: China NGOs in Emergency Rescue*, Wang Ming ed. Social Sciences Academic Press (China), 2009: 108-110.

41. Bian, Wang, Wang, and Feng. *Social Management and Innovation in Disaster Response*: 8-25.

42. Andrew Mertha, "'Fragmented Authoritarianism 2.0': Political Pluralization in the Chinese Policy Process," *The China Quarterly* 200, (December 2009): 995-1012.

43. Zhu Jiangang. "Editor's notes" (卷首语), Philanthropic Studies 5, 2015: 1.

44. For example, Wang Ming has a whole section discussing how the bureaucracy of Federation of the handicapped was not effective at all and used the money mainly on the bureaucratic activities themselves rather than helping the handicapped in need, while the CSO (Can You) with the same mission does a much better job and use money more cost effectively. See Wang Ming, *Oral History for NGOs in China, No.2*, Social Sciences Academic Press (China), 2013: 70-78.

45. 国务院机构改革和职能转变方案 (Plan for the Institutional Restructuring of the State Council and Transformation of Functions Thereof), 2013 http://www.lawinfochina.com/display.aspx?lib=law&id=13554&CGid=, last accessed on 24 June, 2017.

46. 关于支持和规范社会组织承接政府购买服务的通知(Notice on the support and normalize the service purchasing from social organizations by the government), the Ministry of Civil Affairs and the Ministry of Finance, 2014 http://www.mca.gov.cn/article/zwgk/fvfg/mjzzgl/201412/20141200744371.shtml, last accessed on 24 June, 2017.

47. 政府购买服务政策文件选编(Selections from the policy documents of government purchasing services), China Financial and Economic Publishing House, 2014.

48. Jiexiu Wang, *Blue Book of Civil Affairs (2014): Annual Report on Development of China's Civil Affairs* (中国民政发展报告) (2014), China Social Publishing House (中国社会出版社), 2014: 129-131.

49. Chinese People's Political Consultative Conference

50. G. Zheng, *Charity Law of the People's Republic of China: Interpretations and Applications* (《中华人民共和国慈善法》解读与应用) People's Publishing (人民出版社) (2016): 327.

51. J. Han, "Foreign NGO's development and governance since the reform and opening era."

52. There is no systematic calculation of the number of foreign NGOs operating in China given many of them operated in the legal grey area. The China development brief had a directory in 2005 of about 200 selected foreign NGOs in China. Scholars also estimate that the number of foreign NGOs in China would be 1,000 to 6,000. See Shawn Shieh, "The Origins of China's New Law on Foreign NGOs," *ChinaFile*, 2017, https://www.chinafile.com/viewpoint/origins-of-chinas-new-law-foreign-ngos.

53. 云南省规范境外非政府组织活动暂行规定(Interim Provisions on the Regulations of Overseas Non-governmental Organizations in Yunan Province), 2009, http://yunnan.mca.gov.cn/article/mzgz/mjzzgl/zcfg/201303/20130300423225.shtml, last accessed on 24 June, 2017.

54. C. Hsu and J. Teets, "Is China's New Overseas NGO Management Law Sounding the Death Knell for Civil Society? Maybe Not," *The Asia-Pacific Journal* 14, no.4, no.3 (2016): 9.

55. 厦门市人民政府关于印发厦门市台湾经贸社团在厦门设立代表机构备案管理办法的通知(Circulation of the People's Government of Xiamen on printing and distributing the administrative measures for the establishment of representative office for Taiwanese economic and trade associations), 2012 http://xxgk.xm.gov.cn/mzj/zfxxgkml/xxgkzcfg/mjzzgl/201209/t20120906_527029.htm, last accessed on 24 June, 2017.

56. Y. Bao and C. Sun, "改革创新，加快推进我国现代社会组织体制建立:专访民政部民间组织管理局局长王建军，" 中国社会报 (2013); W. Xu, "The trial of overseas NGO Administrative Rule in Beijing" (境外NGO管理法北京试行:三类组织可在中关村), *The Beijing News*, (25 May, 2015).

57. S. Shieh, "The Origins of China's New Law on Foreign NGOs," *ChinaFile*. https://www.chinafile.com/viewpoint/origins-of-chinas-new-law-foreign-ngos, last accessed on 24 June, 2017.

58. X. Jia, "China's implementation of the Overseas NGO Management Law," China Development Brief, (March 2017), http://chinadevelopmentbrief.cn/articles/chinas-implementation-of-the-overseas-ngo-management-law/; By 7 May, there are 69 foreign NGO registrations (some NGOs registered at different provinces and therefore are counted more than once). Majority of those registrations are in the development field (37), with some in economic and trade (25), and a few in education/culture (5), Science and technology (1), and think tank (1). See Shawn Shieh's count at http://ngochina.blogspot.hk/2017/05/more-foreign-ngos-register-in-yunnan.html, last accessed on 25 June, 2017.

Chapter 5

1. G. Deng, *Responding to Wenchuan: An analysis of Relief Mechanism in China,* (Peking University Press, 2009), 1.

2. W. Jin, and C. Wang,《已有近130万人次志愿者参加汶川地震救灾》(Close to 1.3 million volunteers have participated in Wenchuan earthquake relief), Xinhua News Agency, 25 February, 2008, http://www.yn.xinhuanet.com/topic/2008-06 /21/content_13605664.htm.

3. This partially overlapped with the difference-in-difference design in data collection from Southern Sichuan, since this was the original design.

4. USGS, "The Modified Mercalli Intensity Scale," http://earthquake.usgs.gov /learn/topics/mercalli.php

5. USGS, "The Modified Mercalli Intensity Scale: Abbreviated description of the levels of Modified Mercalli Intensity," http://earthquake.usgs.gov/learn/topi cs/mercalli.php.

6. Earthquake Intensity data is not available consistently when under MMI 4.0 thus making it difficult to construct a continuous variable. Thus, the compromise is treating all MMI below 4.0 as one category. Also, the actual effect of the earthquake might be slightly different from the MMI indicator, making a binary variable a safer option to indicate whether there is meaningful earthquake or not, even some information is lost during this recoding.

7. The treatment is the interaction term: date*ludian

8. Interview 09SO22.

9. Interviews 12SJ34 and 12SI36.

10. Interview 145SO01.

11. Interview 15SGO13.

12. Here in this dissertation, being effective means being able to produce results through operating projects.

13. Interview 12SJ34.

14. Interview 12SJ34.

15. Interview 13SN41.

16. Interview 12SJ34.

17. Interview 15SJ17.

18. Interview 12SI38.

19. Interview 13SB35.

20. Interview 14SGO03.

21. Interview 15SGO09.

22. Interview 09SF11.

23. Interview 13SN25.

24. Interview 12SI06.

25. Interview 13SB35.

26. M.W. Foley and B. Edwards, "Civil society and social capital beyond Putnam." *American Behavioral Scientist* 42 (1998): 124-139.

27. X. Zhao, *Annual Report on China's Development of the Governance at the Grass-Roots level (2015),* (Guangzhou: Guangdong Renmin Chubanshe, 2015,) 8.

28. X. Zhao, *Annual Report on China's Development of the Governance at the Grass-Roots level (2015)*, 14.

29. X. Zhao, *Annual Report on China's Development of the Governance at the Grass-Roots level (2015)*, 67.

30. "'Guidelines for the Participation of Social Organizations in the Declaration and Evaluation of Social Service Projects' is published," August 13, 2014, http://www.gongyishibao.com/html/gongyizixun/6844.html.

31. Department of Civil Affairs of Sichuan Province, "Suining published the 'Guidelines and Standards for the Government to Purchase Social Organizations' Home Care Services'," Sept. 5, 2014, https://mzt.sc.gov.cn/Article/Detail?id=1 4745.

32. Department of Civil Affairs of Sichuan Province, "Announcement: Department of Civil Affairs of Sichuan Province Solicit Suggestions from the Public on 'Opinions of Sichuan People's Government regarding Promoting the Healthy Development of Philanthropy (Draft for comments)'," June 3, 2015, https://mzt .sc.gov.cn/Article/Detail?id=15658.

Chapter 6

1. J. Edwards, "All the countries where someone managed to shut down the entire internet—and why they did it," *Business Insider*, June 30, 2019, https:// www.businessinsider.com/countries-internet-shutdown-statistics-2019-6, last accessed on August 22, 2019.

2. N. McCarthy, "The Countries Shutting Down The Internet The Most [Infographic]," *Forbes*, August 28, 2018, https://www.forbes.com/sites/niallmccarthy /2018/08/28/the-countries-shutting-down-the-internet-the-most-infographic/ #46a2acbf1294, last accessed on August 22, 2019.

3. "Facebook removes 652 fake accounts and pages meant to influence world politics," *The Guardian*, August 21, 2018, https://www.theguardian.com/technol ogy/2018/aug/21/facebook-pages-accounts-removed-russia-iran, last accessed on August 22, 2019.

4. C. Lima, "Facebook wades deeper into censorship debates as it bans 'dangerous' accounts," *Politico*, May 2, 2019, https://www.politico.com/story/2019 /05/02/facebook-bans-far-right-alex-jones-1299247, last accessed on August 22, 2019.

5. Daniela Stockmann and Mary Gallagher, "Remote Control: How the Media Sustain Authoritarian Rule in China," *Comparative Political Studies* 44, no. 4 (2011): 436–67, https://doi.10.1177/0010414010394773; Blake Miller, "Automated Detection of Chinese Government astroturfing Using Network and Social Metadata," working paper (Ann Arbor: University of Michigan, 2016).

6. J. Schlæger and M. Jiang, "Official microblogging and social management by local governments in China," *China Information* 28, no. 2 (2014):189–213.

7. M. K. Dimitrov, "Internal Government Assessments of the Quality of Governance in China," *Studies in Comparative International Development* 50, no. 1 (2015): 50–72.

8. S. Wang, M.J. Paul, and M. Dredze, "Social Media as a Sensor of Air Quality and Public Response in China," *Journal of Medical Internet Research* 17, no.3 (March 2015): e22.

9. B. Qin, D. Stromberg, and Y. Wu, "Why Does China Allow Freer Social Media? Protests versus Surveillance and Propaganda," *Journal of Economic Perspectives* 31, no.1 (Winter 2017): 117–140.

10. K.D. Hyun and J. Kim, "The role of new media in sustaining the status quo: online political expression, nationalism, and system support in China," *Information, Communication & Society* 18, no. 7 (2015): 766–781.

11. P. Lorentzen, "China's Strategic Censorship," *American Journal of Political Science* 58, no. 2 (2014): 402–414.

12. Kimberly J. Morgan and Ann Shola Orloff, "Introduction: The Many Hands of the State," Buffett Center for International and Comparative Studies Working Paper no. 14–001 (Northwestern University, December 2014), https://doi.org/10.13140/RG.2.1.2678.6323.

13. Hong Li and Guang Li, "Interactive Development of Government Purchase Service Reform and Social Organizations: An Analysis Based on Motive Mechanism and Determinants," *Journal of Beijing University of Aeronautics & Astronautics, Social Sciences Edition* 33, no. 1 (2020): 84; Chunfu Guo and Zhenchao Zhou, "Practice of Group Organization Participation in Government Public Service Purchase: A Case Study of Chongqing," *Journal of Beijing University of Aeronautics & Astronautics, Social Sciences Edition* 30, no. 4 (2017): 18; Rachel Swaner, "Trust Matters: Enhancing Government Legitimacy through Participatory Budgeting," *New Political Science* 39, no. 1 (2017): 95–108; José M. Alonso, Judith Clifton, and Daniel Díaz-Fuentes, "The Impact of Government Outsourcing on Public Spending: Evidence from European Union Countries," *Journal of Policy Modeling* 39, no. 2 (2017): 333–348.

14. Taiyi Sun, "Earthquakes and the Typologies of State-CSO Relations in China: A Dynamic Framework," *China Information* 31, no. 3 (2017): 304–26, https://doi.org/10.1177/0920203X17720337; also see Adil Najam, "The Four-C's of Third Sector-Government Relations: Cooperation, Confrontation, Complementarity, and Co-optation," *Nonprofit Management & Leadership* 10, no. 4 (2000): 375–396.

15. Martin K. Dimitrov, ed., *Why Communism Did Not Collapse: Understanding Authoritarian Regime Resilience in Asia and Europe* (Cambridge: Cambridge University Press, 2013).

16. A. Rauchfleisch, "Multiple public spheres of Weibo: a typology of forms and potentials of online public spheres in China," *Information, Communication & Society* 18, no. 2, (2015): 139–155.

17. W. R. Hobbs and M.E. Roberts, "How Sudden Censorship Can Increase Access to Information," *American Political Science Review* 112, no. 3 (2018): 621–636.

18. S. Lee, "Surviving Online Censorship in China: Three Satirical Tactics and their Impact," *The China Quarterly* 228, (December 2016): 1061–1080.

19. K. Fu, C. Chan, and M. Chau, "Assessing Censorship on Microblogs in China: Discriminatory Keyword Analysis and the Real-Name Registration Policy," *IEEE Internet Computing* 17, no. 3 (2013):42–50.

20. C. Hiruncharoenvate, "Understanding and circumventing censorship on Chinese social media," dissertation from Georgia Tech (2017).

21. G. King, J. Pan, and M.E. Roberts, "How Censorship in China Allows Government Criticism but Silences Collective Expression," *American Political Science Review* (May 2013): 1–18.

22. S. Shirk, *China: Fragile Superpower: How China's Internal Politics Could Derail Its Peaceful Rise* (New York: Oxford University Press, 2007); Also see M. Whyte, *Myth of the Social Volcano: Perceptions of Inequality and Distributive Injustice in Contemporary China* (Stanford, CA: Stanford University Press, 2010).

23. Min Tang and Huhe Narisong, "Alternative Framing: The Effect of the Internet on Political Support in Authoritarian China," *International Political Science Review* 35, no. 5 (2013): 559–576, https://doi.org/ 10.1177/0192512113501971.

24. Q. Tai, "China's Media Censorship: A Dynamic and Diversified Regime," *Journal of East Asian Studies*, 14, no. 2, (August 2014): 185–210.

25. J. Knockel, "Measuring Decentralization of Chinese Censorship in Three Industry Segments," dissertation from the University of New Mexico (2018), https://digitalrepository.unm.edu/cs_etds/90.

26. D. Wang and G. Mark, "Internet Censorship in China: Examining User Awareness and Attitudes," *ACM Transactions on Computer-Human Interaction (TOCHI)* 22, no. 6, Article no. 31 (December 2015).

27. Adrian Rauchfleisch, "Multiple Public Spheres of Weibo: A Typology of Forms and Potentials of Online Public Spheres in China," *Information, Communication & Society* 18, no. 2 (2015): 139–155, https://doi.org/10.1080/1369118X.2014 .940364; William Hobbs and Margaret Roberts, "Sudden Censorship Can Increase Access to Information," *American Political Science Review* 112, no. 3 (2018): 621–36, https://doi.org/ 10.1017/S0003055418000084.

28. Cheung, Anne SY, and Z. H. A. O. Yun. "An Overview of Internet Regulation in China." *University of Hong Kong Faculty of Law Research Paper* 2013/040 (2013).

29. Guoguang, Wu. "In the name of good governance: E-government, Internet pornography and political censorship in China." In *China's Information and Communications Technology Revolution*, 80–97. Routledge, 2009.

30. Zhao, Jinqiu. "A snapshot of Internet regulation in contemporary China: Censorship, profitability and responsibility." *From Early Tang Court Debates to China's Peaceful Rise* (2009): 141–151.

31. Chu, Cho-Wen. "Censorship or protectionism? reassessing china's regulation of internet industry." *International Journal of Social Science and Humanity* 7, no. 1 (2017): 28.

32. Polyakova, Alina, and Chris Meserole. "Exporting digital authoritarianism: The Russian and Chinese models." *Policy Brief, Democracy and Disorder Series (Washington, DC: Brookings, 2019)* (2019): 1–22.

33. Xuecan, Wu, and Lin Biao. "Turning Everyone into a Censor: The Chinese Communist Party's All-Directional Control over the Media." *Washington: US-China Economic and security review commission, USCC* (2002).

34. J. Knockel, "Measuring Decentralization of Chinese Censorship in Three Industry Segments."

35. Jing Ma, "On the New Media to Challenge for New Young Teachers in Professional Dedication and Countermeasures at Universities," *Studies in Sociology of Science* 6, no.3, (2015): 8–12.

36. Alexandr G. Asmolov and Gregory A. Asmolov, "From We-Media to I-Media: Identity Transformations In the virtual World," *Psychology in Russia: State of the Art* 2, (2009): 101.

37. Professor Quansheng Zhao of American University's School of International Service serves as the chief editor of the publication while I served as the executive editor.

38. Interview 19GO01.

39. Interview 19GO02.

40. Interview 19GO01.

41. Interview 19GO03.

42. See: G. King, J. Pan, and M.E. Roberts, "How Censorship in China Allows Government Criticism but Silences Collective Expression;" D. Bamman, B. O'Connor, and N. Smith, "Censorship and Deletion Practices in Chinese Social Media," *First Monday* 17, no.3–5, (2012).

43. X. Wang, *Social Media in Industrial China*, (London: UCL Press, 2016), 52.

44. Interview 19GO01.

45. Interview 19GO02.

46. X. Ren, "ZuiQianYan: Guojia Wangxingongzuo Chensilu," (最前沿：国家网信工作沉思录), *Xinhua publishing House*, (November 2018), 12.

47. Yuan Li, "The Great Firewall Cracked, Briefly. A People Shined Through," *the New York Times*, February 9, 2021.

48. Xinlang Weibo (Sina Weibo), Wikipedia, https://zh.wikipedia.org/wiki/%E6%96%B0%E6%B5%AA%E5%BE%AE%E5%8D%9A#targetText%3D%E5%8E%86%E5%8F%B2%2C%E2%80%9D%E5%8A%9F%E8%83%BD%EF%BC%8C%E4%BE%9B%E7%94%A8%E6%88%B7%E4%BA%A4%E6%B5%81%E3%80%82, accessed on August 16, 2019.

49. Weixin Gongzhong Pingtai (WeChat Public Platform), Baidu Baike, https://baike.baidu.com/item/%E5%BE%AE%E4%BF%A1%E5%85%AC%E4%BC%97%E5%B9%B3%E5%8F%B0, accessed on August 16, 2019; Jin Ri Tou Tiao, Baidu Baike, https://baike.baidu.com/item/%E4%BB%8A%E6%97%A5%E5%A4%B4%E6%9D%A1/4169373, accessed on December 24, 2021.

50. X. Ren, "ZuiQianYan: Guojia Wangxingongzuo Chensilu," 11.

51. X. Ren, "ZuiQianYan: Guojia Wangxingongzuo Chensilu," 48.

52. Interview 18WSO03.

53. Interview 19GO02.

54. "The seventh census of Zhejiang Province," Zhejiang Provincial Bureau of Statistics, May 13, 2021, last accessed December 26, 2021 http://tjj.zj.gov.cn/art /2021/5/13/art_1229129205_4632764.html.

55. Zhejiang Online Service Platform, "Disclosure of administrative punishment results," The People's Government of Zhejiang Province, last accessed December 26, 2021 https://www.zjzwfw.gov.cn/zjzw/punish/frontpunish/show admins.do?webId=1.

56. See a discussion of state differentiation of CSOs in T. Sun "Deliberate Differentiation for Outsourcing Responsibilities: The Logic of China's Behavior toward Civil Society Organizations," *China Quarterly*, (2019), 1–26.

57. Interview 19GO01.

58. X. Ren, "ZuiQianYan: Guojia Wangxingongzuo Chensilu," 46.

59. Miles Kenyon, "WeChat Surveillance Explained," University of Toronto Citizen Lab, May 7, 2020, https://citizenlab.ca/2020/05/wechat-surveillance-exp lained/.

60. Viola Zhou, "Chinese State Media Want People to Stop Using Internet Slang," *Vice World News*, September 8, 2021.

61. Jason Lee, "Chinese content platforms pledge self-discipline—industry group," *Reuters*, September 11, 2021.

62. Thomas Peter, "China targets online platforms in quest to 'clean up' internet," *Reuters*, December 23, 2021.

63. Liza Lin, "China Fines Weibo for Spreading 'Illegal Information'," *The Wall Street Journal*, December 14, 2021.

64. Tianlei Huang and Nicholas R. Lardy, "China's tech crackdown affects only a small share of its digital economy and total GDP," *PIIE*, October 20, 2021.

65. X. Ren, "ZuiQianYan: Guojia Wangxingongzuo Chensilu," 27.

66. K.D. Hyun and J. Kim, "The role of new media in sustaining the status quo: online political expression, nationalism, and system support in China."

67. "Regulations for the Protection of Computer Information systems Safety in the People's Republic of China," (中华人民共和国计算机信息系统安全保护条例), State Council of People's Republic of China, (1994), https://baike.baidu.com/it em/中华人民共和国计算机信息系统安全保护条例, last accessed on August 16, 2019; also see article 12 of the "People's Police Law of the People's Republic of China," (中华人民共和国人民警察法) National People's Congress, (1995), https:// baike.baidu.com/item/%E7%BD%91%E7%BB%9C%E8%AD%A6%E5%AF%9F /861144?fromtitle=%E7%BD%91%E8%AD%A6&fromid=10819437, last accessed on August 16, 2019.

68. "Temporary Decree on the Management of Computer Information Network International Connectivity in the People's Republic of China," (中华人民共 和国计算机信息网络国际联网管理暂行规定实施办法) State Council of People's Republic of China, (2000), http://www.law-lib.com/law/law_view.asp?id=1 3818, last accessed on August 16, 2019. The law was updated and revised in 2011.

69. "Online police," Wikipedia, https://zh.wikipedia.org/wiki/网络警察, last accessed on August 16, 2019.

70. "Interim Provisions on the Administration of News Service on Internet Sites," (互联网站登载新闻业务管理暂行规定) News office of the state council and the Ministry of Information Industry, (November 7, 2000), http://www.law-lib.com/law/law_view.asp?id=15211, last accessed on August 16, 2019. The formal version of the law was passed the next year and the law was updated in 2017.

71. "Internet Information Service Management Measures in the People's Republic of China," (互联网信息服务管理办法 (2011修订)) State Council, (January 8, 2011), https://www.pkulaw.com/chl/7d533bd9db7539e4bdfb.html, last accessed on August 16, 2019.

72. "Interpretation of the Supreme People's Court Supreme People's Procuratorate on Several Issues Concerning the Application of Laws in the Use of Information Network to Implement Criminal Cases," (最高人民法院最高人民检察院关于办理利用信息网络实施诽谤等刑事案件适用法律若干问题的解释) the Supreme People's Court Supreme People's Procuratorate, (September 10, 2013), http://www.spp.gov.cn/spp/zdgz/201309/t20130910_62417.shtml, last accessed on August 16, 2019.

73. "Interim Provisions on the Development Management of Public Information Services for Instant Messaging Tools," (即时通讯工具公众信息服务发展管理暂行规定) National Cyberspace Affairs Office, (August 7, 2014), Interim Provisions on the Development Management of Public Information Services for Instant Messaging Tools, last accessed on August 16, 2019.

74. "Internet Information Search Service Management Regulations," (互联网信息搜索服务管理规定), Cyberspace Affairs Office, (June 25, 2016), http://www.cac.gov.cn/2016-06/25/c_1119109085.htm, last accessed on August 16, 2019.

75. "People's Republic of China Cyber Security Law," (中华人民共和国网络安全法), National People's Congress, (November 7, 2016), http://www.xinhuanet.com/politics/2016-11/07/c_1119867015.htm, last accessed on August 16, 2019.

76. "Internet News Information Service Management Regulations," (互联网新闻信息服务管理规定), Cyberspace Affairs Office, (June 1, 2017), https://www.cac.gov.cn/2017-05/02/c_1120902760.htm, last accessed on August 16, 2019.

77. "Internet News Information Service License Management Regulations" (互联网新闻信息服务许可管理实施细则), Cyberspace Affairs Office, (June 1, 2017), www.cac.gov.cn/2017-05/22/c_1121015789.htm, last accessed on August 16, 2019.

78. "Interim Provisions on the Development Management of Public Information Services for Instant Messaging Tools," (即时通讯工具公众信息服务发展管理暂行规定), Cyberspace Affairs Office, (August 7, 2017), http://www.piyao.org.cn/2017-08/07/c_129666339.htm, last accessed on August 16, 2019.

79. "Internet Post Comment Service Management Regulations," (互联网跟帖评论服务管理规定), Cyberspace Affairs Office, (August 25, 2017), https://www.cac.gov.cn/2017-08/25/c_1121541842.htm, last accessed on August 16, 2019.

80. "Internet Forum Community Service Management Regulations," (互联网论坛社区服务管理规定), (August 25, 2017), https://www.cac.gov.cn/2017-08/25/c_1121541921.htm, last accessed on August 16, 2019.

81. "Internet Group Information Service Management Regulations," (互联网群组信息服务管理规定), (September 7, 2017), https://www.cac.gov.cn/2017-09/07/c_1121623889.htm, last accessed on August 16, 2019.

82. "Internet User Public Account Information Service Management Regulations," (互联网用户公众账号信息服务管理规定), (September 7, 2019), https://www.cac.gov.cn/2017-09/07/c_1121624269.htm, last accessed on August 16, 2019.

83. "Internet News Information Service Unit Content Management Practitioners Management Measures," (互联网新闻信息服务单位内容管理从业人员管理办法), (October 30, 2017), http://www.cac.gov.cn/2017-10/30/c_1121877917.htm, last accessed on August 16, 2019.

84. "Notice of Public Comment for the State Internet Information Office's 'Cyber Security Review Measures (Revised Draft for Solicitation of Comments)'," *Cyberspace Administration of China*, July 10, 2021.

85. China Law Translate, "Standards and Detailed Rules for the Review of Online Short Video Content (2021)," *China Network Audiovisual Program Service Association*, December, 2021.

86. See similar phenomenon on the Chinese state's treatment of CSOs in T. Sun, "Earthquakes and the Typologies of State-CSO Relations in China: A Dynamic Framework," *China Information* 31 no. 3, (November 2017), 304–326.

87. J. Edwards, "All the countries where someone managed to shut down the entire internet—and why they did it," Business Insider, (Jun. 30, 2019), https://www.businessinsider.com/countries-internet-shutdown-statistics-2019-6, last accessed on August 22, 2019.

88. Y. Hao, "People's stock price triples, mainly due to this new service," *Blue whale Finance*, (April 8, 2019), <http://www.sohu.com/a/306599320_250147>, last accessed on August 16, 2019.

89. Z. Lei, "Ji'Nan, the new capital of online censorship," Journalists' Station, (March 25, 2019), https://chinadigitaltimes.net/chinese/2019/03/%E8%AE%B0%E8%80%85%E7%AB%99%E4%B8%A8%E6%B5%8E%E5%8D%97%EF%BC%8C%E6%96%B0%E7%9A%84%E4%BA%92%E8%81%94%E7%BD%91%E5%AE%A1%E6%A0%B8%E4%B9%8B%E9%83%BD/, last accessed on August 16, 2019.

90. Shen Lu, "Apple exports PRC censorship to Hong Kong and Taiwan, report says," *Protocol*, August 2021.

91. X. Ren, "ZuiQianYan: Guojia Wangxingongzuo Chensilu," (最前沿：国家网信工作沉思录), *Xinhua publishing House*, (November 2018), p.70.

92. *Global China* was banned for a week in September, 2020.

Chapter 7

1. O'Brien, J. Kevin and Lianjiang Li (2006). *Rightful Resistance in Rural China* (Cambridge: Cambridge University Press).

2. Chan, Anita (2001). *China's Workers under Assault: The Exploitation of Labor in a Globalizing Economy*, Armonk, NY: Sharpe; Chen, Feng (2003). "Between the State and Labour: The Conflict of Chinese Trade Unions' Double Identity in Mar-

ket Reform," *China Quarterly*, no. 176: 1006–28; O'Brien, J. Kevin and Lianjiang Li (2004). "Suing the Local State: Administrative Litigation in Rural China," *China Journal*, no. 51: 75–96; Gallagher, Mary Elizabeth (2005). *Contagious Capitalism: Globalization and the Politics of Labor in China*, Princeton: Princeton University Press; Lee, Ching Kwan (2007). *Against the Law: Labor Protests in China's Rustbelt and Sunbelt*, Berkeley: University of California Press; Friedman, Eli (2014). *Insurgency Trap: Labor Politics in Postsocialist China*, Ithaca, NY: Cornell University Press; Gallagher, Mary Elizabeth (2014). "China's Workers Movement and the End of the Rapid-Growth Era," *Daedalus* 143, no. 2: 81–95; Fu, Diana and Greg Distelhorst (2017). "Grassroots Participation and Repression under Hu Jintao and Xi Jinping," *The China Journal*, no.79.

3. Pei, Minxin (1997). "Citizens v. Manandarins: Administrative Litigation in China," *China Quarterly*, no. 152; O'Brien, J. Kevin and Rachel E. Stern (2008). "Studying Contention in Contemporary China," in *Popular Protest in China*, ed. Kevin J. O'Brien, Cambridge, MA: Harvard University Press; Fu, Hualing and Richard Cullen (2008). "Weiquan (Rights Protection) Lawyering in an Authoritarian State: Building a Culture of Public-Interest Lawyering," *China Journal*, no. 59: 111–27; Pils, Eva (2014). *China's Human Rights Lawyers: Advocacy and Resistance*, New York: Routledge; Liu, Sida (2016). "The Changing Roles of Lawyers in China: State bureaucrats, Market Brokers, and Political Activists," in *The New Legal Realism: Studying Law Globally*, ed. Heinz Klug and Sally Engle Merry, (Cambridge: Cambridge University Press), 180–98.

4. Greenhalgh, Susan, "Fresh Winds in Beijing: Chinese Feminists Speak Out on the One-child Policy and Women's Lives," *Signs: Journal of Women in Culture and Society* 26, no. 3 (2001): 847–88; Shen, Yifei "Feminism in China: An Analysis of Advocates, Debates, and Strategies," (Shanghai: Friedrich Eberto Stiftung, 2016).

5. Hassid, Jonathan, "China's Contentious Journalists: Reconceptualizing the Media," *Problems of Post-communism* 55, no. 4 (2008): 52–61.

6. Mertha, Andrew, *China's Water Warriors: Citizen Action and Policy Change*, (Ithaca, NY: Cornell University Press), 2008; Steinhardt, Christoph H. and Fengshi Wu (2016). "In the Name of the Public: Environmental Protest and the Changing Landscape of Popular Contention in China," *China Journal*, no. 75: 61–82.

7. Fewsmith, Joseph. *The Logic and Limits of Political Reform in China*, (Cambridge: Cambridge University Press), 2013.

8. Vala, Carsten T, "Protestant Christianity and Civil Society in Authoritarian China: The Impact of Official Churches and Unregistered Urban Churches on Civil Society Development in the 2000s," *China Perspectives* 3, no. 43 (2012); Koesel, Karrie (2014). *Religion and Authoritarianism: Cooperation, Conflict, and the Consequences* (Cambridge: Cambridge University Press).

9. Yuen, Samson, "Friend or Foe? The Diminishing Space of China's Civil Society," *China Perspectives*, no.3 (2015): 51–56; Loeb, Ketty, "A Grim Outlook for China's Civil Society in the Wake of the 19th Party Congress," *Asia Pacific Bulletin*, Number 402, October 26, 2017.

10. Fu, Diana and Greg Distelhorst, "Grassroots Participation and Repression

under Hu Jintao and Xi Jinping," *The China Journal*, no. 79 (2017); Sun, Taiyi. "Deliberate Differentiation by the Chinese State: Outsourcing Responsibility for Governance." *The China Quarterly* 240 (2019): 880–905.

11. Chen, Feng, "Subsistence Crises, Managerial Corruption, and Labour Protests in China," *China Journal*, no.44 (2002): 41–63; Hurst, William and Kevin J. O'Brien, "China's Contentious Pensioners," *The China Quarterly*, no.170 (2012): 345–60; Chen, Feng, "Between the State and Labour: The Conflict of Chinese Trade Unions' Double Identity in Market Reform," *China Quarterly*, no. 176 (2003): 1006–28; Lee, Ching Kwan, *Against the Law: Labor Protests in China's Rustbelt and Sunbelt*, (Berkeley: University of California Press, 2007).

12. The updated rules can be found at 公安机关处置群体性事件规定, (Gonganjiguan Chuzhi Quntixing Shijian Guiding), http://minli.org/z/201502/184.html, 2015.

13. Yu, Jianrong "Types and Features of Mass Incidents in China Today," 2010, (当前我国群体性事件的类型与特征), http://www.aisixiang.com/data/32027.html, accessed on April 2, 2018.

14. Tong Yanqi, and Shaohua Lei "Large-scale Mass Incidents in China," *East Asian Policy, (2010)*.

15. To get a sense of the scale for the frequency of major "mass incidents" in China, estimates point to around 90,000 incidents in 2006 and 180,000 incidents in 2010 and increasing every year. See Will Freeman, "The Accuracy of China's 'Mass Incidents,'" *Financial Times*, March 2, 2010, https://www.ft.com/content/9ee6fa64-25b5-11df-9bd3-00144feab49a, accessed on 31 March 2018); also see Zhu Zhaogen, *"Xunzhao Zhongguo Zhenggai de JinYaoshi"* (In search for the "Golden Key" to China's Political Reform), *Lianhe Zaobao*, October 14, 2010, http://www.zaobao.com.sg/special/report/politic/cnpol/story20101014-138344, accessed on 31 March 2018; for an overview of large-scale mass incidents in China, see: Tong Yanqi and Lei Shaohua, "Large-scale Mass Incidents in China," *East Asian Policy*, (2010); for an overview of patterns of protests in China at the provincial level, see: Victor Cheung Yin Chan, Jeremy Backstrom, and T. David Mason, "Patterns of Protest in the People's Republic of China: A Provincial Level Analysis," *Asian Affairs: An American Review*, 2014, 41: 91–107.

16. Unger, Jonathan and Anita Chan (1995). "China, Corporatism and the East Asian Model," *Australian Journal of Chinese Affairs* 33: 29–53.

17. Fu, Diana and Greg Distelhorst (2017). "Grassroots Participation and Repression under Hu Jintao and Xi Jinping," *The China Journal*, no.79.

18. O'Brien, J. Kevin and Lianjiang Li, *Rightful Resistance in Rural China*, (Cambridge: Cambridge University Press, 2006); Lee, Ching Kwan, *Against the Law: Labor Protests in China's Rustbelt and Sunbelt*, (Berkeley: University of California Press, 2007); Fu, Diana, *Mobilizing without the Masses: Control and Contention in China*, (Cambridge: Cambridge University Press, 2007).

19. Mertha, Andrew, *China's Water Warriors: Citizen Action and Policy Change*, (Ithaca, NY: Cornell University Press, 2008).

20. Chen, Xi, *Social Protest and Contentious Authoritarianism in China*, (Cambridge: Cambridge University Press, 2012).

21. Teets, Jessica C., Civil Society under Authoritarianism: The China Model, (Cambridge: Cambridge University Press, 2014).

22. Fu and Distelhorst, 2017.

23. Nnajiofor, Peterson, "The New Sharing Economy: Demise of Social and Labor Movements?" *IDEA Research Center*, (2017).

24. Robertson, Graeme "Protesting Putinism: The Election Protests of 2011–2012 in Broader Perspective," *Problems of Post-Communism* 60, no. 2 (2013): 11–23.

25. Dzhygyr, Yuriy, "Why did AutoMaidan become the frontline of Ukraine's civil protest?" Euromaidan Pres, 2013, http://euromaidanpress.com/2014/01/29 /why-auto-maidan-became-the-frontline-of-ukraines-civil-protest/,   accessed April 9, 2018.

26. Collier, Ruth Berins "Labor Platforms and Gig Work: The Failure to Regulate," (Working Paper, University of California Berkeley, 2017).

27. Gobel, Christian and Lynette H. Ong, "Social Unrest in China," Europe China Research and Advice Network, (2012).

28. Horwitz, Josh, "In China, you can now hail a taxi and pay the driver on WeChat." *Tech in Asia*, 2014, https://www.techinasia.com/china-hail-taxi-pay-dr iver-WeChat, accessed April 2, 2018.

29. Gao, Jianghong and Duan Qianqian, "New rules from the ministry of transport on taxi reform: regulate Internet-enabled hires," *21st Century Business Herald*, Guangzhou, October 12, 2015. http://m.21jingji.com/article/20151012/ herald/a8492406309c0d50f70ae03ca7edcdec.html, accessed April 2, 2018 (in Chinese).

30. See China Information Center, *The Annual Report of the Development of China's Sharing Economy*, 2018, http://www.sic.gov.cn/archiver/SIC/UpFile/Files/De fault/20180320144901006637.pdf, accessed April 3 2018.

31. Svensson, Marina, "WeChat: The first Chinese social media product with a global appeal," *Digital China*, 2013, https://digitalchina.blogg.lu.se/WeChat-the -first-chinese-social-media-product-with-a-global-appeal/. accessed April 2, 2018.

32. Tu, Fangjing, "WeChat and civil society in China," *Communication and the Public* I no. 3 (2016): 343–350.

33. Yang, Guobing, *The Power of the Internet in China*, (New York: Columbia University Press, 2011); Tong, Jingrong and Landong Zuo. 'Weibo communication and government legitimacy in China: a computer-assisted analysis of Weibo,' *The Internet, Social Networks and Civic Engagement in Chinese Societies, Information, Communication & Society* 17, no. 1 (2014): 66–85.

34. "Road transportation Regulations of People's Republic of China," (中华人民共和国道路运输条例), The Central People's Government of the People's Republic of China, April 30, 2004, see http://www.gov.cn/zwgk/2005-05/23/content_216 .htm, accessed on October 20, 2019.

35. "Notice on further cracking down on the illegal operation of taxis, such as 'black   cars',"   (关于进一步开展打击"黑车"等非法从事出租汽车经营活动的通知),

General office of the Ministry of Transport, 2013, see http://wcm.mot.gov.cn:90 00/zhuzhan/zhengwugonggao/jiaotongbu/daoluyunshu/201303/t20130318 _1380541.html, accessed on October 20, 2019.

36. "Notice on Promoting the Orderly Development of Taxi Calling Services Such as Mobile Phone Software Calls," (关于促进手机软件召车等出租汽车电召服务有序发展的通知), General office of the Ministry of Transportation, May 26, 2014, see https://baike.baidu.com/item/%E5%85%B3%E4%BA%8E%E4%BF %83%E8%BF%9B%E6%89%8B%E6%9C%BA%E8%BD%AF%E4%BB%B6%E5 %8F%AC%E8%BD%A6%E7%AD%89%E5%87%BA%E7%A7%9F%E6%B1%BD %E8%BD%A6%E7%94%B5%E5%8F%AC%E6%9C%8D%E5%8A%A1%E6%9C %89%E5%BA%8F%E5%8F%91%E5%B1%95%E7%9A%84%E9%80%9A%E7 %9F%A5%EF%BC%88%E5%BE%81%E6%B1%82%E6%84%8F%E8%A7%81 %E7%A8%BF%EF%BC%89, accessed on October 20, 2019.

37. "Taxi management service regulations," (出租汽车经营服务管理规定), The Ministry of Transportation of China, September 30, 2014, see https://baike.baidu .com/item/%E5%87%BA%E7%A7%9F%E6%B1%BD%E8%BD%A6%E7%BB %8F%E8%90%A5%E6%9C%8D%E5%8A%A1%E7%AE%A1%E7%90%86%E8 %A7%84%E5%AE%9A, accessed on October 20, 2019.

38. "Guiding Opinion on Deepening Reform and Further Promoting the Healthy Development of the Taxi Industry," (关于深化改革进一步推进出租汽车行业健康发展的指导意见), The Ministry of Transportation of China, 2015, see http://www.xinhuanet.com/auto/2015-10/10/c_128304499.htm, accessed on April 2, 2018.

39. "Interim Measures for the Management of Online Booking of Taxi Business Services," (网络预约出租汽车经营服务管理暂行办法), The Ministry of Transportation of China, 2016, see http://www.chinanews.com/cj/2015/10-10/7562706. shtml, accessed on April 2, 2018.

40. "Notice on the workflow regarding the appointment of taxi operator to apply for online service capability identification," (关于网络预约出租汽车经营者申请线上服务能力认定工作流程的通知), The Ministry of transportation, November 4, 2016.

41. "Notice of the Ministry of Transportation on Reforming the Qualification Examination for Taxi Drivers," (交通运输部关于改革出租汽车驾驶员从业资格考试有关工作的通知), The Ministry of Transportation, September 4, 2017.

42. "Notice on background check and supervision of taxi drivers," (关于切实做好出租汽车驾驶员背景核查与监管等有关工作的通知), The Ministry of Transportation and the Ministry of Public Security, March 4, 2018.

43. For technology requirements, see "The overall technical requirements for the network reservation taxi supervision information interaction platform (temporary)" (网络预约出租汽车监管信息交互平台总体技术要求 (暂行)), The Ministry of Transpiration, December 20, 2016; also for the overall administrative law on this issue, see "Operation management rules of the supervision of online taxi appointment interactive platforms," (网络预约出租汽车监管信息交互平台运行管理办法), The Ministry of Transportation, February 13, 2018.

44. "Notice on Strengthening the Joint Supervision of the online appointed

Taxi Industry," (关于加强网络预约出租汽车行业事中事后联合监管有关工作的通知), The Ministry of Transportation, June 5, 2018.

Chapter 8

1. Keith Bradsher, "China's Economy Shrinks, Ending a Nearly Half-Century of Growth," *The New York Times*, April 16, 2020, https://www.nytimes.com/2020/04/16/business/china-coronavirus-economy.html.

2. Pei, Minxin, "China's Coming Upheaval: Competition, the Coronavirus, and the Weakness of Xi Jinping," *Foreign Affairs* (May/June 2020).

3. Shoebridge, Michael, "Coronavirus and the death of Xi's 'China Dream'," *The Strategist*, February 28, 2020, https://www.aspistrategist.org.au/coronavirus-and-the-death-of-xis-china-dream/.

4. Zhou, Xudong, "National Health Care System Recognition of 34 deceased doctors, including Li Wenliang," Caixin, March 5, 2020, https://china.caixin.com/2020-03-05/101524345.html.

5. Wang, Haiyan, "After the emergency legislation, there is a race against time for anti-epidemic actions," People's Congress of Shanghai, February .9, 2020, http://www.spcsc.sh.cn/n1939/n4514/n7171/n7196/u1ai205987.html.

6. Provincial Department of Justice Legislation Division I, "The Provincial Department of Justice implements a rapid legislative response mechanism and actively carries out research of epidemic prevention and control legislation," Guangdong Department of Justice, June 18, 2021, http://sft.gd.gov.cn/sfw/fzgz/lfghjhjgzqk/content/post_3569995.html.

7. See the multi-author symposium on Chinese democracy in *Journal of Democracy*, 9 (January 1998).

8. See a brief discussion of this literature in chapter 3.

9. Results presented by Daniela Stockmann at the APSA 2019 conference "Authoritarianism 2.0: The Internet and Authoritarian Rule in China."

10. C. Isidore, "The NBA faces a no-win situation in China. Here's what it stands to lose," *CNN*, October 8, 2019, https://www.cnn.com/2019/10/08/business/daryl-morey-tweet-nba-china/index.html, last accessed on January 4, 2020.

11. E.J. Perry, "Studying Chinese politics: Farewell to revolution?" *China Journal*, Vol.57 (2007): 1–22.

Appendix

1. Taiyi Sun, "Importing Civic Engagement into Authoritarian China," in *Teaching Civic Engagement Globally*, Elizabeth Matto, Alison McCartney, Elizabeth A. Bennion, Taiyi Sun, Alasdair Blair, Dawn Whitehead, and Dick Simpson ed. *American Political Science Association* (2021).

2. Robert Putnam, *Making Democracy Work: Civic Traditions in Modern Italy* (Princeton University Press, 1993).

3. Qingguo Jia, "Let the voice of the Chinese people be heard more conveniently and effectively," *Global China*, October 18, 2021, https://mp.weixin.qq.com/s/s_d1DpeXjukjmy0V2osRgA.

4. Taiyi Sun, "Continue to reduce restrictions on individuals and information exchanges is an important step towards the "four self-confidence," *Global China*, December 7, 2021, https://mp.weixin.qq.com/s/yGw3QRwdVH-NoNK5UqeI_A.

Bibliography

Alonso, José M., Judith Clifton, and Daniel Díaz-Fuentes. "The Impact of Government Outsourcing on Public Spending: Evidence from European Union Countries." *Journal of Policy Modeling* 39, no. 2 (2017): 333–348.

Ang, Y. Y. *How China Escaped the Poverty Trap*. Ithaca, NY: Cornell University Press, 2016.

AONGOMPS. "Statistics on Foreign NGO Registration and Official Events Documentation for the First Nine Months of 2017 in China," *Gongyi cishan zhoukan* (Public Welfare and Charity Week), 37. http://mp.weixin.qq.com/s/WtIa kQgj0sNNQ4wkfFRLfw/, accessed July 31, 2019.

Arai, M., and P. S. Thoursie. "Renouncing Personal Names: An Empirical Examination of Surname Change and Earnings." *Journal of Labor Economics* 27, no. 1 (2009): 127–147.

Asmolov, Alexandr G., and Gregory A. Asmolov. "From We-Media to I-Media: Identity Transformations In the virtual World." *Psychology in Russia: State of the Art* 2 (2009): 101.

Azhar, Haris. "The Human Rights Struggle in Indonesia: International Advances, Domestic Deadlocks." *International Journal on Human Rights* 11, no. 20 (2014): 227–234.

Bamman, D., B. O'Connor, and N. Smith. "Censorship and Deletion Practices in Chinese Social Media." *First Monday* 17, nos. 3–5 (2012).

Bao, Y., and C. Sun. "Reform and Innovation, to Accelerate the Establishment of China's Modern Social Organization System: Interview with Wang Jianjun, Director of the Civil Organization Administration of the Ministry of Civil Affairs" (改革创新，加快推进我国现代社会组织体制建立：专访民政部民间组织管理局局长王建军). *China Social News* (中国社会报) (2013).

Baumgartner, F. R., and B. D. Jones. *Agendas and Instability in American Politics*. Chicago: University of Chicago Press, 1993.

Bertrand, M., and S. Mullainathan. "Are Emily and Greg More Employable Than Lakisha and Jamal: A Field Experiment on Labor Market Discrimination." *American Economic Review* 94, no. 4 (2004): 991–1013.

Bian H., Zhenyao Wang, Puqu Wang, and Yan Feng. *Social Management and Inno-*

vation in Disaster Response (灾害应对重的社会管理创新：绵竹市灾后援助社会资源协调平台项目的探索). China: People's Publishing (人民出版社), 2011, 76–77.

Birkland, T. A. *After Disaster: Agenda Setting, Public Policy, and Focusing Events.* Cambridge: Cambridge University Press, 1997.

Blyth, M. *Great Transformations: Economic Ideas and Institutional Change in the Twentieth Century.* New York: Cambridge University Press, 2002.

Boin, A., and P. T. Hart. "The Crisis Approach." In *Handbook of Disaster Research,* edited by H. Rodriguez, E. L. Quarantelli, and R. R. Dynes, 42–54. New York: Springer, 2007.

Boin, R. A., and M. H. P. Otten. "Beyond the Crisis Window for Reform: Some Ramifications for Implementation." *Journal of Contingencies and Crisis Management* 4, no. 3 (1996): 149–161.

Bowers, Jake, Mark Fredrickson, and Ben Hansen 2014. RItools: Randomization Inference Tools R package version.

Bradsher, Keith. "China's Economy Shrinks, Ending a Nearly Half-Century of Growth." *New York Times,* April 16, 2020, https://www.nytimes.com/2020/04/16/business/china-coronavirus-economy.html/.

Brockman, D. E. "Advance Blacks' Interests: A Field Experiment Manipulating Political Incentives." *American Journal of Political Science* 57, no. 3 (2013): 521–536.

Brownlee, Jason. *Authoritarianism in an Age of Democratization.* New York: Cambridge University Press, 2007.

Butler, D. M., and D. E. Brockman. "Do Politicians Racially Discriminate against Constituents: A Field Experiment on State Legislators." *American Journal of Political Science* 55, no. 3 (2011): 463–477.

Cai, H., and D. Treisman. "Did Government Decentralization Cause China's Economic Miracle?" *World Politics* 58, no. 4 (2006): 505–535.

Capano, G. "Understanding Policy Change as an Epistemological and Theoretical Problem." *Journal of Comparative Policy Analysi* 11, no. 1 (2009): 7–31.

Casey, John J. "Comparing Nonprofit Sectors around the World: What Do We Know and How Do We Know It." *Journal of Nonprofit Education and Leadership* 6, no. 3 (2016): 187–223.

Central Government of the People's Republic of China. "Religious Affairs Regulations." November 30, 2004. http://www.gov.cn/gongbao/content/2005/content_63293.htm.

Central Government of the People's Republic of China. "Religious Affairs Regulations." September 7, 2017. http://www.gov.cn/zhengce/content/2017-09/07/content_5223282.htm.

Central People's Government of the People's Republic of China. "Road Transportation Regulations of People's Republic of China" (中华人民共和国道路运输条例). April 30, 2004. http://www.gov.cn/zwgk/2005-05/23/content_216.htm/, accessed October 20, 2019.

Chan, Anita. *China's Workers under Assault: The Exploitation of Labor in a Globalizing Economy.* Armonk, NY: M. E. Sharpe, 2001.

Chan, H. "Crisis Politics in Authoritarian Regimes: How Crises Catalyse Changes under the State-Society Interactive Framework." *Journal of Contingencies and Crisis Management* 21, no. 4 (2013): 200–210.

Chen, Feng. "Between the State and Labour: The Conflict of Chinese Trade Unions' Double Identity in Market Reform." *China Quarterly*, no. 176 (2003): 1006–1028.

Chen, Feng. "Subsistence Crises, Managerial Corruption, and Labour Protests in China." *China Journal*, no. 44 (2002): 41–63.

Chen, Feng, and Xin Xu. "'Active Judiciary': Judicial Dismantling of Workers' Collective Action in China." *China Journal* 67 (2012): 87–108.

Chen, J., J. Pan, and Y. Xu. "Sources of Authoritarian Responsiveness: A Field Experiment in China." *American Journal of Political Science* 60, no. 2 (2016): 383–400.

Chen, X. "China at the Tipping Point? The Rising Cost of Stability." *Journal of Democracy* 24, no. 1 (2013): 57–64.

Chen, Xi. *Social Protest and Contentious Authoritarianism in China*. Cambridge: Cambridge University Press, 2012.

Cheung, Anne S. Y., and Z.H.A.O. Yun. "An Overview of Internet Regulation in China." University of Hong Kong Faculty of Law Research Paper 2013/040 (2013).

Cheung, Victor, Yin Chan, Jeremy Backstrom, and T. David Mason. "Patterns of Protest in the People's Republic of China: A Provincial Level Analysis." *Asian Affairs: An American Review* 41 (2014): 91–107.

China Information Center. *The Annual Report of the Development of China's Sharing Economy, 2018*. http://www.sic.gov.cn/News/79/8860.htm/, accessed June 13, 2022.

China Internet Network Information Center. "The 48th China Statistical Report on Internet Development." August 28, 2021. http://www.gov.cn/xinwen/20 21-08/28/content_5633876.htm/, accessed December 26, 2021.

China Law Translate. "Standards and Detailed Rules for the Review of Online Short Video Content (2021)." *China Network Audiovisual Program Service Association*, December 2021.

"China Removes Crosses from 500 Churches, Religious Staff Afraid to Cause Trouble." *Gospel Herald* (in Chinese), July 10, 2020. https://chinese.gospelher ald.com/articles/28998/20200710/%E4%B8%AD%E5%9C%8B%E6%8B %86%E4%BA%94%E7%99%BE%E6%95%99%E5%A0%82%E5%8D%81 %E5%AD%97%E6%9E%B6-%E5%82%B3%E9%81%93%E6%96%A5%E7 %A5%9E%E8%81%B7%E4%BA%BA%E5%93%A1%E6%80%95%E6%83 %B9%E4%BA%8B%E5%99%A4%E8%81%B2.htm.

Chu, Cho-Wen. "Censorship or Protectionism? Reassessing China's Regulation of the Internet Industry." *International Journal of Social Science and Humanity* 7, no. 1 (2017): 28.

Chuang, Julia. "China's Rural Land Politics: Bureaucratic Absorption and the Muting of Rightful Resistance." *China Quarterly* 219 (2014): 649–669.

厦门市人民政府关于印发厦门市台湾经贸社团在厦门设立代表机构备案管理办法的
    通知 (Circulation of the People's Government of Xiamen on Printing and
    Distributing the Administrative Measures for the Establishment of Represen-
    tative Office for Taiwanese Economic and Trade Associations), 2012. http://
    xxgk.xm.gov.cn/mzj/zfxxgkml/xxgkzcfg/mjzzgl/201209/t20120906_5270
    29.htm/, accessed June 24, 2017.

Collier, Ruth Berins. "Labor Platforms and Gig Work: The Failure to Regulate"
    (working paper, University of California Berkeley, 2017).

"Cross Removal Returns in Zhejiang Province." *Persecution.org*, July 11, 2020.
    https://www.persecution.org/2020/07/11/cross-removal-returns-zhejiang
    -province/.

Deng, G. *Responding to Wenchuan: An Analysis of Relief Mechanism in China*. Peking:
    Peking University Press, 2009.

Deng, Z., and Y. Jing. "The Construction of the Chinese Civil Society." In *State
    and Civil Society: The Chinese Perspective*, edited by Deng Zhenglai, 25–46.
    Shanghai: World Scientific, 2011.

Department of Civil Affairs of Sichuan Province. "Announcement: Department
    of Civil Affairs of Sichuan Province Solicit Suggestions from the Public on
    'Opinions of Sichuan People's Government Regarding Promoting the
    Healthy Development of Philanthropy (Draft for Comments),'" June 3, 2015.
    https://mzt.sc.gov.cn/Article/Detail?id=15658/.

Department of Civil Affairs of Sichuan Province. "Suining Published the 'Guide-
    lines and Standards for the Government to Purchase Social Organizations'
    Home Care Services,'" September 5, 2014. https://mzt.sc.gov.cn/Article/Deta
    il?id=14745/.

Diamond, L. "Thinking about Hybrid Regimes." *Journal of Democracy* 13, no. 2
    (2002): 21–35.

Dickson, B. J. *Red Capitalists in China: The Party, Private Entrepreneurs, and the Pros-
    pects for Political Change*. Cambridge: Cambridge University Press, 2003.

Dickson, B. J. *Wealth into Power: The Communist Party's Embrace of China's Private
    Sector*. Cambridge: Cambridge University Press, 2008.

Dimitrov, M. K. "Internal Government Assessments of the Quality of Governance
    in China." *Studies in Comparative International Development* 50, no. 1 (2015):
    50–72.

Dimitrov, M. K. "What the Party Wanted to Know: Citizen Complaints as a
    'Barometer of Public Opinion' in Communist Bulgaria." *East European Politics
    and Societies and Cultures* 28, no. 2 (2014): 271–295.

Dimitrov, M. K., ed. *Why Communism Did Not Collapse: Understanding Authoritar-
    ian Regime Resilience in Asia and Europe*. New York: Cambridge University
    Press, 2013.

Ding, I. "Invisible Sky, Visible State: Environmental Governance and Political
    Support in China." PhD diss., Harvard University, Graduate School of Arts
    and Sciences, 2016.

Ding, I. "Performative Governance." World Politics 72, no. 4 (2020): 525–556.

Distelhorst, G., and Y. Hou, "Ingroup Bias in Official Behavior: A National Field Experiment in China.," *Quarterly Journal of Political Science* 9, no. 2 (2013): 203–230.

Dzhygyr, Yuriy. "Why Did AutoMaidan Become the Frontline of Ukraine's Civil Protest?" Euromaidan Press, 2013. http://euromaidanpress.com/2014/01/29 /why-auto-maidan-became-the-frontline-of-ukraines-civil-protest/, accessed April 9, 2018.

Edin, M. "State Capacity and Local Agent Control in China: CCP Cadre Management from a Township Perspective." *China Quarterly* 173 (2013): 35–52.

Edwards, J. "All the Countries Where Someone Managed to Shut Down the Entire Internet—And Why They Did It." *Business Insider,* June 30, 2019. https://www .businessinsider.com/countries-internet-shutdown-statistics-2019-6/, accessed August 22, 2019.

汶川地震8年，600亿捐款都花哪里去了 (Eight Years after the Wenchuan Earthquake, Where Did the 60 Billion Donations Go?), *Wenxuecity news,* 2016. http://www.wenxuecity.com/news/2016/05/12/5198847.html/, accessed June 25, 2017.

Feng, Chongyi. "Preserving Stability and Rights Protection: Conflict or Coherence?" *Journal of Current Chinese Affairs* 42, no. 2 (2013): 21–50.

Feng, Emily. "China Is Removing Domes from Mosques as Part of a Push to Make Them More 'Chinese.'" *NPR*, October 24, 2021. https://www.npr.org/2021 /10/24/1047054983/china-muslims-sinicization/.

Fewsmith, J., and A. Nathan. "Authoritarian Resilience Revisited: Joseph Fewsmith with Response from Andrew J. Nathan." *Journal of Contemporary China* 28, no. 116 (2018): 167–179.

Fewsmith, Joseph. *Blurring the Lines: The Logic and Limits of Political Reform in China.* Cambridge: Cambridge University Press, 2013.

Foley, M. W., and B. Edwards. "Civil Society and Social Capital beyond Putnam." *American Behavioral Scientist* 42 (1998): 124–139.

Freeman, Will. "The Accuracy of China's 'Mass Incidents.'" *Financial Times,* March 2, 2010. https://www.ft.com/content/9ee6fa64-25b5-11df-9bd3-001 44feab49a/, accessed March 31, 2018.

Friedman, Eli. *Insurgency Trap: Labor Politics in Postsocialist China.* Ithaca, NY: Cornell University Press, 2014.

Fu, D. "Disguised Collective Action in China." *Comparative Political Studies* 50, no. 4 (2016): 499–527.

Fu, Diana. *Mobilizing without the Masses: Control and Contention in China.* Cambridge: Cambridge University Press, 2007.

Fu, Diana, and Greg Distelhorst. "Grassroots Participation and Repression under Hu Jintao and Xi Jinping." *China Journal*, no. 79 (2017): 100–122.

Fu, Hualing, and Richard Cullen. "Weiquan (Rights Protection) Lawyering in an Authoritarian State: Building a Culture of Public-Interest Lawyering." *China Journal*, no. 59 (2008): 111–127.

Fu, K., C. Chan, and M. Chau. "Assessing Censorship on Microblogs in China:

Discriminatory Keyword Analysis and the Real-Name Registration Policy."
IEEE Internet Computing 17, no. 3 (2013): 42–50.

Gallagher, M. E. "China: The Limits of Civil Society in a Late Leninist State." In
Civil Society and Political Change in Asia, edited by Muthiah Alagappa, 419–
452. Stanford, CA: Stanford University Press, 2004.

Gallagher, Mary Elizabeth. "China's Workers Movement and the End of the
Rapid-Growth Era." *Daedalus* 143, no. 2 (2014): 81–95.

Gallagher, Mary Elizabeth *Contagious Capitalism: Globalization and the Politics of
Labor in China*. Princeton, NJ: Princeton University Press, 2005.

Gandhi, J. *Political Institutions under Dictatorship*. New York: New York University
Press, 2004.

Gandhi, J., and A. Przeworski, "Cooperation, Cooptation, and Rebellion under
Dictatorship." *Economics and Politics* 18, no. 1 (2006): 1–26.

Gao, H., and A. Tyson, "Administrative Reform and the Transfer of Authority to
Social Organizations in China." *China Quarterly* 232 (December 2017):
1050–1069.

Gao, Jianghong, and Duan Qianqian. "New Rules from the Ministry of Transport
on Taxi Reform: Regulate Internet-Enabled Hires." *21st Century Business Herald*, Guangzhou, October 12, 2015. http://m.21jingji.com/article/20151012/
herald/a8492406309c0d50f70ae03ca7edcdec.html/, accessed April 2, 2018
(in Chinese).

Geddes, Barbara. *Paradigms and Sand Castles: Theory Building and Research Design
in Comparative Politics*. Ann Arbor: University of Michigan Press, 2003.

General Office of the Ministry of Transport. "Notice on Further Cracking Down
on the Illegal Operation of Taxis, Such as 'Black Cars'" (关于进一步开展打击"
黑车"等非法从事出租汽车经营活动的通知), 2013. http://wcm.mot.gov.cn:90
00/zhuzhan/zhengwugonggao/jiaotongbu/daoluyunshu/201303/t201303
18_1380541.html/, accessed October 20, 2019.

General Office of the Ministry of Transportation. "Notice on Promoting the
Orderly Development of Taxi Calling Services Such as Mobile Phone Software
Calls" (关于促进手机软件召车等出租汽车电召服务有序发展的通知), May 26,
2014.   https://baike.baidu.com/item/%E5%85%B3%E4%BA%8E%E4%BF
%83%E8%BF%9B%E6%89%8B%E6%9C%BA%E8%BD%AF%E4%BB%B6
%E5%8F%AC%E8%BD%A6%E7%AD%89%E5%87%BA%E7%A7%9F%E6
%B1%BD%E8%BD%A6%E7%94%B5%E5%8F%AC%E6%9C%8D%E5%8A
%A1%E6%9C%89%E5%BA%8F%E5%8F%91%E5%B1%95%E7%9A%84
%E9%80%9A%E7%9F%A5%EF%BC%88%E5%BE%81%E6%B1%82%E6
%84%8F%E8%A7%81%E7%A8%BF%EF%BC%89/, accessed October 20,
2019.

Gernet, J. *A History of Chinese Civilization*, 2nd ed. New York: Cambridge University Press, 1999.

Gerring, J. *Case Study Research: Principles and Practices*. Cambridge: Cambridge
University Press, 2007.

Gerschewski, Johannes. "The Three Pillars of Stability: Legitimation, Repression, and Co-Optation in Autocratic Regimes." *Democratization* 20, no. 1 (2013): 13–38. https://doi.org/10.1080/13510347.2013.738860/.

Gilbert, C. "Politique et complexite: Les crises sans ennemi." In *Colloque International: Le Cadre Theorique de la Gestion des Crises dans les Societes Complexes: Etat de la Question.* Grenoble, France: CRISE.

Gilbert, C. "Studying Disaster: Changes in the Main Conceptual Tools." In *What Is a Disaster?*, edited by E. L. Quarantelli, 3–12. London: Routledge, 1998.

Gleiss, M. S. "How Chinese Labour NGOs Legitimize Their Identity and Voice." *China Information* 28, no. 3 (2014): 362–381.

Gobel, Christian, and Lynette H. Ong. "Social Unrest in China." *Long Briefing, Europe China Research and Advice Network (ECRAN)* (2012), https://euecran.eu/Long%20Papers/ECRAN%20Social%20Unrest%20in%20China_%20Christian%20Gobel%20and%20Lynette%20H.%20Ong.pdf.

Gold, T. B. "The Resurgence of Civil Society in China." *Journal of Democracy* 1, no. 1 (1990): 18–31.

Gongyi, Shangming. http://www.512ngo.org.cn, accessed June 24, 2017.

Gongyi, Xieli. http://www.ixieli.org/, accessed June 24, 2017.

Gould, S. J., and N. Eldredge. "Punctuated Equilibria: The Tempo and Mode of Evolution Reconsidered." *Paleobiology* 3, no. 1 (1977): 115–151.

Greenhalgh, Susan. "Fresh Winds in Beijing: Chinese Feminists Speak Out on the One-Child Policy and Women's Lives." *Signs: Journal of Women in Culture and Society* 26, no. 3 (2001): 847–888.

Guo, Chunfu, and Zhenchao Zhou. "Practice of Group Organization Participation in Government Public Service Purchase: A Case Study of Chongqing." *Journal of Beijing University of Aeronautics and Astronautics, Social Sciences Edition* 30, no. 4 (2017): 18.

Guoguang, Wu. "In the Name of Good Governance: E-Government, Internet Pornography, and Political Censorship in China." In *China's Information and Communications Technology Revolution*, edited by Xioling Zhang and Yongnian Zheng, 80–97. London: Routledge, 2009.

Han, H. "Legal Governance of NGOs in China under Xi Jinping: Reinforcing Divide and Rule." *Asian Journal of Political Science* 26, no. 3 (2018): 390–409.

Han, J. "Foreign NGO's Development and Governance since the Reform and Opening Era" (改革开放以来在华NGO的发展及其治理). In *Blue Book of Philanthropy: Annual Report on China's Philanthropy Development (2013)*, edited by Yang Tuan. China, Social Sciences Academic Press, 2013, 188.

Han, Rongbin. "Cyber Nationalism and Regime Support under Xi Jinping: The Effects of the 2018 Constitutional Revision." *Journal of Contemporary China* (2021): 1–17.

Hao, T. "Benign Violation of the Constitution" (论良性违宪). *Faxue yanjiu* 18, no. 4 (1996).

Hao, Y. "People's Daily's Stock Tripled Mainly Due to This New Service" (人民网股价暴涨三倍，背后最大的"功臣"是这个新业务). *Sohu.com*, April 8, 2019. https://baijiahao.baidu.com/s?id=1630327893388838887&wfr=newsapp/.

Hasmath, R., and J.Y.J. Hsu. "Isomorphic Pressures, Epistemic Communities, and State-NGO Collaboration in China." *China Quarterly* 220 (December 2014): 936–954.

Hassid, Jonathan. "China's Contentious Journalists: Reconceptualizing the Media." *Problems of Post-Communism* 55, no. 4 (2008): 52–61.

He, B., and A. J. Nathan. "China's Changing of the Guard: Authoritarian Resilience." *Journal of Democracy* 14, no. 1 (2003): 6–17.

He, B., and S. Thogersen. "Giving the People a Voice? Experiments with Consultative Authoritarian Institutions in China." *Journal of Contemporary China* 19, no. 66 (2010): 675–692.

He, L. "Deng Zihui: the Pioneer and Trail Blazer of Rural Reform in China" (中国农村变革的先驱和开拓者邓子恢). Party History Lyceum (党史文苑), 2008, no. 23, http://news.ifeng.com/history/zhongguoxiandaishi/detail_2012_11/13/19099395_0.shtml/.

Heilmann, S. "Policy Experimentation in China's Economic Rise." *Study of Comparative and International Development* 43 (2008): 1–26.

Heilmann, S. "Policy-Making through Experimentation: The Formation of a Distinctive Policy Process." In *Mao's Invisible Hand: The Political Foundations of Adaptive Governance in China*, edited by Sebastian Heilmann and Elizabeth J. Perry, 62–101. Cambridge, MA: Harvard University Press, 2011.

Hermann, C. F. "Some Consequences of Crisis Which Limit the Viability of Organizations." *Administrative Science Quarterly* 8, no. 1 (1963): 61–82.

Heurlin, C. *Responsive Authoritarianism in China*. New York: Cambridge University Press, 2016.

Hildebrandt, T. *Social Organization and the Authoritarian State in China*. New York: Cambridge University Press, 2013.

Hiruncharoenvate, C. "Understanding and Circumventing Censorship on Chinese Social Media." PhD diss., Georgia Tech University, 2017.

Hobbs, William, and Margaret Roberts. "How Sudden Censorship Can Increase Access to Information." *American Political Science Review* 112, no. 3 (2018): 621–636. doi:10.1017/S0003055418000084.

Hogan, J., and D. Doyle. "A Comparative Framework: How Broadly Applicable Is a 'Rigorous' Critical Junctures Framework?" *Acta Politica* 44, no. 2 (2009): 211–240.

Horwitz, Josh. "In China, You Can Now Hail a Taxi and Pay the Driver on WeChat." *Tech in Asia*, January 6, 2014. https://www.techinasia.com/china-hail-taxi-pay-driver-WeChat/, accessed April 2, 2018.

Hsu, C. "Beyond Civil Society: An Organizational Perspective on State-NGO Relations in the People's Republic of China." *Journal of Civil Society* 6, no. 3 (2010): 259–277.

Hsu, C., and J. Teets. "Is China's New Overseas NGO Management Law Sounding the Death Knell for Civil Society? Maybe Not." *Asia-Pacific Journal* 14, issue 4, no. 3 (2016): 9.

Hsu, C. L., and Y. Jiang. "An Institutional Approach to Chinese NGOs: State Alliance versus State Avoidance Resource Strategies." *China Quarterly* 221 (March 2015): 100–122.

Huang, Tianlei, and Nicholas R. Lardy. "China's Tech Crackdown Affects Only a Small Share of Its Digital Economy and Total GDP." *PIIE*, October 20, 2021, https://www.piie.com/research/piie-charts/chinas-tech-crackdown-affects -only-small-share-its-digital-economy-and-total.

Hurst, William, and Kevin J. O'Brien. "China's Contentious Pensioners." *China Quarterly*, no. 170 (2012): 345–360.

Hwang, D., and J. D. Lichtenthal. "Anatomy of Organisational Crises." *Journal of Contingency and Crisis Management* 8, no. 3 (2000): 129–140.

Hyun, K. D., and J. Kim. "The Role of New Media in Sustaining the Status Quo: Online Political Expression, Nationalism, and System Support in China." *Information, Communication, and Society* 18, no. 7 (2015): 766–781.

Ingram, H., A. Schneider, and P. deLeon. "Social Construction and Policy Design." In *Theories of the Policy Process*, 2nd ed., edited by Paul Sabatier, 93–128. Boulder, CO: Westview Press, 2007.

民办非企业单位登记管理暂行条例 (The Interim Regulations on Registration Administration of Private Non-Enterprise Units), 1998. http://www.pkulaw .cn/fulltext_form.aspx?Db=chl&Gid=21052/, accessed June 24, 2017.

Isidore, C. "The NBA Faces a No-Win Situation in China. Here's What It Stands to Lose." *CNN*, October 8, 2019. https://www.cnn.com/2019/10/08/business/ daryl-morey-tweet-nba-china/index.html/, accessed on January 4, 2020.

Jenkins-Smith, H., and P. Sabatier. "The Dynamics of Policy-Oriented Learning." In *Policy Change and Learning: An Advocacy Coalition Approach*, edited by Paul Sabatier and Hank Jenkins-Smith, 41–56. Boulder, CO: Westview Press, 1993.

Jia, Qingguo. "Let the Voice of the Chinese People Be Heard More Conveniently and Effectively." *Global China*, October 18, 2021. https://mp.weixin.qq.com /s/s_d1DpeXjukjmy0V2osRgA/.

Jia, X. "China's Implementation of the Overseas NGO Management Law." China Development Brief, March 2017. http://chinadevelopmentbrief.cn/articles/ chinas-implementation-of-the-overseas-ngo-management-law/, accessed on June 25, 2017.

Jin, W., and C. Wang. 《已有近130万人次志愿者参加汶川地震救灾》(Close to 1.3 Million Volunteers Have Participated in Wenchuan Earthquake Relief). Xinhua News Agency, June 21, 2008. http://www.gov.cn/jrzg/2008-06/21/conte nt_1023208.htm/.

Jin Ri Tou Tiao. Baidu Baike. https://baike.baidu.com/item/%E4%BB%8A%E6 %97%A5%E5%A4%B4%E6%9D%A1/4169373, accessed December 24, 2021.

Johnson, T. "Extending Environmental Governance: China's Environmental State and Civil Society." PhD thesis, University of Glasgow, 2009.

Johnston, Hank, and Sheldon X. Zhang. "Repertoires of Protest and Repression in Contemporary China." *Mobilization: An International Quarterly* 25, no. SI (2020): 601–622.

Kang, X., and H. Han, "Graduated Controls: The State-Society Relationship in Contemporary China." *Modern China* 34, no. 1 (2008): 36–55.

Keeler, J.T.S. "Opening the Window for Reform: Mandates, Crises, and Extraordinary Policymaking." *Comparative Political Studies* 25, no. 4 (1993): 433–486.

Kelly, David, and X.I.N. Gu. "New Conservatism: Ideological Program of a 'New Elite.'" In *China's Quiet Revolution: New Interactions between State and Society*, edited by David S. Goodman and Beverly Hooper, 219–233. Melbourne: Longman Cheshire, 1994.

Kenyon, Miles. "WeChat Surveillance Explained." University of Toronto Citizen Lab, May 7, 2020. https://citizenlab.ca/2020/05/wechat-surveillance-explained/.

King, G., J. Pan, and M. E. Roberts. "How Censorship in China Allows Government Criticism but Silences Collective Expression." *American Political Science Review* 107, no. 2 (2013): 1–18.

King, G., J. Pan, and M. E. Roberts. "Reverse Engineering Chinese Censorship: Randomized Experimentation and Participant Observation." *Science* 345, no. 6199 (2014): 1–10.

Kingdon, J. *Agendas, Alternatives, and Public Policies*. Amsterdam: Longman, 1995.

Knockel, J. "Measuring Decentralization of Chinese Censorship in Three Industry Segments." PhD diss., University of New Mexico, January 31, 2018. https://digitalrepository.unm.edu/cs_etds/90/.

Koesel, Karrie. *Religion and Authoritarianism: Cooperation, Conflict, and the Consequences*. Cambridge: Cambridge University Press, 2014.

中华人民共和国公益事业捐赠法 (Law of the People's Republic of China on Donations for Public Welfare). http://www.lawinfochina.com/display.aspx?lib=law&id=6238&CGid=, accessed June 24, 2017.

Lee, C. "Daily Active Users for WeChat Exceeds 1 Billion." *ZDNet*, January 9, 2018. https://www.zdnet.com/article/daily-active-user-of-messaging-app-wechat-exceeds-1-billion/.

Lee, Ching Kwan. *Against the Law: Labor Protests in China's Rustbelt and Sunbelt*. Berkeley: University of California Press, 2007.

Lee, Jason. "Chinese Content Platforms Pledge Self-Discipline—Industry Group." *Reuters*, September 11, 2021.

Lee, S. "Surviving Online Censorship in China: Three Satirical Tactics and Their Impact." *China Quarterly* 228 (December 2016): 1061–1080.

Lei, Z. "Ji'Nan, the New Capital of Online Censorship." Journalists' Station. *China Digital Times*, March 25, 2019. https://chinadigitaltimes.net/chinese/2019/03/%E8%AE%B0%E8%80%85%E7%AB%99%E4%B8%A8%E6%B5%8E%E5%8D%97%EF%BC%8C%E6%96%B0%E7%9A%84%E4%BA%92%E8%81%94%E7%BD%91%E5%AE%A1%E6%A0%B8%E4%B9%8B%E9%83%BD/, accessed on August 16, 2019.

Lewis, O. A. "Net Inclusion: New Media's Impact on Deliberative Politics in China." *Journal of Contemporary Asia* 43, no. 4 (2013): 678–708.

Li, Hong, and Guang Li. "Interactive Development of Government Purchase Service Reform and Social Organizations: An Analysis Based on Motive Mechanism and Determinants." *Journal of Beijing University of Aeronautics and Astronautics, Social Sciences Edition* 33, no. 1 (2020): 84.

Li, L. "The Direct Registration of Four Types of Social Organizations: Halting Unnecessary Procedures." For the Ministry of Civil Affairs of the People's Republic of China, December 2013. http://www.mca.gov.cn/article/mxht/mtgz/201312/20131200556602.shtml/.

Li, Yuan. "The Great Firewall Cracked, Briefly: A People Shined Through." *New York Times*, February 9, 2021.

Li, Z., and A. Ong. *Privatizing China: Socialism from Afar*. Ithaca, NY: Cornell University Press, 2008.

Lima, C. "Facebook Wades Deeper into Censorship Debates as It Bans 'Dangerous' Accounts." *Politico*, May 2, 2019. https://www.politico.com/story/2019/05/02/facebook-bans-far-right-alex-jones-1299247, accessed on August 22, 2019.

Lin, Liza. "China Fines Weibo for Spreading 'Illegal Information.'" *Wall Street Journal*, December 14, 2021.

Liu, P. "Experimentation Based on the Center's Selective Control" (基于中央选择性控制的试验—中国改革"实践"机制的一种新解释), *kaifang shidai*, no. 4 (2010).

Liu, Sida. "The Changing Roles of Lawyers in China: State Bureaucrats, Market Brokers, and Political Activists." In *The New Legal Realism: Studying Law Globally*, edited by Heinz Klug and Sally Engle Merry, 180–198. Cambridge: Cambridge University Press, 2016.

Loeb, Ketty. "A Grim Outlook for China's Civil Society in the Wake of the 19th Party Congress." *Asia Pacific Bulletin*, no. 402, October 26, 2017, https://scholarspace.manoa.hawaii.edu/server/api/core/bitstreams/548835d5-ccd8-4a31-a47f-4a900304f3b6/content.

Lorentzen, P. "China's Strategic Censorship." *American Journal of Political Science* 58, no. 2 (2014): 402–414.

Lorentzen, P. "Regularizing Rioting: Permitting Public Protest in an Authoritarian Regime." *Quarterly Journal of Political Science* 8, (2013): 127–158.

Lu, Shen. "Apple Exports PRC Censorship to Hong Kong and Taiwan, Report Says." *Protocol*, August 2021, https://www.protocol.com/china/apple-china-engraving-censorship.

Lu, X., and P. F. Landry. "Show Me the Money: Interjurisdiction Political Competition and Fiscal Extraction in China." *American Political Science Review* 108, no. 3 (2014): 706–722.

Luebbert, G. M. *Liberalism, Fascism, or Social Democracy*. New York: Oxford University Press, 1991.

Luehrmann, L. M. "Facing Citizen Complaints in China, 1951–1996." *Asian Survey* 43, no. 5 (2003): 845–866.

Ma, J. "On the New Media to Challenge for New Young Teachers in Professional Dedication and Countermeasures at Universities." *Studies in Sociology of Science* 6, no.3 (2015): 8–12.

Ma, Q. "Defining Chinese Nongovernmental Organizations." *International Journal of Voluntary and Nonprofit Organizations* 13, no. 2 (2002): 113–130.

Magaloni, B., and J. Wallace. "Citizen Loyalty, Mass Protest, and Authoritarian Survival." Paper presented at the conference on "Dictatorships: Their Governance and Social Consequences," Stanford University, California, April 25–26, 2008.

Marquis, Christopher, and Yanhua Bir. "The Paradox of Responsive Authoritarianism: How Civic Activism Spurs Environmental Penalties in China." *Organization Science* 29, no. 5 (2018): 948–968.

Mattingly, D. C. *The Art of Political Control in China*. Cambridge: Cambridge University Press, 2019.

McCarthy, N. "The Countries Shutting Down the Internet the Most [Infographic]." *Forbes*, August 28, 2018. https://www.forbes.com/sites/niallmccart hy/2018/08/28/the-countries-shutting-down-the-internet-the-most-infogra phic/#46a2acbf1294/, accessed on August 22, 2019.

McConnell, A. "Overview: Crisis Management, Influences, Responses, and Evaluation." *Parliamentary Affairs* 56, no. 3 (2003): 393–409. Meng, T., J. Pan, and P. Yang. "Conditional Receptivity to Citizen Participation: Evidence from a Survey Experiment in China." *Comparative Political Studies* 50, no. 4 (2014): 399–433.

Mertha, A. "'Fragmented Authoritarianism 2.0': Political Pluralization in the Chinese Policy Process." *China Quarterly* 200 (December 2009): 995–1012.

Mertha, Andrew. *China's Water Warriors: Citizen Action and Policy Change*. Ithaca, NY: Cornell University Press, 2008.

Migdal, J. S. *State in Society: Studying How States and Societies Transform and Constitute One Another*. Cambridge: Cambridge University Press, 2004.

Miller, Blake. "Automated Detection of Chinese Government Astroturfing Using Network and Social Metadata." Working paper, University of Michigan, 2016.

Ming, Wang. "On Improving the Mechanisms of Social Supervisors" (关于完善社会监督员机智的建议案). In *Reports on the Civil Society Action in Wenchuan Earthquake: China NGOs in Emergency Rescue*, edited by Wang Ming, 108–110. China: Social Sciences Academic Press, 2009.

Ming, Wang. *Oral History for NGOs in China, No. 2*. China: Social Sciences Academic Press, 2013, 70–77.

Ministry of Civil Affairs and the Ministry of Finance. 云南省规范境外非政府组织活动暂行规定 (Interim Provisions on the Regulations of Overseas Non-governmental Organizations in Yunan Province), 2009. http://mzj.km.gov.cn/c/2010-05-18/1542895.shtml /, accessed June 13, 2022.

Ministry of Civil Affairs and the Ministry of Finance. 关于支持和规范社会组织承接政府购买服务的通知 (Notice on the Support and Normalize the Service Purchasing from Social Organizations by the Government), 2014. http://www.mca.gov.cn/article/zwgk/fvfg/mjzzgl/201412/20141200744371.shtml/, accessed June 24, 2017.

Ministry of Transportation. "Notice on Strengthening the Joint Supervision of the Online Appointed Taxi Industry" (关于加强网络预约出租汽车行业事中事后联合监管有关工作的通知), June 5, 2018.

Ministry of Transportation. "Notice on the Workflow Regarding the Appointment of Taxi Operators to Apply for Online Service Capability Identification"

(关于网络预约出租汽车经营者申请线上服务能力认定工作流程的通知), November 4, 2016.

Ministry of Transportation. "Operation Management Rules of the Supervision of Online Taxi Appointment Interactive Platforms" (网络预约出租汽车监管信息交互平台运行管理办法), February 13, 2018.

Ministry of Transportation of China. "Guiding Opinion on Deepening Reform and Further Promoting the Healthy Development of the Taxi Industry" (关于深化改革进一步推进出租汽车行业健康发展的指导意见), 2015. http://www.xinhuanet.com/auto/2015-10/10/c_128304499.htm/, accessed April 2, 2018.

Ministry of Transportation of China. "Interim Measures for the Management of Online Booking of Taxi Business Services" (网络预约出租汽车经营服务管理暂行办法), 2016. http://www.chinanews.com/cj/2015/10-10/7562706.shtml/, accessed April 2, 2018.

Ministry of Transportation of China. "Notice of the Ministry of Transportation on Reforming the Qualification Examination for Taxi Drivers" (交通运输部关于改革出租汽车驾驶员从业资格考试有关工作的通知), September 4, 2017.

Ministry of Transportation of China. "Taxi Management Service Regulations" (出租汽车经营服务管理规定), September 30, 2014. https://baike.baidu.com/item/%E5%87%BA%E7%A7%9F%E6%B1%BD%E8%BD%A6%E7%BB%8F%E8%90%A5%E6%9C%8D%E5%8A%A1%E7%AE%A1%E7%90%86%E8%A7%84%E5%AE%9A, accessed October 20, 2019.

Ministry of Transportation. "The Overall Technical Requirements for the Network Reservation Taxi Supervision Information Interaction Platform (Temporary)" (网络预约出租汽车监管信息交互平台总体技术要求 [暂行]), December 20, 2016.

Ministry of Transportation and the Ministry of Public Security. "Notice on Background Check and Supervision of Taxi Drivers" (关于切实做好出租汽车驾驶员背景核查与监管等有关工作的通知), March 4, 2018.

Montinola, G., Y. Qian, and B. R. Weingast. "Federalism, Chinese Style: The Political Basis for Economic Success." *World Politics* 48, no. 1 (1996): 50–81.

Morgan, Kimberly J., and Ann Shola Orloff. "Introduction: The Many Hands of the State." Buffett Center for International and Comparative Studies Working Paper no. 14–001. Northwestern University, December 2014. doi:10.13140/RG.2.1.2678.6323.

Najam, Adil. "The Four-C's of Third Sector–Government Relations: Cooperation, Confrontation, Complementarity, and Co-optation." *Nonprofit Management and Leadership* 10, no. 4 (2000): 375–396.

Nathan, A. "China's Challenge." *Journal of Democracy* 26, no. 1 (2015): 156–170.

Nathan, A. J. "Authoritarian Resilience." *Journal of Democracy* 14, no. 1 (2003): 6–17.

Nathan, A. J. *China's Transition*. New York: Columbia University Press, 1997.

National Cyberspace Administration of China. "Notice of Public Comment for the State Internet Information Office's 'Cyber Security Review Measures (Revised Draft for Solicitation of Comments),'" July 10, 2021.

National Cyberspace Affairs Office. "Interim Provisions on the Development Management of Public Information Services for Instant Messaging Tools" (即时通讯工具公众信息服务发展管理暂行规定), August 7, 2017. http://www.piyao.org.cn/2017-08/07/c_129666339.htm/, accessed August 16, 2019.

National Cyberspace Affairs Office. "Internet Forum Community Service Management Regulations" (互联网论坛社区服务管理规定), August 25, 2017. https://www.cac.gov.cn/2017-08/25/c_1121541921.htm/, accessed August 16, 2019.

National Cyberspace Affairs Office. "Internet Group Information Service Management Regulations" (互联网群组信息服务管理规定), September 7, 2017. https://www.cac.gov.cn/2017-09/07/c_1121623889.htm/, accessed August 16, 2019.

National Cyberspace Affairs Office. "Internet Information Search Service Management Regulations" (互联网信息搜索服务管理规定), June 25, 2016. http://www.cac.gov.cn/2016-06/25/c_1119109085.htm/, accessed August 16, 2019.

National Cyberspace Affairs Office. "Internet News Information Service License Management Regulations" (互联网新闻信息服务许可管理实施细则), June 1, 2017. www.cac.gov.cn/2017-05/22/c_1121015789.htm/, accessed August 16, 2019.

National Cyberspace Affairs Office. "Internet News Information Service Management Regulations" (互联网新闻信息服务管理规定), June 1, 2017. https://www.cac.gov.cn/2017-05/02/c_1120902760.htm/, accessed August 16, 2019.

National Cyberspace Affairs Office. "Internet News Information Service Unit Content Management Practitioners Management Measures" (互联网新闻信息服务单位内容管理从业人员管理办法), October 30, 2017. http://www.cac.gov.cn/2017-10/30/c_1121877917.htm/, accessed August 16, 2019.

National Cyberspace Affairs Office. "Internet Post Comment Service Management Regulations" (互联网跟帖评论服务管理规定), August 25, 2017. https://www.cac.gov.cn/2017-08/25/c_1121541842.htm/, accessed August 16, 2019.

National Cyberspace Affairs Office. "Internet User Public Account Information Service Management Regulations" (互联网用户公众账号信息服务管理规定), September 7, 2019. https://www.cac.gov.cn/2017-09/07/c_1121624269.htm/, accessed August 16, 2019.

National People's Congress. Article 12 of the "People's Police Law of the People's Republic of China" (中华人民共和国人民警察法), 1995. https://baike.baidu.com/item/%E7%BD%91%E7%BB%9C%E8%AD%A6%E5%AF%9F/861144?fromtitle=%E7%BD%91%E8%AD%A6&fromid=10819437/, accessed August 16, 2019.

National People's Congress. "People's Republic of China Cyber Security Law" (中华人民共和国网络安全法), November 7, 2016. http://www.xinhuanet.com/politics/2016-11/07/c_1119867015.htm/, accessed August 16, 2019.

National Religious Affairs Administration. "Measures for the Management of Religious Groups," February 1, 2020. http://www.sara.gov.cn/ywdt/322201.jhtml/.

Neumark, D., R. J. Bank, and K. D. Van Nort. "Sex Discrimination in Restaurant Hiring: An Audit Study." *Quarterly Journal of Economics* 111, no. 3 (1996): 915–941.

News Office of the State Council and the Ministry of Information Industry. "Interim Provisions on the Administration of News Service on Internet Sites" (互联网站登载新闻业务管理暂行规定), November 7, 2000. http://www.law-lib .com/law/law_view.asp?id=15211/, accessed August 16, 2019.

98洪水的损失及外来的捐款 (Damages and Donations from the 98 Flood), 2009. http://news.xilu.com/2009/0909/news_112_14702.html/, accessed June 25, 2017.

Nnajiofor, Peterson. "The New Sharing Economy: Demise of Social and Labor Movements?" *IDEA Research Center* (2017), http://www.net4dem.org/mayglo bal/Documents/The%20New%20Sharing%20Economy_Peterson%20Nnaji ofor.pdf.

Nohrstedt, D., and C. M. Weible. "The Logic and Policy Change after Crisis: Proximity and Subsystem Interaction." *Risk, Hazards, and Crisis in Public Policy* 1, no. 2 (July 2010): 1–32.

North, Douglass C. *Institutions, Institutional Change, and Economic Performance.* Cambridge: Cambridge University Press, 1990.

O'Brien, K., and L. Li. *Rightful Resistance in the Chinese Countryside.* New York: Cambridge University Press, 2006.

O'Brien, K. J. "Rightful Resistance Revisited." *Journal of Peasant Studies* 40, no. 6 (2013): 1051–1062.

O'Brien, Kevin J., and Yanhua Deng. "Preventing Protest One Person at a Time: Psychological Coercion and Relational Repression in China." *China Review* 17, no. 2 (2017): 179–201.

O'Brien, Kevin J., and Lianjiang Li. *Rightful Resistance in Rural China.* Cambridge: Cambridge University Press, 2006.

O'Brien, Kevin J., and Lianjiang Li. "Suing the Local State: Administrative Litigation in Rural China." *China Journal*, no. 51 (2004): 75–96.

O'Brien, Kevin J., and Rachel E. Stern. "Studying Contention in Contemporary China." In *Popular Protest in China*, edited by Kevin J. O'Brien, 11–25. Cambridge, MA: Harvard University Press 2008.

Ong, Lynette H. "Thugs and Outsourcing of State Repression in China." *China Journal* 80, no. 1 (2018): 94–110.

"Online Police." *Wikipedia.* https://zh.wikipedia.org/wiki/网络警察, accessed August 16, 2019.

Ostergaard, Clemens. "Citizens, Groups, and Nascent Civil Society in China: Towards an Understanding of the 1989 Student Demonstrations." *China Information* 4 (1989): 28–41.

Ostrom, E. *Understanding Institutional Diversity.* Princeton, NJ: Princeton University Press, 2005.

Pei, Minxin. "China's Coming Upheaval: Competition, the Coronavirus, and the Weakness of Xi Jinping." *Foreign Affairs* (May/June 2020).

Pei, Minxin. "Citizens v. Manandarins: Administrative Litigation in China." *China Quarterly*, no. 152 (1997): 82.

Pepinsky, T. B. *Economic Crises and the Breakdown of Authoritarian Regimes: Indonesia and Malaysia in Comparative Perspective*. New York: Cambridge University Press, 2009.

Perry, E. *Challenging the Mandate of Heaven: Social Protests and State Power in China*. Armonk, NY: M.E. Sharpe, 2002.

Perry, E. "A New Rights Consciousness?" *Journal of Democracy* 20, no. 3 (2009): 17–20.

Perry, E. "Trends in the Study of Chinese Politics: State-Society Relations." *China Quarterly* 139 (1994): 704–713.

Perry, E. J. "Studying Chinese Politics: Farewell to Revolution?" *China Journal* 57 (2007): 1–22.

Peter, Thomas. "China Targets Online Platforms in Quest to 'Clean Up' Internet." *Reuters*, December 23, 2021.

Pils, Eva. *China's Human Rights Lawyers: Advocacy and Resistance*. New York: Routledge, 2014.

国务院机构改革和职能转变方案 (Plan for the Institutional Restructuring of the State Council and Transformation of Functions Thereof), 2013. http://www.lawinfochina.com/display.aspx?lib=law&id=13554&CGid=, accessed June 24, 2017.

Polyakova, Alina, and Chris Meserole. "Exporting Digital Authoritarianism: The Russian and Chinese Models." *Policy Brief, Democracy, and Disorder Series*. Washington, DC: Brookings Institution, 2019, 1–22.

Provincial Department of Justice Legislation Division I. "The Provincial Department of Justice Implements a Rapid Legislative Response Mechanism and Actively Carries Out Research of Epidemic Prevention and Control Legislation." Guangdong Department of Justice, June 18, 2021. http://sft.gd.gov.cn/sfw/fzgz/lfghjhjgzqk/content/post_3569995.html/.

外国商会管理暂行规定 (Provisional Regulations for the Administration of Foreign Chambers of Commerce in China, 1989), accessed June 24, 2017. http://www.mca.gov.cn/article/gk/fg/shzzgl/201507/20150700847911.shtm/.

Putnam, Robert. *Making Democracy Work: Civic Traditions in Modern Italy*. Princeton, NJ: Princeton University Press, 1993.

Qiaoan, Runya, and Jessica C. Teets. "Responsive Authoritarianism in China—A Review of Responsiveness in Xi and Hu Administrations." *Journal of Chinese Political Science* 25, no. 1 (2020): 139–153.

Rauchfleisch, Adrian. "Multiple Public Spheres of Weibo: A Typology of Forms and Potentials of Online Public Spheres in China." *Information, Communication, and Society* 18, no. 2 (2015): 139–155. https://doi.org/10.1080/1369118X.2014.940364.

基金会条例 (Regulation on Foundation Administration), 2004. http://www.lawinfochina.com/display.aspx?lib=law&id=3463&CGid=/, accessed June 24, 2017.

社会团体登记管理条例 (Regulation on Registration and Administration of Social Organizations), 1989.

Reilly, James. *Strong Society, Smart State*. New York: Columbia University Press, 2011.

Ren, X. "ZuiQianYan: Guojia Wangxingongzuo Chensilu" (最前沿：国家网信工作沉思录). Xinhua Publishing House, November 2018.

Reny, Marie-Eve. *Authoritarian Containment: Public Security Bureaus and Protestant House Churches in Urban China*. New York: Oxford University Press, 2018.

Robertson, Graeme. "Protesting Putinism: The Election Protests of 2011–2012 in Broader Perspective." *Problems of Post-Communism* 60, no. 2 (2013): 11–23.

Roland, Gerard. *Transition and Economics: Politics, Markets, and Firms*. Cambridge: MIT Press, 2000.

Rosenbaum, P. R. *Design of Observational Studies*, Springer Series in Statistics. New York: Springer Verlag, 2010.

Rosenthal, U., and A. Kouzmin. "Crises and Crisis Management: Toward Comprehensive Government Decision Making." *Journal of Public Administration Research and Theory* 7, no. 2 (1997): 277–304.

Saich, Tony. "What Explains the Resilience of Chinese Communist Party Rule?" *Brown Journal of World Affairs* 27 (2020): 105.

Saurugger, S., and F. Terpan. "Do Crises Lead to Policy Change? The Multiple Streams Framework and the European Union's Economic Governance Instruments." *Policy Sciences* 49, no. 1 (2016): 35–53.

Schlæger, J., and M. Jiang. "Official Microblogging and Social Management by Local Governments in China." *China Information* 28, no. 2 (2014): 189–213.

Schmitter, P. C. "Still the Century of Corporatism?" *Review of Politics* 36, no. 1 (1974): 85–131.

政府购买服务政策文件选编 (Selections from the Policy Documents of Government Purchasing Services), China Financial and Economic Publishing House, 2014.

Shen, Y., and J. Yu. "Local Government and NGOs in China: Performance-Based Collaboration." *China: An International Journal* 15, no. 2 (2017): 177–191.

Shen, Yifei. "Feminism in China: An Analysis of Advocates, Debates, and Strategies." Shanghai: Friedrich Eberto Stiftung, 2016.

Shieh, Shawn. "The Origins of China's New Law on Foreign NGOs." *ChinaFile*. https://www.chinafile.com/viewpoint/origins-of-chinas-new-law-foreign -ngos/, accessed June 24, 2017.

Shih, V. C. *Economic Shocks and Authoritarian Stability: Duration, Financial Control, and Institutions*. Ann Arbor: University of Michigan Press, 2020.

Shirk, S. *China: Fragile Superpower: How China's Internal Politics Could Derail Its Peaceful Rise*. New York: Oxford University Press, 2007..

Shoebridge, Michael. "Coronavirus and the Death of Xi's 'China Dream.'" *The Strategist*, February 28, 2020. https://www.aspistrategist.org.au/coronavirus -and-the-death-of-xis-china-dream/.

Shue, V. "Legitimacy Crisis in China?" In *Chinese Politics: State, Society, and the*

Market, edited by Peter Hays Gries and Stanley Rosen, 41–68. New York: Routledge, 2010.

Shue, V. *The Reach of the State: Sketches of the Chinese Body Politic.* Stanford, CA: Stanford University Press, 1988.

Sichuan Women's Federations. "Report on the Work of the Mass Organizations Social Service Centers in Sichuan Province" (四川省基层群团组织社会服务中心工作汇报), 2015. http://www.scfl.org.cn/Article/ShowArticle.asp?ArticleID =8302/.

Simon, K. *Civil Society in China: The Legal Framework from Ancient Times to the "New Reform Era."* New York: Oxford University Press, 2013.

Slater, D. *Ordering Power: Contentious Politics and Authoritarian Leviathans in Southeast Asia.* New York: Cambridge University Press, 2010.

Smith, J., and D. Wiest. *Social Movements in the World-System: The Politics of Crisis and Transformation.* New York: Russell Sage Foundation, 2012.

Solon, Olivia. "Facebook Removes 652 Fake Accounts and Pages Meant to Influence World Politics." *The Guardian,* August 21, 2018. https://www.theguardian.com/technology/2018/aug/21/facebook-pages-accounts-removed-russia -iran/, accessed August 22, 2019.

Song, C., S. Wang, and P. Kristen. "All Roads Lead to Rome: Autonomy, Political Connections, and Organisational Strategies of NGOs in China." *China: An International Journal* 13, no. 3 (2015): 72–93.

Spires, A. J. "Contingent Symbiosis and Civil Society in an Authoritarian State: Understanding the Survival of China's Grassroots NGOs." *American Journal of Sociology* 117, no. 1 (2011): 1–45.

State Council. "Internet Information Service Management Measures in the People's Republic of China" (互联网信息服务管理办法 (2011修订)), January 8, 2011.   https://www.pkulaw.com/chl/7d533bd9db7539e4bdfb.html/, accessed August 16, 2019.

State Council of People's Republic of China. "Regulations for the Protection of Computer Information systems Safety in the People's Republic of China" (中华人民共和国计算机信息系统安全保护条例), 1994. https://baike.baidu.com/item/中华人民共和国计算机信息系统安全保护条例, accessed August 16, 2019.

State Council of People's Republic of China. "Temporary Decree on the Management of Computer Information Network International Connectivity in the People's Republic of China" (中华人民共和国计算机信息网络国际联网管理暂行规定实施办法), 2000. http://www.law-lib.com/law/law_view.asp?id=13 818/, accessed August 16, 2019.

Steinhardt, Christoph H., and Fengshi Wu. "In the Name of the Public: Environmental Protest and the Changing Landscape of Popular Contention in China." *China Journal,* no. 75 (2016): 61–82.

Stockmann, Daniela, and Mary Gallagher. "Remote Control: How the Media Sustain Authoritarian Rule in China." *Comparative Political Studies* 44, no. 4 (2011): 436–67. https://doi.org/10.1177/0010414010394773.

Stockmann, Daniela. "'Authoritarianism 2.0': The Internet and Authoritarian Rule in China." APSA 2019 Conference session. August 30, 2019.

Stockmann, Daniela. *Media Commercialization and Authoritarian Rule in China.* Cambridge: Cambridge University Press, 2013.

Stromberg, Qin D., and Y. Wu. "Why Does China Allow Freer Social Media? Protests versus Surveillance and Propaganda." *Journal of Economic Perspectives* 31, no. 1 (2017): 117–140.

Su, Yang, and Xin He. "Street as Courtroom: State Accommodation of Labor Protest in South China." *Law and Society Review* 44, no. 1 (2010): 157–184.

Sullivan, L. "The Emergence of Civil Society in China, Spring 1989." In *The Chinese People's Movement: Perspectives on Spring 1989,* edited by Tony Saich, 126–144. Armonk, NY: M. E. Sharpe, 1990.

Sun, T. "Deliberate Differentiation for Outsourcing Responsibilities: The Logic of China's Behavior toward Civil Society Organizations." *China Quarterly* (2019): 1–26.

Sun, T. "Earthquakes and the Typologies of State-CSO Relations in China: A Dynamic Framework." *China Information* 31, no. 3 (2017): 304–326.

Sun, Taiyi. "The Continuation of Reducing Restrictions on Individuals and Information Exchanges Is an Important Step towards the 'Four Self-Confidence.'" *Global China,* December 7, 2021. https://mp.weixin.qq.com/s/yGw3QRwd VH-NoNK5UqeI_A/.

Sun, Taiyi. "Deliberate Differentiation by the Chinese State: Outsourcing Responsibility for Governance." *China Quarterly* 240 (2019): 880–905.

Sun, Taiyi. "Importing Civic Education into Authoritarian China." In *Teaching Civic Engagement Globally,* edited by Elizabeth C. Matto, Allison Rios Millett McCartney, Elizabeth A. Bennion, Alasdair Blair, Taiyi Sun, and Dawn Michele Whitehead, 53–72. Washington, DC: American Political Science Association, 2021.

Supreme People's Court Supreme People's Procuratorate. "Interpretation of the Supreme People's Court Supreme People's Procuratorate on Several Issues Concerning the Application of Laws in the Use of Information Network to Implement Criminal Cases" (最高人民法院最高人民检察院关于办理利用信息网络实施诽谤等刑事案件适用法律若干问题的解释), September 10, 2013. http://www.spp.gov.cn/spp/zdgz/201309/t20130910_62417.shtml/, accessed August 16, 2019.

Svensson, Marina, "WeChat: The First Chinese Social Media Product with a Global Appeal." *Digital China,* 2013. https://digitalchina.blogg.lu.se/WeChat -the-first-chinese-social-media-product-with-a-global-appeal/, accessed April 2, 2018.

Swaner, Rachel. "Trust Matters: Enhancing Government Legitimacy through Participatory Budgeting." *New Political Science* 39, no. 1 (2017): 95–108.

Tai, J. W. "Embedded Civil Society: NGO Leadership and Organizational Effectiveness in Authoritarian China." PhD dissertation, George Washington University, 2012. https://scholarspace.library.gwu.edu/concern/gw_etds/8s45q8 86t/.

Tai, Q. "China's Media Censorship: A Dynamic and Diversified Regime." *Journal of East Asian Studies* 14, no. 2 (2014): 185–210.

Tang, Min, and Huhe Narisong. "Alternative Framing: The Effect of the Internet on Political Support in Authoritarian China." *International Political Science Review* 35, no. 5 (2013): 559–76, https:doi.org/10.1177/0192512113501971.

Tang, Wenfang. *Populist Authoritarianism: Chinese Political Culture and Regime Sustainability*. New York: Oxford University Press, 2016.

Teets, J. *Civil Society under Authoritarianism: The China Model*. New York: Cambridge University Press, 2014.

Teets, J. "The Test of a Civilization: Social Management and the Future of Philanthropy in China." Paper presented at the conference on "Chinese Philanthropy: Past, Present and Future," Fudan University, Shanghai, June 9–10, 2015.

Thogersen, S. "Giving the People a Voice? Experiments with Consultative Authoritarian Institutions in China." *Journal of Contemporary China* 19, no. 66 (2010): 675–692.

Tocqueville, A. D. *Democracy in America*. New York: Penguin Books, 2003.

Tong, Jingrong, and Landong Zuo. "Weibo Communication and Government Legitimacy in China: A Computer-Assisted Analysis of Weibo Messages ono Two 'Mass Incidents.'" *Information, Communication, and Society* 17, no. 1 (2014): 66–85.

Tong, Yanqi and Shaohua Lei. "Large-Scale Mass Incidents and government responses in China." *International Journal of China Studies* 1, no2 (2010): 487–508.

Tong, Z. "One Should Not Affirm the Concept of 'Benign Violation of the Constitution'" (良性违宪"不宜肯定—对郝铁川同志有关主张的不同看法). *Faxue yanjiu* 18, no. 6 (1996).

Truex, R. "Consultative Authoritarianism and Its Limits." *Comparative Political Studies* 50, no. 3 (2014): 329–361.

Truex, R. "The Returns to Office in a 'Rubber Stamp' Parliament." *American Political Science Review* 108, no. 2 (2014): 235.

Tsai, K. S. *Capitalism without Democracy: The Private Sector in Contemporary China*. Ithaca, NY: Cornell University Press, 2007.

Tsai, L. *Accountability without Democracy: Solidary Groups and Public Goods Provision in Rural China*. New York: Cambridge University Press, 2007.

Tsai, Wen-Hsuan, and Nicola Dean. "Experimentation under Hierarchy in Local Conditions: Cases of Political Reform in Guangdong and Sichuan, China." *China Quarterly* 218 (2014): 339–358.

Tsou, Tang. *The Cultural Revolution and Post-Mao Reforms: A Historical Perspective*. Chicago: University of Chicago Press, 1986.

Tu, Fangjing, "WeChat and Civil Society in China." *Communication and the Public* I, no. 3 (2016): 343–350.

Unger, Jonathan, and Anita Chan. "China, Corporatism, and the East Asian Model." *Australian Journal of Chinese Affairs* 33 (1995): 29–53.

United States Geological Survey. "The Modified Mercalli Intensity Scale." https://www.usgs.gov/programs/earthquake-hazards/modified-mercalli-intensity -scale/.

Vala, Carsten T. "Protestant Christianity and Civil Society in Authoritarian China: The Impact of Official Churches and Unregistered Urban Churches on Civil Society Development in the 2000s." *China Perspectives* 3, (2012): 43–52.

Wakeman, F., Jr. "The Civil Society and Public Sphere Debate: Western Reflections on Chinese Political Culture." *Modern China* 19, no. 2 (1993): 108–138.

Wallace, J. L. "Information Politics in Dictatorship." In *Emerging Trends in the Social and Behavioral Sciences: An Interdisciplinary, Searchable, and Linkable Resource*, edited by Robert Scott and Stephen Kosslyn, 1–11. Hoboken, NJ: Wiley and Sons, 2015.

Wang, D., and G. Mark. "Internet Censorship in China: Examining User Awareness and Attitudes." *ACM Transactions on Computer-Human Interaction (TOCHI)* 22, no. 6, article no. 31 (December 2015).

Wang, Haiyan. "After the Emergency Legislation, There Is a Race against Time for Anti-Epidemic Actions." People's Congress of Shanghai, February 9, 2020. http://www.spcsc.sh.cn/n1939/n4514/n7171/n7196/u1ai205987.html/.

Wang, Jiexiu. *Blue Book of Civil Affairs (2014): Annual Report on Development of China's Civil Affairs* (中国民政发展报告) (2014). China: Social Publishing House (中国社会出版社), 2014, 129–131.

Wang, Juan. "Managing Social Stability: The Perspective of a Local Government in China." *Journal of East Asian Studies* 15, no. 1 (2015): 1–25.

Wang, Q. "Co-Optation or Restriction: The Differentiated Government Control over Foundations in China." China Nonprofit Review, October 2, 2016. https://papers.ssrn.com/sol3/papers.cfm?abstract_id=2846635#/.

Wang, S. "Learning through Practice and Experimentation: The Financing of Rural Health Care." In *Mao's Invisible Hand: The Political Foundations of Adaptive Governance in China*, edited by Sebastian Heilmann and Elizabeth J. Perry, 102–137. Cambridge, MA: Harvard University Press, 2011.

Wang, S., M. J. Paul, and M. Dredze. "Social Media as a Sensor of Air Quality and Public Response in China." *Journal of Medical Internet Research* 17, no. 3 (2015): e22.

Wang, X. *Social Media in Industrial China*. London: UCL Press, 2016.

Weatherley, R., and Q. Zhang. *History and Nationalist Legitimacy in Contemporary China: A Double-Edged Sword*. London: Palgrave Macmillan, 2017.

Weber, Max. "Politics as a Vocation." In *From Max Weber: Essays in Sociology*, edited by H. H. Gerth and C. Wright Mills, 77–128. New York: Oxford University Press, 1946.

Weiss, Jessica Chen. "Authoritarian Signaling, Mass Audiences, and Nationalist Protest in China." *International Organization* 67, no. 1 (2013): 1–35.

Weixin Gongzhong Pingtai (WeChat Public Platform). Baidu Baike. https://baike.baidu.com/item/%E5%BE%AE%E4%BF%A1%E5%85%AC%E4%BC%97%E5%B9%B3%E5%8F%B0/, accessed August 16, 2019.

Wheeler, N. "Nurturing Civil Society: A Joint Venture." In *The Role of American NGOs in China's Modernization: Invited Influence*. New York: Routledge, 2012, 168.

Whyte, M. *Myth of the Social Volcano: Perceptions of Inequality and Distributive Injustice in Contemporary China*. Stanford, CA: Stanford University Press, 2010.

Wood, G. "New Partners or Old Brothers? GoNGOs in Transnational Environmental Advocacy in China." *China Environmental Series* 5 (1996): 45–58.

Wu, F., and K. Chan. "Graduated Control and Beyond: The Evolving Government-NGO Relations." *China Perspective*, no. 3 (2012): 9–17.

Wu, Xuecan, and Lin Biao. "Turning Everyone into a Censor: The Chinese Communist Party's All-Directional Control over the Media." Washington, DC: US-China Economic and Security Review Commission, USCC, 2002.

Xinlang Weibo (Sina Weibo). *Wikipedia*. https://zh.wikipedia.org/wiki/%E6%96
%B0%E6%B5%AA%E5%BE%AE%E5%8D%9A#targetText%3D%E5%8E
%86%E5%8F%B2%2C%E2%80%9D%E5%8A%9F%E8%83%BD%EF%BC
%8C%E4%BE%9B%E7%94%A8%E6%88%B7%E4%BA%A4%E6%B5%81
%E3%80%82/, accessed August 16, 2019.

Xu, B. *The Politics of Compassion: The Sichuan Earthquake and Civic Engagement in China*. Stanford, CA: Stanford University Press, 2017.

Xu, W. "The Trial of Overseas NGO Administrative Rule in Beijing" (境外NGO管理法北京试行：三类组织可在中关村). *Beijing News*, May 25, 2015.

Yang, D. *Beyond Beijing: Liberalization and the Regions in China*. London: Routledge, 2002.

Yang, G. "The Internet and Civil Society in China: A Preliminary Assessment." *Journal of Contemporary China* 12, no. 36 (2003): 453–475.

Yang, Guobing. *The Power of the Internet in China*. New York: Columbia University Press, 2011.

Yang, Hongxing, and Dingxin Zhao. "Performance Legitimacy, State Autonomy, and China's Economic Miracle." *Journal of Contemporary China* 24, no. 91 (2015): 64–82.

Yi, Zou. "Trade Unions Should Firmly Grasp the Advanced Nature and Keep Pace with the Times" (工会要牢牢把握先进性 与时俱进). *Trade Union's Half Month Paper* 20, 2015, Hangzhou. http://www.hzgh.org/byt/view.aspx?id=29005/.

Yinger, J. "Measuring Racial Discrimination with Fair Housing Audits: Caught in the Act." *American Economic Review* 76, no. 5 (1986): 881–893.

Yu, Jianrong. "Types and Features of Mass Incidents in China Today" (当前我国群体性事件的类型与特征), 2010. http://www.aisixiang.com/data/32027.html/, accessed April 2, 2018.

Yuen, Samson. "Friend or Foe? The Diminishing Space of China's Civil Society." *China Perspectives*, no. 3 (2015): 51–56.

Zaharidis, N. "The Multiple Streams Framework: Structure, Limitations, Prospects." In *Theories of the Policy Process*, 2nd ed., edited by Paul Sabatier, 65–92. Boulder, CO: Westview Press, 2007.

Zeng, J. "Did Policy Experimentation in China Always Seek Efficiency? A Case Study of Wenzhou Financial Reform in 2012." *Journal of Contemporary China* 24, no. 92 (2014): 338–356.

Zhan, X., and S. Tang. "Understanding the Implications of Government Ties for

Nonprofit Operations and Functions." *Public Administration Review* 76, no. 4 (2016): 589–600.

Zhang, J. "Didi by the Numbers: Ride-Hailing Firm Covered More Miles in 2018 Than 5 Earth-to-Neptune Round-Trips." *South China Morning Post*, January 23, 2019. https://www.scmp.com/tech/start-ups/article/2181542/didi-numbers-ride-hailing-firm-covered-more-miles-2018-5-earth/.

Zhang, J. "Will the Government 'Serve' the People: The Development of Chinese E-Government." *New Media and Society* 4, no. 2 (2002): 163–184.

Zhang, L. "A Commentary on 'Beyond Civil Society.'" *Journal of Civil Society* 7, no. 1 (2011): 119–122.

Zhao, Jinqiu. "A Snapshot of Internet Regulation in Contemporary China: Censorship, Profitability, and Responsibility." In *From Early Tang Court Debates to China's Peaceful Rise*, edited by Friederike Assandri and Dora Martins, 141–151. Amsterdam: Amsterdam University Press, 2009.

Zhao, Suisheng. *A Nation-State by Construction: Dynamics of Modern Chinese Nationalism*. Stanford, CA: Stanford University Press, 2004.

Zhao, X. *Annual Report on China's Development of the Governance at the Grass-Roots Level (2015)*. Guangzhou: Guangdong Renmin Chubanshe, 2015.

Zhao, Yuezhi. *Communication in China: Political Economy, Power, and Conflict*. Lanham, MD: Rowman and Littlefield Publishers, 2008.

Zhaogen, Zhu. *"Xunzhao Zhongguo Zhenggai de JinYaoshi"* (In Search for the "Golden Key" to China's Political Reform). *Lianhe Zaobao*, October 14, 2010. http://www.zaobao.com.sg/special/report/politic/cnpol/story20101014-13 8344/, accessed March 31, 2018.

Zhejiang Online Service Platform. "Disclosure of Administrative Punishment Results," People's Government of Zhejiang Province. https://www.zjzwfw. gov.cn/zjzw/punish/frontpunish/showadmins.do?webId=1/,   accessed December 26, 2021.

Zhejiang Provincial Bureau of Statistics. "The Seventh Census of Zhejiang Province," May 13, 2021. http://tjj.zj.gov.cn/art/2021/5/13/art_1229129205_463 2764.html/, accessed December 26, 2021.

Zheng, G. *Charity Law of the People's Republic of China: Interpretations and Applications* (《中华人民共和国慈善法》解读与应用). China: People's Publishing (人民 出版社), 2016, 327.

Zhi, X. 中国各朝人口数量 ("Zhongguo Gechao Renkou Shuliang: Chinese Population in Each Dynasty"). https://wenku.baidu.com/view/cc5c7e91941ea76e5 9fa040b.html/.

"Zhonghua Renmin Gongheguo Guowuyuan Ling di 492 Hao: Zhonghua Renmin Gongheguo Zhengfu Xinxi Gongkai Tiaoli." Open Government Information Ordinance, April 2007. http://www.gov.cn/zwgk/2007-04/24/conte nt_592937.htm/, accessed July 31, 2019.

"Zhonghua Renmin Gongheguo Jingwai Feizhengfu Zuzhi Jingnei Huodong Guanlifa" (Law of the Management of Foreign NGOs in the PRC). http:// www.npc.gov.cn/npc/xinwen/2017-11/28/content_2032719.htm/, accessed July 31, 2019.

Zhou, Viola. "Chinese State Media Want People to Stop Using Internet Slang." *Vice World News*, September 8, 2021.

Zhou, X. "Unorganized Interests and Collective Action in Communist China." *American Sociological Review* 58, no. 1 (1993): 54–73.

Zhou, Xudong. "National Health Care System Recognition of 34 Deceased Doctors, Including Li Wenliang." *Caixin*, March 5, 2020. https://china.caixin.com/2020-03-05/101524345.html/.

Zhu, Jiangang. "Editor's notes" (卷首语). *Philanthropic Studies* 5 (2015): 1.

Index

Note: Page numbers in italics indicate tables and figures.

Donations Law, 82
dual management system, 38, 82, 96
Dujiangyan, 87

earthquakes, 20, 26, 90–91, 99, 128, 132, 178. *See also* Ludian earthquake (2014); Sichuan earthquakes; Wenchuan earthquake
economic growth, 15, 25, 76, 78, 169, 188, 196, 198, 201. *See also* industrial innovations; job creation
The Economist, 165
Edwards, Bob, 129
elections: county level, 83, 221n25; free elections, 153; local elections, 171; Russian influence on US, 133; township level, 83, 221n25; village level, 83, 221n25; voting, 197
elites: civil society building and, 31; controlling power of, 7, 9, 57; expectations of rulers, 29; legalization without institutionalization and, 76, 197; political exchanges and conflicts of, 204; repressive actions and, 165
entrapment, 168, 169–70, 175, 177, 179–80, 181, 183, 187, 188, 206
equilibrium, 17, 19, 127
ethnicity, 4, 22, 210

Facebook, 33, 133, 138, 176
Fang, Fang, 194
Federation of the Handicapped, 231n44
Federation of Trade Unions, 89
Fewsmith, Joseph, 203, 204
fieldwork tips: about, 203–4; building social capital, 207–9; interviewee treatment, 204–6; language and empathy, 206–7; learning from pioneers, 210–11; local support/local networks, 209–10; no response/censorship as data, 211; original data, 212; speaking out, 212–13
512 NGO Services Center, 85, 87–89, 98, 230n31
Foley, Michael, 129
Ford Foundation, 81
Foreign NGO (Non-governmental Organization) Law (2016): CSOs and, 13, 25; differentiation and, 79; CSO funding and, 70, 71; interactive experimentation and, 97, 98, 99–100; legalization and, 26, 80, 96–97, 106, 130; overseas NGOs and, 39

foreign NGOs' activities, 232nn52,58; Step 1: tolerate, 94; Step 2: governments participate and take initiatives, 95; Step 3: promote successful models, further replication, and top-down disruption, 95–96; Step 4: legalization, 96–97
Foundation Regulations (2004), 38, 81, 82
foundations: charitable organizations as, 93; collaborations, 89; CSOs registered as, 32; foreign foundations, 81; Foundation Regulations (2004), 38, 82; funding and, 49, 50, 70, 123; GZ's GONGO and, 86; legalization and, 98
fragmented repression, 171
Fredickson, Mark, 63
Fu, Diana, 171
funding: cutting off CSO's funding, 11; foundations and, 49, 50, 70, 123; of Futian institution, 28; Sichuan earthquakes and, 26; usage of, 231n44
Futian institution, 28

G20, *149*
Gansu province, *21*
Geddes, Barbara, 5
geopolitical events: effects on three-stage process, 15–16. *See also* internet censorship; ride-sharing sector; Sichuan earthquakes
Global China: ban on, 240n94; censorship and, 132, 166; data and, 139–40, 212; differentiation and, 157, 159; *Inside the Beltway* and, 150, 151, 152, *153*, 154; legalization and, 163; speaking out, 213; toleration and, 155, 156; on WeChat, 141–50
GONGOs (government-organized nongovernmental organizations), 70, 85, 86, 89, 92
good governance: civic participation increase and, 6; as explanation for authoritarian resilience, 5; policymaking process and, 6
governance: Confucian approach to, 29; levels of, 35–37, 36; of nascent civil society of China, 28–90, 35–40; regional differences and, 35; Sichuan earthquake and constraints of, 19, 20; strengthening capacity of, 15; tested organizations maintained for future usefulness to effective, 4; testing of effectiveness of, 3;

vices (2016), 187; Measures for the Management of Religious Groups (2020), 4; "Regulations of Foreign Chambers of Commerce" (1989), 186; Religious Affairs Regulations of 2017, 4. *See also* internet censorship; legalization
Lee, Teng-hui, *149*, 150
legal gray zones, 44, 52, 78, *80*, 94, 161, 164, 172, 173–75, 187, 189
legalization: in case studies, *26*; Charity Law (2016), *26*; civil society organizations (CSOs) and, *26*; cross-removal campaigns and, 4; Foreign NGO (Nongovernmental Organization) Law (2016), *26*; institutionalization and, 13; interactive experimentation and state-organized, 97–101; ride-sharing sector and, *26*; ride-sharing sector and, 186–87; self-media and, *26*; Sichuan earthquakes and, *26*; as third stage of interactive authoritarianism, 101–2, 196; transition triggers and, 15; in virtual spaces, 161–64; WeChat and, *26*
legalization without institutionalization: about, 76–79; divide and rule, 79; domestic CSOs' activities, 83–94; foreign NGOs' activities, 94–97; initial conditions and institutional disruptions, 79–83, 196; state-organized legalization and, 97–101; as third stage, 10; as third stage of interactive authoritarianism, 13, 101–2
legal status, 11
legitimacy: charismatic, 5; drivers in China, 6; as explanation for authoritarian resilience, 5; improving state's, 10–11, 196–97; rational-legal, 5; traditional, 5
Li, Keqiang, 148, *149*
Li, Liguo, 37, 228n60
Li, Wenliang, 194
lineage systems, 29
Liu, Shaoqi, 29
local government, 5, 10, 14, 29. *See also* village governments
lower response rate, 227n42
low risk toleration, 45–48
Lu, Qibin, 209
Ludian earthquake (2014), 22, 105, 106, 107, 108–12, 112–14, 131
Lushan earthquake (2013), *21*, 47, 48, 70, 89, 95, 105, 112–14, 125, 131

Macau, 81
MacFarquhar, Roderick, 203, 208
Mao, Zedong, 29–30, 51, 77, 133–34, *149*, 201
market demand, *26*
market revenue return, *26*
Marxist-Leninism, 77
mass incidents, 170–72, 182, 184, 185–86, 242n15
Mass Organizations Conference, 90
May 4th Movement, 146
McKinsey and Company, 88
Measures for the Management of Religious Groups (2020), 4
media field, 19. *See also* self-media; social media
Meituan, 35
memorandums of understanding (MOUs), 88
methodology: conducting fieldwork in China, 203–13, 230n28; data and, 20–27, 227n43; data collection, 20, 233n3, 233n6; data inclusion, 219n76; institutional disruption and, 16–19; participant observation, 20; research design on deliberate differentiation, 57–62; response rates, 227n39, 227n42; results and analysis, 62–67, 227n44, 227n46, 227n47
Mexico, 5, 194
Mianyang, 91
Mianzhu, *80*, 87, 88, 90
Mianzhu post-disaster social resources coordination platform, *80*, 88, 89, 90, 98
military branch, 35
Ming Dynasty, 220n2
Ministry of Civil Affairs, 37, 38, 46, 81, 82–83, 92, 96, 97, 99, 228n60
Ministry of Ecology and Environment, 36
Ministry of Finance, 81, 92
Ministry of Foreign Affairs, 81
Ministry of Foreign Trade and Economic Cooperation, 81
Ministry of Internal Affairs, 37
Ministry of Public Security, 38–39, 96, 97, 100, 170, 185
Ministry of Transportation, 186
Moon, Jae-In, *149*
mosques, 4
most-different-case design, 25, *26*, 32, 198–99

Mullainathan, Sendhil, 210
municipal government, 36, 37, 56, 83, 163,
　221n24

Nanjing, 176
nascent civil society of China: activities
　within, 18; corporatism and, 30–32;
　democratization and, 30; emergence of,
　30–31; governing of, 28–30, 35–40; inter-
　active authoritarian approach and, 15;
　key player categories of, 32–35; as
　severely constrained, 25; state-society
　interactions in, 4–5, 30–32. See also
　CSOs; ride-sharing sector; self-media
Nathan, Andrew, 193
National Basketball Association (NBA),
　200
national environments, 26
nationalism, 5
Nationalists, 77
national level government, 130
National People's Congress (NPC), 35, 36,
　92, 93, 146
National Religious Affairs Administration,
　4
National Security Commission, 96, 207
nature: as institutional disruption, 26;
　institutional disruption from, 19, 20. See
　also earthquakes
newly-formed organizations, 24
new media, 139
New Tang Dynasty TV, 149
NGO Disaster Preparedness Center
　(NGODPC), 87
NGOs (nongovernmental organizations):
　as subgroup of CSOs, 33; term usage, 33.
　See also foreign NGOs' activities
Ningbo, 90
Nnajiofor, Peterson, 172
noncommunist single-party regimes, 5
non-enterprise units, 82, 98
non-market CSOs, 32
non-regime-challenging CSOs, 44, 201
non-response category, 227n39
non-state players, 9, 14–15, 32, 77
norms: institutional adaptability theory,
　15; institutions as instruments theory,
　15; to prolong regime, 6; Sichuan earth-
　quake and alteration in, 19
North, Douglass, 16, 19
North Korea, 132, 146

North Korean Labor Party, 149
not-for-profit CSOs, 32–33
"Notice on Further Cracking Down on the
　Illegal Operation of Taxis, Such as 'Black
　Cars'" (2013), 186
"Notice on Promoting the Orderly Devel-
　opment of Taxi Calling Services Such as
　Mobile Phone Software Calls," 186
"Notice on the Support and Normalize the
　Service Purchasing from Social Organi-
　zations by the Government" (2014), 92
not-yet-censored keywords, 148, 149
Nu River, 95

O'Connor, Brendan, 144
Office of the Central Cyberspace Affairs
　Commission, 36, 37
Offices of Civil Affairs, 38
Offices of Cyberspace Affairs, 37, 39, 40
Olympic Game (2022 Beijing Winter), 165
online communities, 26
"Opinions of Sichuan People's Govern-
　ment Regarding Promoting the Healthy
　Development of Philanthropy (Draft for
　Comments)" (2015), 130
origin, 39, 187, 222n28
outcomes: in case studies, 26; civil society
　organizations (CSOs) and, 26; ride-
　sharing sector and, 26; self-media and,
　26; Sichuan earthquakes and, 26; simi-
　larity of, 27; WeChat and, 26
outsourcing, 10, 13, 15

Pan, Jennifer, 67, 144, 203, 226n39, 227n42
Panzhihua, 85, 86
participant observation, 20, 24
patch regulations, 80, 81, 186
patrimonial regimes, 5
Paypal, 33, 138
peak associations, 31
Pence, Mike, 148, 149
Peng, Shuai, 161
people-run non-enterprises, 32, 93
People's Daily, 40, 166, 204
performance legitimacy, 5, 6, 53, 229n7
performative legitimacy, 5, 52, 53, 77,
　229n7
Perry, Elizabeth, 210–11
personalist regimes, 5
physical spaces, 6, 26 fig., 27
Pillsbury, Michael, 159